SCANDINAVIAN INSTITUTE OF ASIAN STUDIES
STUDIES ON ASIAN TOPICS
GENERAL EDITOR: KARL REINHOLD HAELLQUIST

ISLAM: STATE AND SOCIETY

T0348033

SCANDINAVIAN INSTITUTE OF ASIAN STUDIES

STUDIES ON ASIAN TOPICS

STUDIES ON ASIAN TOPICS NO. 12

ISLAM: STATE AND SOCIETY

Edited by
KLAUS FERDINAND
and
MEHDI MOZAFFARI

RoutledgeCurzon
Taylor & Francis Group
LONDON AND NEW YORK

SCANDINAVIAN INSTITUTE OF ASIAN STUDIES
Njalsgade 84, DK-2300 Copenhagen S, Denmark

First published 1988 in the United Kingdom by
RoutledgeCurzon, 2 Park Square, Milton Park,
Abingdon, Oxon, OX14 4RN

Transferred to Digital Printing 2006

ISBN 0 7007 0194 X

Exclusively distributed in India by
Allied Publishers Pvt. Ltd.
13-14 Asaf Ali Road, New Delhi-110002
and at
Ahmedabad Bangalore Bombay Calcutta
Hyderabad Lucknow Madras

CONTENTS

PART III
SECULARIZATION: NATION-STATE AND MODERNIZATION

CONTRIBUTORS

MOHAMMED ARKOUN
Institut d'Etudes Arabes et Islamiques, Université de la Sorbonne, Paris III

ASGER CHRISTENSEN
Institute of Ethnology and Anthropology, University of Copenhagen

HICHEM DJAÏT
University of Tunis

KLAUS FERDINAND
Institute of Ethnography and Social Anthropology, Moesgaard — University of Aarhus

MAHMOOD A. GHAZI
Islamic Research Institute, Islamabad

JAN HJÄRPE
University of Lund

GASYM MAMED OGLU KERIMOV
Institute for Scientific Atheism, Academy of Social Sciences, Moscow

ANN K. S. LAMBTON
Professor Emeritus, University of London

TUOMO MELASUO
Department of Political History, University of Turku

MEHDI MOZAFFARI
Institute of Political Science, University of Aarhus

MAJA NAUR
University of Odense

NIELS HENRIK OLESEN
Copenhagen

GORM RYE OLSEN
Institute of Political Science, University of Aarhus

ANNIKA RABO
Department of Social Anthropology, University of Stockholm

JØRGEN BÆK SIMONSEN
Institute of History, University of Copenhagen

CHRISTOPHER TOLL
Institute of Semitic Philology, University of Aarhus

NOTE

In editing this book, the individual preferences of the contributors concerning spelling and style have been observed, and so no attempt has been made towards a standardized presentation throughout the work. Uniformity within each paper has, however, been the objective.

PREFACE

In 1982, the Danish Research Council for the Humanities initiated a research programme on "Contemporary Islamic Studies" (Islam i Nutiden). The objective of this programme was to promote and develop Islamic research in Denmark.

The background to this initiative was the appreciably growing cultural, social and political importance of Islam within the Muslim societies and in the international arena. Denmark has long-standing historical relations with the Muslim countries. The works of Carsten Niebuhr (1733 – 1815) still constitute a valuable source of acquaintance with this part of the world, which continue to inspire the research of many specialists from different disciplines. Since the 1960s, a new chapter has been opened in Danish-Islamic relations. During this period the Muslim countries have become politically and economically more and more important; Denmark, as an "exporting country", has consequently taken an interest in ameliorating its knowledge of the cultural, societal, political and religious character of its Muslim partners. In addition to that, a significant number of Muslims, especially people coming from Turkey, Pakistan, Yugoslavia and North Africa, had established themselves in Denmark in the 1960s and 1970s. As a result, Islam has become the country's second-largest religion after Christianity.

The research programme started in 1982 with the project "Islam: State and Society", in which an interdisciplinary group of researchers took part. It was also under this project that an international symposium was held at the University of Aarhus 30 August – 1 September 1984. The present volume contains the revised papers of this symposium. Much to our regret, we could not integrate the paper of Dr. John Duke Anthony into this volume. His paper was entitled "Islam and Society in the Persian Gulf".

As organisers of the symposium, we would like to express our deep gratitude to all participants, and especially to the authors and discussants. We feel particularly indebted to Professor Ann K. S. Lambton, who has taken the trouble to read all the manuscripts and write an enlightening foreword to this volume. We are grateful, too, to the University of Aarhus for housing the symposium and to the Danish Research Council for the Humanities for its financial support to the symposium, including the publication of papers. Finally we want to express our thanks to the Scandinavian Institute of Asian Studies for facilitating the appearance of this book.

The system of transliteration is, with modifications, the one adopted by the Royal Asiatic Society.

Klaus Ferdinand   Mehdi Mozaffari

INTRODUCTION

A. K. S. LAMBTON

Islam is grounded in history. Traditionally it encompassed all aspects of social and political life and formulated norms of conduct. *Ḥadīth*, forged or otherwise, contributed to the emergence of a common pattern of thought. The literate and illiterate were familiar with the Qur'ān and it was at the finger-tips of every chronicler, every historian, every writer. Chancery practice was full of Quranic quotations and the application of these themes to government.

The relation of the past to the present may take a variety of forms in human experience. For some it may be a creative source of vitality and change. For others it may be dead and have lost all relevance, while for yet others the past may be living and its impact so vivid that past and present seem to be mingled and hope for the future determined by faith in the living past. Paradoxically, however, a living past may also have a deadening effect by dampening the fire of contemporary creativity.[1] A study of state and society and the nature of authority in Islam must take into account the various experiences of the past; an obsession with passing trends must not be allowed to obscure the longer perspective of truth. No full understanding of the questions that agitate the Islamic world today is possible unless they are traced to their sources in earlier times.

The Islamic community, the *umma*, was believed to be instituted by divinity itself and its government came to be seen as a divine gift, and hence the population a divine trust. But an institution can be worked only by men. Personalities of necessity figure prominently in Islamic history as in the history of the non-Islamic world. Charged with the application and execution of the idea or ideas embodied in the institution of the *umma*, men were both shaped and guided by the institution itself and also, perhaps more importantly, themselves shaped and guided the institution. As Professor Butterfield states, "It is men who make history."[2] Unfortunately for the early and medieval period of Islamic history sources which tell us what people really thought are rare. Nevertheless the importance of personality in the unfolding of Islamic history and behind the development of Islamic institutions cannot be neglected. Events are the result of complex situations in which a variety of people participate.

It has been said that the web of history is seamless.[3] Its division into periods makes it more manageable, but to some extent distorts. Elements of continuity in different aspects of life will be found even in periods of violent change. Men act and write within the framework of the complex of antecedent ideas and customs handed down through successive generations; and in relation to this framework men see and understand themselves.

Those who would know how the world of classical Islam was transformed into the world of medieval Islam must start their investigations in the early centuries. Equally, if they would understand the institutions and ideas which have persisted into the modern period long after the circumstances that had engendered them had passed away, they must look back to the medieval period and beyond. The contributions of both the early centuries and medieval times are of lasting importance: in religion, law, philosophy, science, art and literature. But at the same time it must be remembered that the tradition handed down is not necessarily the same for all parts of the Islamic world. Popular practice varied and reflected different social realities.

Besides the real and profound contributions of early and medieval Islam as they actually were, there is also the indirect contribution of the idealized early centuries of Islam, "magnified, mirrored and roseate" in the thought of the Islamic middle ages and of modern times. This idealized picture, different for Sunnīs and Shī'īs, for Arabs, and Persians and Turks, is none the less real because it is indirect and ideal. It moved the mind and stirred the spirit of Muslims in the past and still does so in modern times.

The authority of the Prophet was based on belief in a divine revelation, and a combination of divine knowledge or wisdom (*hikma*, *'ilm*) and authority (*mulk*) was attributed to him. He was regarded as the seal of the prophets and hence this combination of prophethood and political authority was not transmitted to his successors. Further, since he left no clear-cut instructions for the choice of his successor, different groups and individuals were able to claim the right to rule on various grounds of legitimacy. In the last resort, the question of legitimacy was decided by force, but even force had to have an ideological basis. Nobility, Islamic seniority and nearness of kin to the Prophet were the crucial factors in the debate at the time of the Prophet's death, qualities which were held to belong to the Quraysh in general and the *muhājirūn* in particular. The authority of the orthodox caliphs rested basically on seniority in Islam and the consensus of believers. The Shī'īs, on the other hand, rested the claim to legitimacy primarily on the principle of kinship and nomination by *naṣṣ* or designation.[4]

The early disputes within the community were over the person and functions of its head; and it was over his person and the method of his choice that the sects separated. Early Islam made the individual's allegiance depend upon the doctrinal legitimacy of the ruler, but this was not because of any rights the individual possessed, but simply because it was a Quranic requirement. Later jurists were to demand absolute obedience to the caliph as a religious obligation defined in terms of the *sharī'a* and justified by the Quranic obligation, "Obey God, obey the Prophet and those in authority amongst you"; and this obligation the community came to recognize as essential for the maintenance of authority and the prevention of anarchy and disorder.

From the very beginning religion and state were one and this has remained a characteristic of Islam down to modern times. To interpret Islamic thinkers in terms of the modern western antithesis of church and state is to distort their thought. The *sharī'a*, the divinely revealed law of God, had absolute authority. It preceded the state and was its law. There could, therefore, be no question of the law embodying the consent of those to whom it applied. The individual had no rights against the state but merely the right to expect that the leader of the community, the *imām* or caliph, would act in conformity with the law. The *imām*'s duty was to maintain and enforce the law.

Obedience to the ruler, since the source of his authority was God and the law which he administered was God's law, was a religious obligation. Disobedience to him was a sin and a crime to be punished in this world and the next. Civil war and internal disturbances were considered to be fundamentally rebellion against the divine law. The series of events which include the murder of 'Uthmān, the designation of 'Alī as *imām*, the battle of Ṣiffīn, the development of both the Shī'at 'Alī and the Khārijī schisms and the seizure of power by Mu'āwiya, all of which had implications for the legitimacy of the *imām* and therefore bearing on the values of the faith, are often called "the first *fitna*" or "the great *fitna*". Later the term *fitna* (pl. *fitan*) was applied to any period of disturbance inspired by schools or sects which broke away from the majority of believers. Every "innovator", every man guilty of innovation (*bid'a*) was potentially an instigator of *fitna*. According to al-Ḥasan al-Baṣrī the `ahl al-sunna wa'l-jamā'a, the people of the "authoritative" tradition and the community, had the strict duty to obey the legitimate sovereign so long as his orders did not run counter to the Qur'ān, and to shun all *fitna*.[5]

By the 5th/11th century the jurists had elaborated a comprehensive legal system concerning the qualifications, investiture and functions of the *imām*, though there were some differences among them over the nature of his authority.[6] By this time, both the caliph and the sultan were felt to be necessary for the government of the world. On the day of judgment, sultans would have to render account for the trusts which caliphs or divinity had granted to them in the shape of temporal power. The jurists did not, however, admit the existence of the state as an institution in its own right and considered the emergence of a temporal state as a separate institution to be a usurpation due to the intrusion of elements of corruption into the community. The state, although possessed of temporal power, lacked any intrinsic authority of its own.[7] This did not, however, mean that men should withdraw from participation in the state — though some did. Ibn Taymiyya, writing after the fall of the caliphate, states "It is a duty to consider the exercise of power as one of the forms of religion, as one of the acts by which man draws near to God."[8]

When the 'Abbāsid caliphate was finally extinguished by the Mongols in 656/1258, the jurists had to find a new basis for the authority of rulers, so that Islamic institutions might be maintained in the absence of the caliph, regardless of political divisions. The prevailing view came to be that the seizure of government itself gave authority: even if a government was vicious, it was to be obeyed because obedience to it was a lesser evil than anarchy. Sometimes the ruler sought to validate his claim to sovereignty by a declaration that he was a *mujāhid*,[9] i.e. that he led the faithful in holy war (whether this was against infidels or rebel Muslims). This underlines the change which had taken place; it was no longer the origin of political power which gave legitimacy but its use. For most Muslims the basis of identity was Islam, and it was Islam, not the state or nation, that constituted the main claim to their loyalty. Muslim rulers tended to refer to themselves as lords of Islam or of the Muslims and to their territories as Islamic lands.[10] Ethnic or territorial designations of sovereignty were rare until modern times.

Heresy was disloyalty and apostasy treason, and with this went the assumption that the stability of the state was bound up with right religion (though the interpretation of right religion might vary). The problem of the justification of power did not arise, but if a ruler did not administer God's law he became a usurper and the duty of obedience to him was replaced by the duty (not the right) of disobedience. A large body of literature grew up over the centuries as Muslim jurists and theologians discussed the question of legitimacy and the circumstances in which a ruler ceased to be legitimate. They also discussed at length the question of rebellion and the regulations of warfare against rebels.[11] Both Sunnīs and Shī'īs hedged submission to an unlawful government by various conditions, but from time to time the sharp edges of the problem were blunted by compromise and expediency as dictated by the political circumstances of the day.

It is significant that whenever and wherever there have been popular outbreaks against governments these have expressed themselves in

Islamic terms, whatever the social or economic causes which in part gave rise to them. This was the case not only of movements in classical and medieval times but also of the first major movements of resistance to European expansion into Islamic lands in the nineteenth century, that led by Ahmad Brelwi in India, the movement of Shāmī in Dāghistān, and that of 'Abd al-Qādir in Algeria. The latter, to quote Mr. Hourani, won support by a characteristically Muslim blend of piety and political skill.[12] Movements of revolt in the past were movements within Islam and not against Islam and were attempts to solve internal problems. Their aim was usually a return to an ideal past. The natural and spontaneous form of expression used by Muslims to voice their criticisms and aspirations continues to be Islamic, even if Islam is not the only reality underlying their criticisms and guiding their aspirations.[13] The spread of western civilization into Islamic lands in recent years has been accompanied by disillusion with their own rulers, whose power was seen to rest on the use of a hated and alien culture. This disillusion, coupled with a rejection of western civilization, has been expressed in the traditional idiom, often with great popular force, as witness the Persian revolution of 1978−9.

Islam is not, however, monolithic. Apart from the major split between Sunnīs and Shī'īs, there were also different doctrinal tendencies, traditionalist, fundamentalist and, in the nineteenth and twentieth centuries, "modernist".[14] There is also the interplay between dogmatic religion, Sufism and popular piety, "official" Islam and "popular" Islam, with its expectation of a *mahdī*. All these movements have this in common, that they sought and seek, in one way or another, to promote the cause of Islam. All Muslims share one faith, but the social structures in which their common Islamic sentiment developed differed as also did their political experiences. Further, in recent years the problems of nationality and national liberation, and economic and social upheaval have brought new dimensions, while ideological debates have often centred round concepts related to secular and materialist ideologies such as socialism, communism, liberation from imperial domination and so forth.

At one extreme there is "official" Islam, to be seen in consultations between Islamic governments in summit conferences, in regional co-operation, Islamic banks, and development organizations. At the other extreme there are fundamentalist movements, sometimes underground, bent on the renewal of society by ending the rule of alien infidels and domestic apostates and a return to what they see to be a pure and authentic Islamic order. They believe the overthrow of impious rulers and western materialism to be prerequisites to the establishment of God's kingdom on earth.[15]

The papers presented to the conference, written from the standpoint of a variety of disciplines and ranging over a wide spectrum in time and space, contain new insights into the history of state and society in Islam and the problem of authority. Professor Arkoun, while convinced that the basic documents — the Qur'ān, the Traditions, and the ''orthodox'' sources claimed by each great tradition of Islam, Sunnī, Shī'ī and Khārijī — are still alive and active as an ideological system of beliefs and knowledge shaping the future, asks, in a stimulating paper, for a new evaluation of authority in Islamic thought. He is critical both of the *islāḥī 'ulamā'* for their projection of the demands and needs of contemporary Muslim societies on to the fundamental texts and of European and American scholars for an exclusively narrative and philological approach to these texts and lack of philosophical perspective in their discussions of the theory of authority in Islam. He insists upon the need for human beings to have access to some means of knowledge other than religion concerning their nature and destiny, however difficult and imperfect the apprehension of that knowledge may be. He would seem to be implicitly concerned with the problem of the deadening impact of the living past on contemporary creativity, and also with a fundamentalism (of whatever religion, Islamic, Jewish or Christian) which, in its assertion that the received text consists of a set of eternal living truths, has an in-built guarantee of infallibility which avoids the need for a creative re-interpretation of the faith.

Seeking for some new and creative source of vitality and change, Professor Arkoun suggests that this is to be found in ''the theory of knowledge''. ''The problem of authority'', he states, ''does not today depend on any religious or secular institution; in so far as reason has established its autonomy *vis-à-vis* outside authorities (revelation, church, *sharī'a*, state) it must constitute knowledge as a sphere of authority . . . independent of ideologies, able to explain their formation and master their impact.''

This raises the question of secularism. Professor Arkoun pleads for a revision of ideas concerning the place of secularism in Islam and the attitude of official Islam towards secularism. He points out that Islamic societies are involved in secular history and have adopted the attributes of material modernity; even the so-called fundamentalist movements ''are themselves secular in their daily life, their professions and their basic needs; the majority of the militants come from the lower classes, cut off from the traditional culture, unable to reach the modern urban culture; they rightly ask for more justice, less brutal oppression, possibilities to participate in the new history; but they express these basically secular hopes in a religious language, the only one at their disposal.'' The development or spread of secularism in Islam, if it is to be fruitful, depends, in his view, upon what he calls "intellectual modernity". Without such he sees no possibility of a fruitful encounter between secularism and a religious world view. From such an encounter and the discovery of secularism as a new dimension of thought, he envisages the development of a new theory and practice of authority — a process which he considers necessary not only in Islamic societies but also in western. Alleging that both classical orientalist discourse and so-called revolutionary Islamic discourse are "prisoners of the image of a provincial, ethnographic Islam, locked into its classsical formulations inadequately and poorly reformulated in contemporary ideological slogans", he calls for a new approach to the rich experience hidden in the living core of Islam.[16]

Clearly, the orientalist when writing about Islamic civilization is, or should be, engaged in a dialogue with his materials, but he can interpret them only within the limits set by his evidence. The questions he asks will be those suggested by the evidence, and, as I am sure Professor Arkoun would agree, he must employ the proper rules of evidence and reason.[17] Legitimate questions must be asked of the evidence. Without evidence there can be no meaningful questions — though it is possible that no orientalist has been bright enough to ask the right questions. This is, I think, Professor Arkoun's point.

Professor Toll discusses the purpose of oriental and Islamic studies. Predictably, he refers to Professor Said's attack on orientalists and part of his paper is devoted to an urbane refutation of Professor Said's attack. He touches lightly on the early foundation of Arabic chairs in European universities and points out that the encouragement of oriental studies was due to a diversity of motives. The outlook of one scholar differed from that of another, but their common motive was intellectual curiosity and their common tradition the use of scholarly methods. He considers that the intrinsic and ultimate purpose of oriental studies in all their variety — as of all studies in the humanities — is to contribute to human culture. Scholarship for him is a creative art and the scholar an artist. In the light of this perception, he suggests that what the orientalist contributes is his picture of Islam and Islamic civilization, a picture based on substantial fact but created out of his imagination. He sees the orientalist as an explorer driven by intellectual curiosity, striving to find out what was unknown before he made it known, an imaginative artist, creating what nobody had created before him in order to obtain prestige, fame and worldly immortality. This is a somewhat idiosyncratic view. An imaginative understanding, however desirable, will tend towards uncertainty unless it is controlled by precise learning. The freedom of exploration must also be circumscribed by the reality of the past. The orientalist ought, no doubt, to be an artist, but more importantly, he must be governed by the techniques of his particular craft. He needs an imaginative and sympathetic understanding, but he must also be taught to be critical and with this, I have no doubt, Professor Toll would agree. Those engaged in oriental studies, as all engaged in intellectual investigations, seek the truth within the confines of their particular province, and the quality of their work is to be judged on purely intellectual grounds.

Several of the papers, in addition to that of Professor Arkoun, draw attention to the direct and indirect contributions of the past. Dr. Djaït's paper mades a valuable and stimulating contribution to an understanding of the origins of the Islamic state seen against the background of pre-Islamic Arabia. He distinguishes various phases in its emergence and describes the factors that gave it cohesion. He argues that from the beginning the idea of war was present and that the Islamic state was a ''warrior'' state. He traces the way in which Muhammad became heir to Qurayshī authority and the Quraysh the defenders of the Islamic state. He also shows that the new state was riddled with latent conflicts deriving from two different systems of value, that of the Jāhiliyya and that of Islam, tensions which continued to exist in the Islamic state in later years.

Dr. Naur traces the relevance of consensus in Islam and shows how this tendency enabled the trade union movement in Libya to become part of the state apparatus, even though state ideology was no longer legitimised by reference to Islam.

Mr. Simonsen, in an examination of the terms *dhimma* and *jizya* in early Islam, shows how historical tradition was made to serve an ideology. Dr. Hjärpe analyses certain controversial points in the Muslim discussion of human rights. At one extreme there was an enthusiastic acceptance of the UN declaration on human rights as a genuine expression of Islamic values and principles formed by the conditions of contemporary society, just as the Quranic revelation was governed by the conditions of Arab society at the time of the Jāhiliyya, and at the other extreme total rejection of the declaration as being incompatible with the eternal and unchangeable law of God.

In a paper entitled 'Islam and civil society', Dr. Mozaffari discusses secularization in terms of the national state and political movements in Egypt and Iran and Islam's relationship to the nation state and civil society. He notes the changes Islam has undergone in history and draws a distinction between the conception and the reality of Islam. In this connection he examines the case of the Islamic revolution in Iran and attempts to explain its causes and the reasons for Khomeini's success.

Dr. Rabo seeks to construct a model, based on the experience of Syria, to resolve the contradictions between modern secular politics and the re-emergence of the influence of Islam in politics. He rests his discussion on the assumption that the state is crucial in the development of Middle Eastern nations and that state policies and official rhetoric are at the centre of political controversies. Tracing the evolution of the Ba'th regime in Syria, he sees it as the mediator between the different classes. He also examines how the Syrians themselves analyse their political economy, the symbolic language of politics and the use of both Islamic and secular rhetoric, and the political myth of a welfare state on the one hand and a just caliphate on the other in which the *umma* would fulfil the aspirations of all Muslims.

Dr. Gorm Rye Olsen challenges the popular concept of the impact of Islam on social development in Islamic countries. His thesis, taking as his examples Egypt and Saudi Arabia, is that Islam has no impact on the development of the economic structures of capitalism or on changes in class structure. The significance of Islam, he maintains, is limited to the sphere of ideology, to the legitimizing of the political and economic power of whatever class or group happens to be in control. A conviction of the basic importance of economic development and changes in class structure would seem to be implicit in his perception of societal development. These are, no doubt, important in their own right, but civilization is not only economics and class change. He discusses the changing role of Islam in Egypt during the past thirty years but maintains that ideology followed rather than determined events, though it had an important function in legitimizing the policies of successive governments. Saudi Arabia presents a rather different picture to Egypt, but in this case also Dr. Olsen's opinion is that Islam has had no effect on the economic development of the country or on its class structure. He considers that the House of Saud, in using Islam and the *'ulamā'* to legitimize its claim to government, has shown itself skilful in adopting traditional values and institutions to the requirement of a modernizing state.

Several of the papers bring into relief the diversity of the different regions in the world of Islam and reveal class structures of great complexity, dichotomies between townsmen and countrymen and between nomads and settled people, with their many subdivisions and cross-classifications. Three papers examine tribal concepts of authority and identity. Their authors illustrate something of the complexity involved in the problem of authority in Islamic society, and show that it might also revolve round national and tribal identity. Dr. Asta Olesen traces the emergence of the state of Afghanistan over the last hundred years. She describes tribal concepts of authority and legitimacy, ultimately derived from God but mediated through the tribe whose authority was rooted in Pakhtunwali and the internal equality of the *jirga*. This is clearly a different system and concept of authority from that prevailing in the central lands of the Islamic world. Dr. Olesen also remarks on the mixture of loyalties — religious, tribal, ethnic, regional and ideological — found among the various resistance groups of the present day. Her account underlines the impossibility of any attempt to generalize about the nature of local resistance in Afghanistan. Dr. Asger Christensen writes with insight on the different meanings of Muslim identity in contemporary Afghanistan, the heterogeneous nature of Islam in Afghanistan, the schism between the Pakhtun and other ethnic groups and the relationship between Pakhtunwali and Islam.

Dr. Melasuo, in a wide-ranging paper, discusses the question of the cultural identity of the Berbers, the self-image of Algerian society and the political implications of the cultural debate proceeding in Algeria. He suggests that the rapid structural and economic transformation since the Second World War has led to a crisis between "modernization" and cultural identity among people throughout the world. In the case of the Berbers the debate centres on first the recognition of the Berber language and culture, secondly recognition of Algerian popular culture, thirdly a reinterpretation of Algerian history, the role of the Berbers in this and the importance of the Arabs and Arab civilization, and fourthly basic civil liberties. He shows that this debate, since 1980, has also had political implications for the nature and content of Algerian socialism and for development strategies. He also touches briefly on the marabout movement, changing attitudes towards Islam and the position of women.

Lastly, Professor Kerimov discusses modern Muslim missionary activity and the work of Islamic centres in Europe, the USA, Canada, Australia, Latin America and Japan. He considers the two main aspects of this activity to be first propaganda for Islamic cultural values, Islamic ways of life and Islamic moral standards, and secondly attempts to combat the penetration of western ideas into Muslim countries.

PART I
ON CONTEMPORARY ISLAMIC STUDIES

1

THE PURPOSE OF ISLAMIC STUDIES

Christopher Toll

It can be presumed that studies in Arabic took place in the Near East for different purposes before the rise of Islam. Thus, when the Arabs learned about the Jewish and Christian faiths we can suppose that the Jews and the Christians had learned enough Arabic to be able to carry on commerce with the Arabs or to do missionary work among them. We know that there was much business activity in Arabia, where the caravan routes crossed each other, and that Christian missionaries followed these caravan routes. Likewise, we are acquainted with the Jewish colonies in Madīna, Khaybar and Taymā' and in South Arabia. We are also aware that the mission was used by the Byzantine emperor and the Sasanian king for political purposes.

Also, with the rise of Islam and Islamic culture, there was still more reason for the Aramaic or Greek-speaking neighbours to learn Arabic in order to meet the demands of the Arabs for an arabization of the administration under the caliph and for translations of scholarly works. One example is St. John of Damascus, who knew Arabic as well as Greek. He was an official of the Umayyad caliphs and the first Christian thinker to have made a study of Islam and who did not use polemics but serious theological arguments.[1] Another is Ḥunayn b. Isḥāq, the bilingual Syrian Christian from al-Ḥīra in Abbasid times. Only through studies in Arabic could he have been enabled to create a scientific Arabic language with a new terminology and a more flexible syntax by means of which complicated abstract notions could be expressed. Among the works translated by Ḥunayn we find philosophical and medical treatises.[2]

Thus, at this early stage we already find some of the motives which have given rise to the study of Arabic, and later on Islam, in the West, namely, the desire to profit from business, the desire to conduct missions and the desire for knowledge and its practical use.

The earliest scholarly studies of Arabic and of Islam are, of course, those carried out by the Islamic scholars themselves. These studies are outside the scope of this paper — their purpose is more or less self-evident, whereas the purpose of Islamic studies in the West is a matter worthy of some deliberation.

Before I proceed to this deliberation I wish to add that the works of the Islamic scholars have from the beginning been not only an object of study but also an indispensable help — I only need to mention Arabic grammars and dictionaries or the commentaries of the Qur'ān and of the Classical poetry, on which Western scholarship still heavily leans. When the roles were reversed and Europe had to learn from the Arabs, translations were no longer made into Arabic but from Arabic into Latin, and European scholars had to take up Arabic studies.

Latin manuscripts of the tenth century on the astrolabe with Arabic terminology seem to show that Arabic studies had started in Catalonia, having been influenced by Cordoba and, in turn, influenced Christian Europe. The twelfth century marked the beginning of the great period of translations from Arabic by Christian scholars. Works to be translated were chosen mainly from the fields of medicine, mathematics and astronomy, and show that the aim was to acquire practical knowledge. There was, however, also an interest in Arabic philosophical works.

Arabic science, or classical scholarship as transmitted by the Arabs, gave rise to European universities. In Salerno a medical school was founded, and in Bologna, Padua, Montpellier and Paris philosophy, botany, zoology, physics and alchemy were studied according to Arab tradition.

The Crusades promoted the study of the Arabic language in Europe in order to facilitate the mission among the Muslims. In 1311 the Council of Vienna decided to create chairs in Oriental languages at the University of Paris, Salamanca, Rome, Oxford and Bologna.

When the Qur'ān was edited by Hinckelmann in Hamburg in 1694 the editor tells us in the preface the reasons for his edition: first that one must know the Qur'ān in order to combat Islam and propagate Christendom, but then he adds that Arabic is related to Hebrew and therefore important for Biblical and comparative studies and that also the poetical and scientific works of the Arabs are worthy of consideration.

This interest in Arabic in connection with Biblical studies was a result of the Reformation and led to the creation of chairs in Oriental languages, among them Arabic, at the universities of Northern Europe.

In the sixteenth century the rise of the Ottoman empire furthered the political and commercial interests of European countries in the Near East. The spirit of Humanism inspired an accompanying interest in Islamic culture, and scholars were often among the members of diplomatic missions to Islamic countries. Scholars were also sent to the East to learn languages and to collect manuscripts.

The first to break with the tradition of putting Arabic studies at the service of mission and theology was Joseph Scaliger, who was an historian and used all the means of historical research — texts, inscriptions, numismatics, chronology — to arrive at the historical facts. Scaliger died in Leiden in 1609.

The Age of Enlightenment brought an interest in the Orient for its own sake — one of the first results of this undogmatic interest was Bartholomé d'Herbelot's *Bibliothèque orientale* of 1697, a forerunner of our *Encyclopaedia of Islam*. The romantic world of the "Arabian Nights", made known at the beginning of the eighteenth century by the French translation of Antoine Galland, was a different and more attractive world than that of the false prophet and of the menacing Turks.

When, after the French revolution, the establishment of chairs in Arabic, Persian and Turkish was proposed in the French National Assembly, the motive was "l'importance des langues Orientales pour l'extension du commerce et le progrès des lettres et des sciences", and the author of the proposal stressed the practical utility of the living languages for business and politics.

The first incumbent of the chair of Arabic, Silvestre de Sacy, did not, however, concentrate on the proposed practical utility of Arabic but on scholarly studies of Classical Arabic. He was particularly interested in Arabic grammar.

Another important Orientalist in the nineteenth century was the Austrian Joseph v. Hammer-Purgstall, but his importance was more cultural than scholarly. He wanted to present the Oriental world to Europe by means of his immensely rich journal *Fundgruben des Orients* which influenced among others Goethe and Rückert.

In the following generation began the critical treatment of historical texts — suffice it to mention in this context Dozy and his work on the history of Muslim Spain.

This outline of Orientalist scholarship in Europe[3] will suffice to show the diversity of motives and interests that have governed Oriental studies.

Edward Said, in his book *Orientalism* (1978) has looked upon these motives from a rather negative angle. He accuses the Orientalist scholars, particularly those of England, France and the United States, of treating the Orient as an object, of recreating it, of looking upon the Orient as something foreign, something opposed to Christianity, something to be judged, of studying the Orient in order to gain power over it and thus of helping the colonial states to dominate the Orient.

What Said has to say about Orientalism is, of course relevant to our issue.

Said reproaches Orientalists for their support of colonialism. As the reviewer of Said's *Orientalism* in *Arabica* has pointed out,[4] colonialism also existed without Oriental studies and Oriental studies have existed and continue to exist without colonialism.

Denmark and Sweden, for instance, could hardly be called colonial powers and it is improbable that Danish and Swedish Orientalists have had imperialistic motives for their studies. It could be argued that Scandinavian scholars have followed the English and French traditions, but I think that the German tradition was stronger in Scandinavian Orientalism, and colonialism was scarcely a major part of that tradition. Besides, colonialism cannot be less painful to the oppressed peoples if it is accompanied by ignorance of their culture. Interest in and knowledge of their culture ought rather to be a redeeming feature. In any case, whatever harm colonialism has done, it has contributed to an increased interest in and knowledge of the culture of the peoples of Islam.

The same could probably be said about missions, commercialism and politics: that missionizing is more agreeable, commercialism mutually more fruitful and politics more inclined to be understanding if they are not coupled with ignorance, and that every contact between cultures could contribute to increasing mutual interest and knowledge (this applies even to wars, such as those of the Crusades).

Said is right in saying that the Crusades and the Christian missions have contributed to show how the Orient is thought of in Europe, and it may have been the case also in Scandinavia, but when Said mentions the Ottoman peril, he is not aware of the fact that this peril was not felt in all European countries. In Sweden the Turks were considered not as enemies, but as allies against common foes, the Austrians and the Russians.

To most Europeans, however, the Orient is foreign, and many people feel repelled by what is foreign. But if, instead, you feel attracted by a foreign people, then it is hardly because you dislike them. Even if Said quotes instances of harsh judgements on Islam, its Prophet or the Arabs, I doubt if it is correct to conclude from them that Orientalists in general are negative in their view of the Orient.

Moreover, the Orient is not wholly foreign to the European. Islam is a Biblical religion related to Christianity, and a Swedish scholar, Tor Andrae, the biographer of the Prophet Muḥammad, and himself a bishop of the Church of Sweden, said about the Islamic mystics: "Confronted by their words I have had a remarkable experience of something at the same time new and alien and yet well known. I have looked into the features of a stranger which yet belonged to a kinsman. I have met sayings which have forced me deliberately and inquiringly to scrutinize my own belief. I have seen rays from a source of light which I know well but refracted through a new medium".[5] A similar feeling inspired my teacher, H. S. Nyberg in Uppsala, whose fascination for the relations between Christian and Islamic mysticism is apparent in his thesis on the *Kleinere Schriften des Ibn al-'Arabī*.[6]

Now if Said is wrong in speaking about English and French Orientalism as representative of European Orientalism as a whole, he is also wrong in speaking of Orientalists in general — Orientalists are individuals and their attitude to Oriental studies and to the Orient is an individual one. We have seen that Tor Andrae was moved by a feeling of kinship, that his studies were a challenge to him, not to dominate the Muslims and to judge their faith, but to learn from them.

Another example of a highly individual approach to Islam is that of Louis Massignon. In Albert Hourani's words — and I quote from Hourani on purpose, because he is one of the few Orientalists not criticized by Said — Massignon's "thought about Islam begins from that point at which his own life was transformed: a sudden apprehension of the existence of God and of a debt owed to Him, at a moment of despair in Iraq in 1908. The experience had come to him in Muslim country, through the medium of Arabic, the language of Islam, and perhaps it was this which gave him the abiding sense of the divine origin of Islam which posed the problems to which he remained faithful for more than another half century of life." And Hourani adds: "This vision of the redemption of Islam, urged in a language of great beauty, and not only in words but in acts — of pilgrimage and of political protest, wherever the human dignity of Muslims seemed to him threatened — has left its mark on French life and on its literature, its theology and its mission as well as its Islamic scholarship."[7]

Now if these scholars, as belonging to a Christian tradition, could still not be trusted, I would like to adduce Ignaz Goldziher, the Hungarian Jew, with his Talmudic background, whose first book was inspired by the desire to refute Renan's racial theory. But that fact does not prevent Said from packing those two together as "Orientalists — from Renan to Goldziher" and considering Goldziher's appreciation of Islam's tolerance towards other religions as undercut by his dislike of Muhammad's anthropomorphism and Islam's too exterior theology and jurisprudence.

But even if you could find a lot to criticize in the individual scholar's work — and in which scholar's work is there nothing to criticize? — he and his scholarship are to be judged not only on account of their shortcomings but also according to their merits. I would like to confront the harsh judgement that Said makes about Gibb in many places in his book with the following words of Hourani,[8] when he said about Gibb's aims and motives: "One of his lasting concerns was to rescue Oriental studies from their marginal position in the universities and insert them into the central stream of intellectual life from which they had first emerged. . . . His intellectual curiosity began with language and literature. . . In all this there was something of the pure self-moving curiosity of the scholar — a strange and passionate imagination".

I shall return to this curiosity and this imagination of the scholar. These examples might suffice, however, to show that outlook and motives vary from one individual scholar to another and that it is impossible to treat all Orientalists alike.

I would like to add that these different individual approaches of the scholars, by their diversity, contribute to an advance of scholarship towards some sort of objectivity, as expressed by J. D. J. Waardenburg[9] in the following words: "On pourrait reprocher à la position prise, et la manière d'envisager l'Islam, qui en découle: à Goldziher une vision trop exclusivement historique de l'Islam; à Snouck Hurgronje l'accent mis peut-être trop exclusivement encore sur le système juridique musulman; à Becker une vue, trop purement soucieuse d'humanisme, sur la civilisation musulmane; à Macdonald une insistance trop lourde sur la considération de la réalité invisible dans l'Islam; à M. Massignon, de voir l'Islam de façon trop purement mystique. Mais mieux vaut apprécier les découvertes apportées par chacun à notre connaissance, le progrès graduel de l'approche du "mystère" de la religion islamique, le raffinement et la pénétration de la recherche toujours plus spécialisée, et surtout la prise de conscience croissante du travail qui est en train de se faire, de son point de départ et de son but. Il y a un progrès, aussi bien scientifique qu'humain dans la recherche et la découverte." If there is a common motive it is rather that of intellectual curiosity, and if there is a common tradition, it is rather in the use of scholarly methods.

That brings me to another criticism of Said's contention. The methods used in Oriental studies are hardly very different from those used in other fields, e.g., in Classical studies. Several Orientalists have, from Scaliger onwards, also been Classical philologists. Others have used the methods of the sciences of religion, history, literature etc. If the results of these methods are not worthy of blame outside Oriental studies — why should they be, when concerned with the Orient?

As an example I would like to present the outline of a theory relevant to the theme of this book. It has been shown that the rise of commerce in Italy in the *quattrocento* and *quinquecento* and in Holland in the seventeenth century originated in the establishment of free markets and the absence of mercantilism and the guild system and was followed by a flourishing culture supported by rich merchants, by patrons who not only paid, but possessed imagination and a discerning understanding of what to pay for. It could perhaps be argued that the decline of our own culture, manifested by a lack of imagination and original art, is caused by the disappearance of a rich, educated and imaginative upper class following standardization, a new guild system in the form of trade unions, heavy taxes, and so on. Such a theory could be opposed but hardly on Said's grounds that it aims at a domination of the countries or the civilizations involved.

Now if I use the same theory in our field, the Islamic world, I ask: Could the rise of Islamic culture have been furthered by the disappearance of trade barriers and the creation of a class of rich merchants[10] following the spread of the Caliphate? And could the decline of Islamic culture be the result of the division of the Caliphate into smaller states with more frontiers, more trade barriers, more taxes and fewer rich, refined and imaginative people to further culture? What role did the *waqf* institution and the guild system, the *ḥisba*, play in the decline of Islamic culture?

When I ask these questions I make the Orient, Islamic culture and society, the object of my interest, but how could anything one studies be other than an object? (A sociological study of professors would make objects of us — would that matter?) And this object is foreign to me, because if it were familiar, if I knew it already, there would be no need to ask questions, no need to subject it to study. But I cannot understand how by being foreign it should arouse any feelings in me but those of curiosity, the wish to know if my questions are pertinent, if there are answers to them which could help me to understand the reasons for the rise and decline of Islamic culture. I cannot see that any judgement is involved. If I find the answers, I cannot see that they could be used to dominate the Islamic world any more than the same questions and answers concerning Europe would aim at dominating Europe. Thus, if theories and methods used by historians of economy, religion, history, literature when studying European countries are legitimate, why shouldn't they be if used when studying Oriental countries?

When I say, contrary to Said, that no judgement is involved I do it with reservation, not only because many Orientalists have pronounced judgements on the Orient, on Islam, on the Prophet, but also because a certain measure of judgement is involved in any activity. In the words of the German Manès Sperber, "Man appraises when observing, he observes tendentiously and according to a principle of selection, he appraises when thinking, judging, acting. Thus all human activity is an appraising one."[11] But this is part of the human condition and is not particular to Oriental studies — they have it in common with all scholarship. And the judgements will be corrected. As Hourani says, in the course of time the process of judgement on Islam by Christians has been permeated by something else: by a process of study and understanding of what Islam is in itself. By the end of the eighteenth century this increased understanding of Islam has affected the judgement passed on Islam by the secular thinkers.[12]

Said also reproaches the West for not giving any attention to the basic questions: why Middle East studies? and for whom?[13] Since he himself does not answer these questions we now leave him and go back to our subject which consists more or less of these questions.

As we have seen, the main purposes of Islamic studies have been several:

to obtain knowledge about Islamic science or culture for practical use, e.g., in medicine, or for knowledge's own sake,
to refute Islam and facilitate missionary work,
to support biblical studies,
to satisfy a romantic attraction,
to gain political influence, or
to profit from business.

Of these, Said has stressed the refutation of Islam and the wish to gain political influence and to create a European Orient, whereas I have tried to show that to emphasize these motives in such a general way is unjust.

Still, much of what Said contends is worthy of being taken in earnest. In my example of a theory explaining the rise and decline of Islamic culture, from economical causes, I pointed out the importance of a rich, refined and imaginative upper class able to judge what kind of culture to support, i.e., the importance of the role of the patron. Today the patrons are mostly politicians and officials, a fact that obviously influences culture.

Now scholarship also has to be paid for, and that makes the scholar to some extent dependent on his patrons for material support, promotion and prestige in society. When the purpose of scholarly studies diverges from his own in the view of national assemblies and governments, ministries and university councils, and the public, the scholar might feel tempted, at least outwardly, to adhere to a purpose foreign to him.

Thus Said may be right when he accuses scholars of being in the service of the powers that be, of supporting colonialism, of using their knowledge in the service of extrinsic causes. It is easy to add to Said's examples. Said himself in several places mentions the so-called "area studies" where Orientalists and other scholars do "interdisciplinary" work together.

"Area studies" and "interdisciplinary" are but new words for the usual Oriental studies, as all Orientalists must be aware of, and if they use them themselves it is only to make their studies more important in the eyes of the public. Oriental studies *are* "area studies" and have always been, the area being the Oriental country or countries involved. Likewise, Islamic studies have never been concerned only with Islamic religion but with the whole civilization including, of course, the languages in which this civilization has expressed itself. And these studies have always been "interdisciplinary" since Oriental philology is concerned with all kind of texts: religious, historical, social, scientific etc. The problem is not that the Orientalists have not been willing to work together with other scholars; the problem is that other scholars usually are not able to read the texts, and thus the Orientalist is himself forced to be also an historian, etc.

I have mentioned texts. Said reproached Orientalists for being text-centred. But how could you study Islam except by the texts, written or to a lesser extent oral? Even if you study the behaviour of people or their artefacts you can hardly do it without any written or spoken comments, i.e., without texts.[14] And when you have no direct access to the texts, when you do not know their language, your information will be only selective, and for that selection you will be dependent on translations by others — you will not be able to select your information yourself.

Another instance of opportune lip-service on the part of the Orientalists is when they stress the importance of their knowledge for trade with Oriental states which often goes together with the advocating of area studies. The idea of preferring university studies that have business value is nothing new. In Sweden in 1750 mercantilism led the authorities to propose the abolition of Oriental studies at Uppsala University in favour of a new chair in physics which was considered more useful. The University Council however, opposed this proposition and succeeded in preserving the Oriental studies.

There is nothing to be said against trade with Oriental and other states, and if knowledge of the culture of the peoples with which we trade can smooth the path, which I am sure it can, we should all help to spread such knowledge. But what ought to be stressed is that the *purpose* of Arabic or Islamic or Oriental studies is *not* to promote trade, any more than it is to facilitate missionary work or to support Biblical studies or even to influence present-day politics. Islamic studies could do all that too, if you wish, but that is not its principal aim, and it is rather silly of the Orientalists to try to build their existence on such changing and ephemeral grounds.

What then *is* the purpose of our studies if not a commercial, not a missionary or Biblical and not a political one? It is, of course, a scholarly one: the purpose of scholarship is to create knowledge, also knowledge that is of no practical use, knowledge irrespective of any eventual use, all the more so as you do not know, what knowledge will turn out to be practically useful.

One classical example is the thesis on Islamic water-wheels which was scorned as typical of useless scholarship, but soon turned out to a valuable tool to ameliorate irrigation in many countries.[15] Another example is my edition of al-Hamdānī's book on gold and silver which is now used by the Geological Survey of North Yaman for prospecting purposes.[16]

On the other hand, the results of studies carried out for a specific practical purpose may nevertheless be of scholarly importance. An old and a recent example will show this. When, at the beginning of the sixteenth century, Pedro de Alcalá published a dictionary and a grammar of the spoken language of Granada, he added such texts that a missionary among the Muslims needed most, but the solid philological method he used made his work independent of the extrinsic cause for its production.[17] And when the chair in Semitic languages at the University of Göteborg was changed into a chair in Modern Arabic — whatever that may be[18] — and the importance of spoken Arabic was stressed, the intention was clearly to improve relations with the Arab world — not least the commercial ones — but the outcome was the scholarly study of Arabic dialects, of little practical use but of scientific value since the dialects are rapidly changing and maybe even disappearing.

Thus, I repeat: the purpose of our studies is to create knowledge, irrespective of any eventual use. This can be done only in freedom. The reason why we study the Orient, Islam, the Arab world, is that if we did not know anything about the languages, the religions and the civilizations of the Orient, our knowledge would not be universal: there would be big gaps in our general knowledge of religion, languages, history, literature, history of learning etc.

Scholarship is an integral part of our culture. I said that it *creates* knowledge. Scholarship is thus a creative art, and the scholar is an artist. By means of his creative imagination which is fed on his previous knowledge he is able to see something new that nobody has seen before him and that he tries to present to the world, as an original creation, just as any other work of art.

In the same way as many artists have tried to imagine and recreate the picture of, e.g., the Virgin Mary with her Child or mourning at the foot of the cross, many scholars have tried to imagine the picture of Muhammad as a prophet and a statesman. The differences in view of Muhammad in Western scholarship range from total rejection to total acceptance. Which picture is the true one? You cannot tell. They are all — and Said blames their authors for this — not truth but representations.

But you can say: this picture impresses me and others than me, this picture bears witness to imaginative understanding, this picture is convincing. Today we would say that the picture of the Prophet Muhammad, created by Tor Andrae, a sympathetic portrait showing a man who inspires confidence in men of strength and integrity, a man readily moved to smile, a kind man, gentle also towards his enemies, is more true than those earlier ones showing Muhammad as a false prophet and a bad man, because it seems more likely that the man who was instrumental in creating one of the world's most important religions had great positive qualities rather than the opposite. But as for the really *true* picture of the Prophet — *Allāhu a'lam*.

Said is right when he says that the Orient is a creation of the Orientalists, but he is wrong when he blames them for it, because how could it be otherwise? Scholarship does not aim at truth.[19] Apart from the fact that it is often impossible to arrive at the truth since our understanding of a foreign language and background, distant in time and space, is incomplete and our sources often unreliable, final truth would stifle all discussion, as Lessing argued, or as the Tunisian scholar Hichem Djaït says today: "L'idée de perfection bloque tout processus de perfectionnement."[20] Scholarship aims at contributing new ideas to a continuing discussion, in the words of H. S. Nyberg, "in making clear our own positions in a discussion that will perhaps always remain undecided".[21] New truths will oust old ones, as Umberto Eco says: "Le uniche verità che servono sono strumenti da buttare."[22] And even a blatantly bad idea might be of value when it calls forward as a refutation another better idea which would perhaps otherwise never have seen the light.

Of course the Orient, or rather the idea of the Orient, is different for a Dane than for an Arab, just as Denmark, or the idea of Denmark, is different for an Arab than for a Dane. Again, Denmark means something else also to a Swede. You cannot blame the Swedes because they have a different picture of Denmark than the Danes have, because to them Denmark is an object, something they judge in another way than the Danes can do. Even if the picture is not just, it might serve a purpose, as Albert Hourani says: "... it may have been this harsh judgement which enabled Lammens to distinguish so clearly certain important aspects of early Islamic history".[23]

There is no reason why only Orientals should study and judge the importance of the Orient, any more than that only Swedes should study and judge the importance of, e.g., the Swedish eighteenth century scholar Linnaeus. He belongs as much to, say, the English, who have their Linnaean Society, or to the world at large.

A South Arabian counterpart of Linnaeus is al-Hamdānī, who lived in the tenth century. As a philosopher, historian, geographer and poet, he belongs to the culture of South Arabia of his time but also to the culture of modern Yaman, he belongs to the culture of the Arabs and to the culture of Islam. But not only that: he is also an heir to Greek, Iranian and Indian culture. Since his works have been edited, translated and studied in Europe,[24] he now also belongs to our culture, and European scholarship, Scandinavian scholarship, have contributed to a better knowledge of al-Hamdānī also in the Arab world. Thus, Orientals and Europeans have mutually contributed to each other's culture. This means that the Muslim and Arab, al-Hamdānī, and his works now belong to our universal human culture in the same way as the Christian and Swede, Linnaeus, does.

This interaction has another side. Not only has Orientalist scholarship and its picture of the Orient enriched European culture in many ways from the Middle Ages onwards, but as Said points out already at the beginning of his book (p. 6): Europe's own culture gained in strength and identity by setting itself off against the Orient. Today, when Western technology seems to efface many of the differences between the cultures, the question of cultural identity is probably more actual than before, and the importance of foreign cultures as a help to look upon our own has consequently increased.

Conversely: The fact that Europeans look upon the Orient and its peoples with the eyes of Europeans is of particular value to the Orientals who are thus able to compare their own view with ours. If we looked upon the Orient with the same eyes as the Orientals, if our view of the Orient were identical with theirs — what interest would this view have, what could it teach the Orientals? With only their own picture of the Orient the Orientals would be considerably poorer.[25]

Returning to the conception of scholarship as art, this also means that scholars are artists. They are moved by intellectual curiosity, they are people of imagination, creating new ideas, discovering new coherences — I now disregard the diligence in collecting and the exactitude and lucidity in presenting the facts which are also necessary[26] — and this newness of their conceptions makes them uncertain of their value. If you do what other people do you are not open to criticism, but if you do something on your own, that has not been done before, you do not know if it will be approved.

Therefore, great scholars, as great artists, are often very unsure of themselves. This uncertainty shows itself in polemics and sensitiveness to criticism. It shows itself in their need of appreciation and recognition. Great scholars, as great artists, are vain. Vanity can be taken as a sign of creative imagination, since signs of recognition such as honours, rank, titles, academicals and other marks of distinction were not invented by small and insignificant people but since time immemorial by the intelligent and creative to assure themselves of their value to society. And this value, the value of the artists, scholars, painters, authors etc. and their works is great, indeed, because, after all, as human beings we live *by* useful knowledge but we live *for* culture, and when we are gone, our age will be judged not so much by its politics and commerce with their transient results, as by its culture, the creations of which will remain.

Consequently the real, intrinsic and ultimate purpose of Islamic studies — as of all studies in the humanities — is to contribute to human culture, and what we contribute is our pictures of Islam and of Islamic civilization from the beginning to this day, pictures which are created out of our imagination but based on substantial facts, at best original creations attracting onlookers by their beauty and coherence, their simplicity and logic, their boldness and originality.

Professor Rundgren in Uppsala in 1972, and before him the Swedish Archbishop Söderblom in 1920 in lectures called "Scholarship as a way of life", talked about the scholar as a pure, unselfish man who solely seeks the truth without a thought of utility or renown.[27] Said's picture shows a biased Westerner and bigoted Christian hostile to Islam and the Orientals and striving to dominate the east.

I look upon the scholar as a human being, not always as free, independent and sincere as one could wish but, at best, an explorer, driven by intellectual curiosity, striving to find out what was unknown before he made it known, an imaginative artist, creating what nobody has created before he did, to obtain prestige, fame and worldly immortality.

The first picture is worthy of being held up to us as an ideal, the second one seems distorted, the third one is surely more realistic, more human, more fascinating, and showing more of what no culture could do without and thus, I think, more true.

2

THE CONTEMPORARY DEBATE IN THE MUSLIM WORLD ON THE DEFINITION OF "HUMAN RIGHTS"

Jan Hjärpe

In contemporary use, the term "Human Rights" has received its connotations and its concrete meaning from the *UN Declaration on Human Rights* of 10 December 1948 and the later Conventions intended for its explication and application. This Declaration and the content of the prevailing concept of Human Rights stem from the European history of ideas and its conceptual categories, implications and assumptions. These categories and premises are often regarded as self-evident, but they are rooted in European legal tradition and its development in history.[1]

The UN Declaration has its specific background in the experiences of World War II. I use the term, "Human Rights" as defined in the UN Declaration.

In regions of the world where, despite a dominant westernized culture, other experiences, traditions, cultures and ideas exist, some of the points in the UN Declaration, and in the Western concept of Human Rights, can be regarded as controversial. But the impact of the dominant Western culture is still strong enough to necessitate that the terminology and categorization of the UN Declaration be repeated and reflected in the texts intended to criticize it and to supplant it. (The "apologetical pitfall": one is influenced by that which one is criticizing.)

In the Muslim world, the concept of Human Rights is discussed intensively, and many attempts have been made by individuals and organizations to determine and declare what an Islamic content of the concept of Human Rights should be. The mere existence of the debate shows that the content of the UN Declaration is regarded as controversial, at last in some respects.

The very basis of these discussions and alternative declarations is that the UN Declaration is seen as not entirely compatible with the Islamic Sharīʿa or even with its foundation, the Qurʾān and the Prophet's Sunna. This incompatibility — be it real or imagined — becomes problematic when the Sharī'a and its bases are not interpreted historically, but are regarded as independent of historical conditions, and when the Sharī'a, regarded as the absolute Law of God, is *objectified* and proclaimed as the Law of society, the juridical basis of the State in all fields of jurisprudence, and not simply as a system of rules or moral values limited to the community of *believers*, i.e., when the Divine Law is regarded as existent and valid independent of those who believe in it.

However, even the most "integristic" groups are eager to use the term "Human Rights" and to incorporate it in their own cognitive universes.[2]

Opinions in the Muslim world differ considerably as to the purpose, scope, fields of competence, and principles of interpretation and application of the Islamic Sharī'a and the nature of its relation to the legislation of the State. This produces different attitudes towards the UN Declaration. We find on the one hand an enthusiastic *acceptance* of it where the UN Declaration is regarded as a genuine expression of Islamic values and principles, an expression formed by the conditions of contemporary society, just as the Qur'ānic revelation was formed under conditions of Arab society at the time of al-Jāhiliyya. But we also find the total *rejection* of it as incompatible with the eternal and unchangeable Law of God, and, as a document of purely *human* origin, utterly devoid of any interest or importance.[3]

In order to systematize these controversial points, I have chosen to describe the attitude that rejects some of the UN Declaration, but which remains within its framework, uses its terminology, and has the intention of providing an alternative to it seen as applicable in a contemporary society.[4] This attitude we could perhaps call "moderate integrism".

I will first enumerate the points in the UN Declaration which are debated, explicitly or implicitly, in the contemporary Muslim discussion.

Even the *UN Charter*, in its first article, is problematic when it stipulates one of the goals of the organization to be:

> To achieve international co-operation. . . in promoting and encouraging respect for human rights and for fundamental freedoms for all *without distinction* as to race, *sex*, language, or *religion*.

(Note the formulation: not "equally" but the much more precise "without distinction". Thus one's sex or religion must not be regarded as a matter of any consequence from a legal point of view.)

This is repeated in the Declaration, Article 2. Then we have the following points:

Art. 4 with its prohibition of slavery.

Art. 5 "No one shall be subjected to torture or to *cruel, inhuman or degrading* treatment *or punishment.*"

Art. 7 "*All are equal before the law* and are entitled without discrimination to equal protection of the law. All are entitled to *equal protection against any discrimination in violation of this Declaration* and against any incitement to such discrimination"

Art. 8 and 10 treating the *equality* for everyone "to a fair and public hearing by an independent and *impartial tribunal*".

Art. 11:2 against retroactive application of laws.

Art. 16:1 "Men and women of full age, *without any limitation* due to race, nationality *or religion*, have the right to marry and to found a family. They are entitled to *equal rights* as to marriage, *during marriage and at its dissolution.*"

Art. 18 "Everyone has the right to freedom of thought, conscience and religion: *this right includes freedom to change his religion or belief. . .*"

Art. 19 Treating freedom of opinion and expression.

Art. 21:2 "Everyone has the right of *equal access to public service* in his country."

Art. 21:3 "*The will of the people shall be the basis of the authority of government. . .*"

These points in the Declaration are underlined in subsequent international conventions. Still more stress is there laid on the equality of men's and women's rights.

The implicit premise

The UN Declaration of Human Rights is built on an unstated premise: *secularism*. Society is secular, religion must not be defined as an order for the society/state. Laws are secular in the sense that they are independent of the authority of a specific religion. A law has its legal force by the human acceptance of it (=legislation), and it is thus possible to mention a date when a law begins or comes into force; it is not of divine or sacred character and outside the category of Time. The file of competence belonging to *religion* lies exclusively in *individual* free choice (cf. the formulation of Art. 18), and to *family* decisions (cf.

Art. 26:3 and the right of parents to choose in regard to the education of their children), but this is not true for *the law*, as the law shall be applied to all equally, without distinction as to religion. The basis of *the authority* of government is the *will of the people*, i.e. human sovereignty, not divine.

The root of the conflict between the notions of Human Rights in the UN Declaration, and the "Muslim alternatives" to it, is this implicit premise of secularism.

The points mentioned above become problematic in two ways: first, when they are seen as incompatible with Islamic Sharī'a regarded as a Divine Law, of heavenly origin and authority, and not, as in the UN Declaration, of human origin and authority; secondly, when this Divine Law is regarded not only as a code for the indidvidual believer for his/ her family, and for the group of believers, but is objectified[5] as normative for society, seen as a legal system of divine authority valid and applied regardless of the individual's (or the majority's) degree of acceptance or belief in it.

In what ways can the points mentioned above be regarded as contrary to the Sharī'a? (Sharī'a in the sense of a traditional interpretation of it. I shall not discuss the differences between the madhāhib in traditional fiqh, or the contemporary use of ijtihād and the current application of Sharī'a laws in different Muslim countries.)[6]

(*Art. 2*) When religion (not only Islam but "religion" in general) is regarded as normative for society and a system of jurisprudence, the consequence must be that "freedom of religion" includes the right *not* to be equal before the law, in the sense that one has the right to apply different laws, at least in part, according to the individual's religious affiliation ("affiliation", not "belief", as the personal belief of the individual is not decisive for his "religion" in the legal sense; cf. below).

Muslims and non-Muslims have — according to traditional Sharī'a interpretation — different legal status, e.g. as witnesses in court, besides the differences in family law. Likewise, traditionally interpreted Sharī'a differentiates between men and women in rank, functions, competence as witnesses in court (in the proportion 2 to 1), etc.

(*Art. 4*) The more extreme traditionalists maintain that slavery cannot be prohibited as a principle, as the Qur'ān contains rules as to slaves, slaves' rights, slave trade etc. It can of course be abolished in practice; but the non-slave status is in itself not a "Human Right".

(*Art. 5*) From our point of view the traditional Sharī'a punishments (ḥudūd, the "limits") with amputations, flogging, stoning, and also the application of *lex talionis* (qiṣāṣ) in cases of murder or infliction of corporal injuries, must be regarded as "cruel, inhuman or degrading treatment or punishment".

(*Art. 7, 8 and 10*) Traditional Sharī'a implies differences (i.e., makes distinctions) between the status of Muslims and non-Muslims in legal matters, in the function of the court, and in the degree of legal protection: e.g. there are differential punishments in the *lex talionis* for the murder of a Muslim and of a non-Muslim Dhimmī (in the proportion 10 to 1 for the diya, or "wergild", due to be paid) as well as between men and women (2 to 1). These traditional rules for ḥudūd, qiṣāṣ and diya are now applied in practice in the Islamic Republic of Iran, and (although much less stringently) in the Sudan after the law reforms of 1983.

(*Art. 16:1*) Traditional Sharī'a family law prohibits marriage between a Muslim woman and a non-Muslim man, and it gives the man (but not the woman) an unconditional right to divorce. It also stipulates different rights and duties in the family for men and women. They are perhaps regarded as of "equal value", but not as equals in the sense of having the same rights and duties. These are not "without distinction".

(*Art. 18*) The traditional Sharī'a gives certain non-Muslims (Jews, Christians, Zoroastrians, and — dependent on the interpretation — other groups too) the right to practise their own religions, also as a jurisdictional system, but it prohibits, customarily by capital punishment, apostasy from Islam (i.e. *change* of religion *from* Islam to another religion or to atheism). This means that the legal affiliation of a person to a religion, especially to Islam, does not necessarily imply his belief in it. Freedom of religion is not general, as it is applicable in principle only to those who are given *dhimmī* status (as they are classified as "people of the Book").

(*Art. 21:2*) Affiliation to Islam is often regarded as a condition for certain higher posts in the administration of the state.

In most parts of the Muslim World there exists, as a legacy from the colonial era, a more or less secular legal system applied in nearly all the domains. The common exception is Family Law. Some states (Saudi Arabia, Iran, Sudan etc) apply Sharī'a law, although with very different interpretations. Others regard "the principles of Islam Sharī'a" as a source, or even as "the primary source of legislation",[7] i.e., the Sharī'a is *not* the law of the land but a source of inspiration for the human legislators.

In several countries we can see a tendency, due to pressure from the "integrists", to *adapt* legislation to the Sharī'a laws, but without abandoning the principle that the state *institutes* the laws. Opinions differ as to what this adaptation of the laws will mean in practice, how the Sharī'a is to be interpreted, and *to whom* the authority of interpretation belongs.

Examples from the Constitutions

The concepts of Sharī'a play a role even when a state declares itself secular and secularistic, as Turkey has done. The repudiation of the notion of religion as a legal system and as a social order means a setting aside of what we regard as Human Rights.

The Turkish constitution of 1982, Art. 24, prohibits the notion of religious law as a law for society. All propaganda in that direction is also prohibited and liable to severe punishment. There are also laws against the use of certain titles, garments and outfits, Dervish convents, and the law of marriage etc. (Art. 174). These things can be seen as contrary to Art. 18 in the UN Declaration (freedom of opinion and religion). But simultaneously the purpose of these articles in the Turkish constitution is to safeguard that which is the implicit and necessary premise of the Declaration, i.e. secularism.

We can compare Turkey's constitution with that of Egypt. The latter is also a secular constitution in the sense that it expresses *human sovereignty* (Art. 3), the State has a *legislation*, laws are instituted by the People's Assembly. Its character as a legislating body is not questioned by Art. 2 which points to Islamic Sharī'a as "the primary source of legislation", as it is the Assembly which interprets it and enforces the laws. The Board of 'Ulamā' is only consultative. In practice this means that the laws are identical with or very close to the Western secular legal tradition, although in the field of family law a certain reverence is shown for religious rules. This is in accordance with the explicit concept in the UN Declaration of religion as of special relevance to family life (cf. above). The question of men's and women's equality is obviously seen as somewhat problematic in that respect:

> The State guarantees the co-ordination between the woman's duties to the family and her career in society, the equality with men in the fields of political, social, cultural and economic life . . . *without any violation of the rules of Islamic Sharia.*

It is of course of special interest to study the Iranian Constitution of 1979, as it explicitly claims to represent Islamic Sharī'a (in accordance with the Ja'farī madhhab) as applied to a contemporary society, while at the same time trying to translate that legal tradition in the terms and concepts of Western legal tradition, and especially into the prestigious terminology of the UN Declaration of Human Rights. Here follow a few selected examples.

The basis is formulated in the Constitution's Art. 2:4. The State is based on belief in the "justice of God *in creation* and in *Divine Law*". This means a belief that it is natural that human beings, the creations of God, obey the Law of God, i.e. the Sharī'a. The *authority to decide* what God's Law is, that is to interpret it, is given entirely to the 'Ulamā', the "religious specialists" (Art. 2:iia and Art. 4, cf. Art. 72 and 91 – 9).

"Absolute sovereignty over the World and mankind is God's" (Art. 56). The sovereignty belongs to God, which *in practice* means the 'Ulamā', who decide what God's Law is, not the people (cf. Art. 57).

It is laid down that Islamic Sharī'a shall be applied in all fields, and according to the Ja'farī madhhab. The exception is family law, where Art. 12 establishes that Muslims of other madhāhib, and dhimmīs (i.e. Jews, Christians and Zoroastrians, the only three permitted non-Muslim religions) follow their own rules. This means that the differences in family law between members of the different religions, and between the sexes in Sharī'a law, are constitutional.

Let us quote some of the Articles in the Iranian Constitution, which are related to the Articles of the UN Declaration mentioned above.[8]

Art. 19: "The people of Iran, regardless of their ethnic, family and tribal origin, shall enjoy equal rights. Colour, race, language and the like shall not be cause for privilege."

We may notice that the world *"religion"* is *not* mentioned (cf. Art. 2 in the UN Declaration).

Art. 20: "All citizens of the nation, whether men or women, are equally *protected* by the law. They also enjoy *human*, political, economic and cultural *rights according to Islamic standards.*"

All are "equally protected by the law", but it is not said that they are "equal before the law". Likewise the term "human rights" is qualified by the phrase "according to Islamic standards", i.e. they are not defined by the UN Declaration. This qualification (or limitation) is repeated frequently:

Art. 21: "The government shall guarantee the rights of women in all areas *according to Islamic standards . . .*"

Art. 24: "Publications and the press may express ideas freely, *except when they are contrary to Islamic principles. . .*" (cf. Art 175).

This limitation of the freedom of expression and of the press is total, as no field in society is exempt from the authority of the Sharī'a and of the 'Ulamā' (institutionalized in the wilāyat-i faqīh).

We continue the comparison with the UN Declaration by quoting from the Iranian Constitution:

Art. 28: "Every person has the right to choose the profession he wishes, *provided it is not contrary to the principles of Islam.*"

Art. 38: "Any form of torture *to obtain confession or acquire information* is forbidden. . ."

This means that only torture intended for the purpose mentioned is prohibited. Flogging, amputations and stoning as *punishments* (or as legal retaliations) are constitutional, and applied in Iran's Criminal code in accordance with Art. 61 of the Constitution.

Art. 61: "The judicial power. . . shall establish *punishment according to the Law of God"*.

In this connexion I quote the protest which the Director General of the Foreign Press Department in Tehran wrote to *Time* magazine [9] this year (1984):

> Your article 'Torture: a Worldwide Epidemic' [April 16] makes two references to my country, which has been subjected to a campaign by the Western press to tarnish its image and reputation. In Iran, stoning is not a form of torture but a punishment officially sanctioned by Iran's new penal code based on the holy Koran and Islamic Sharia. It is not used against political offenders but against ordinary criminals guilty of serious offenses such as adultery and pederasty. . .

The rituals and procedures of the Tribunals as to proofs, evaluations of witnesses and oaths etc., follow the patterns designed by the Ja'farī tradition and thus differ considerably from the procedure in Western courts. It is Western jurisprudence which forms the basis of the UN Declaration.

As to the retroactive force of the laws, we can quote:

Art. 49: "The Government shall confiscate wealth derived from usury, . . ., *gambling,* . . . from the establishment of *places of corruption,* and from other *illegitimate* sources. . ."

The crimes against the Sharī'a laws will thus be punished although these laws did not exist before the revolution.

It can be of some interest to see how Yassin Omer al-Imam, a leader of the Muslim Brotherhood in the Sudan, comments on the Western — and international — criticism of the amputations, floggings and stonings in Sudan after the enforcement of Sharī'a ḥudūd laws in 1983:

> In the Islamic Sharia, Hudud (penal laws) enjoy the strongest constitutional force; being definite, expressed in the texts with absolute certainty and

related to God and His boundaries [hudūd!] over which man should not exercise any discretion. Technically they are what lawyers call the 'law above the laws'. God, the Creator of man, has so engineered these basic laws *as to protect all human rights* (*sic*) and provide ultimate justice within human societies.[10]

The Law of God is above all other laws, God is the Creator of Man, thus His Law must be "Human Rights" by definition. Then since these punishments are included in the Law of God they cannot be against "Human Rights". On the contrary they actually constitute "Human Rights", or at least they protect them.

This reasoning shows clearly that the premise is entirely different from the premises of the UN Declaration of Human Rights. The term "Human Rights" here assumes a meaning which is totally different from the concept of Human Rights in the UN Declaration; the difference between "divine law" and "human right". And this holds true even when we find similarities between the Articles of the UN Declaration and the texts proposed by various Muslim bodies. It is the very premises which are incompatible.

The Dhaka Declaration

At the 14th Islamic Conference of Foreign Ministers in 1983 in Dhaka the text of a proposed declaration on "Human Rights" was discussed. The Conference did not accept the proposed text, with the exception of the Preamble. But in this Preamble we can read:

> The member states of the Organisation of the Islamic Conference affirm their belief in Allah, Lord of all the worlds . . who created man . . . [and] made him his *vicegerent* on earth to develop it, entrusted him with duties. . .

Man is the "vicegerent" of God, His khalīfa. The text alludes to the Qur'ān (2:30/28). The meaning here is that as Man is the vicegerent, or steward of God on Earth, he is obliged to follow God's "instructions" for that stewardship, i.e. God's Law. Sovereignty belongs to God alone (which in practice means to those who are considered official interpreters of the Qur'ān and the Sunna of Islam).

The member states also expressed that they

> . . .believe in *fulfilling the injunctions of the unchanging Islamic Shari'ah* . . . which is universal in its applicability. . .

and

> . . . reaffirm the cultural and historical role of the Islamic Ummah . . . *to guide all humanity*. . . and to affirm [man's] freedom and right to a dignified *life in accordance with the Islamic Shari'ah* . . .

"Human Rights" not compatible with the rules of the Sharī'a are thus by definition not to be called "Human Rights".

> The member-states . . . believe that *fundamental rights and freedom according to Islam (sic)* are an integral part of the Islamic faith and that *no one* . . .

(i.e. not even the UN or any other authority)

> . . . shall have the right to abolish them either in whole or in part or to violate them . . . they are *binding divine commands (sic)*, which are contained in his revealed books, and *which were sent through the last of his prophets* . . .

> (The member states) ". . . believe that all human beings . . . being the descendants of Adam, . . . are *equal in dignity and basic duties* . . ."

"In dignity and basic duties " — as defined by the authorities of the Sharī'a — but not necessarily equal in other respects.

Apart from the Preamble the text of the Declaration was not accepted by the Conference as it would have conflicted with the existing laws in many of the member states. Nevertheless, its content is of interest. It reflects the continuing debate and the pressure from those trying to promote a more "integristic" interpretation of Islam in society. I quote here from the account of it in the Muslim magazine *Impact International*.[11] The magazine propounds this concept of "integrism", and thus presents the content in a very positive way.

One should note especially the *modifications* in comparison with the UN Declaration. Themes and terminology are very much those of the UN Declaration, so every addition or omission can be regarded as a reservation against that which the UN Declaration says or implies. (In the quotation below I have omitted that which agrees with the UN Declaration and have only quoted what disagrees in some way or other.)

> *All human beings* [come] from one family *united by their subordination to Allah*. All men are *equal in dignity and basic duties* and responsibilities . . . The family is the foundation of society and marriage is its basis and no obstacle based on *race, colour or nationality* shall prevent exercise of this right. . . .

We may notice that "or religion" is omitted!

> . . . Woman is equal to man *in human dignity* and *has her own rights* to enjoy *as well as duties* to perform. Woman has *her* civil rights and financial independence and the right to retain her name and lineage. [The] *Husband* is responsible for the maintenance and welfare of the family.

It is thus stated here, although in positive terms, that women and men have *different* duties and rights.

> Everyone shall have the *right to follow the religion of Allah* and *no one shall be compelled to change* his religion to another or to atheism.

Freedom of religion is here defined as freedom to follow "the religion of Allah", which we may suppose means that it is limited to Ahl al-Kitāb (Muslims, Jews, Christians, Zoroastrians, and other groups accorded dhimmī status). This freedom of religion included the right not be be compelled to change religion. Note the point: The *right to change* religion, or to be without one, is thus *not* regarded as a Human Right.

> Man is born free and no one has the right to humiliate, oppress or exploit him. There can be *no subjugation but to Allah the Almighty*.
> Everyone is entitled to own propety individually or in partnership with others *in accordance with the Shari'ah*. . .
> Confiscation of property is prohibited in all cases except in accordance with the Shari'ah. . .
> It is not permitted to arrest an individual, to restrict his freedom, to exile *or punish him without legal reasons*. . .
> Right to freedom of opinion and expression by every means *within the principles of the Shari'ah* is guaranteed.
> *Individuals are equal before Shari'ah* (justice). *There is no difference between the ruler and the ruled, in this respect.*

The freedoms and rights mentioned here are qualified with the phrase "according to Sharī'a". The Sharī'a is above all human legislation. Over the legislating body, the people and the authority of the State stand the authorities representing the Divine Law. Individuals are not equal before the laws, but "equal before Sharī'a". Sovereignty does not belong to the people, it is not a "Human Right", but a divine prerogative.

The "Dhaka Declaration" as a whole (including the parts not quoted here) can be characterized as a summary of Abū A'lā Mawdūdī's "Human Rights in Islam", since 1975.

Conclusions

1. The themes and even the formulations of the UN Declaration of Human Rights are regarded as important and prestigious. One is well aware of its role in international opinion. The alternatives presented follow its pattern in many ways. When Islamic Sharī'a is interpreted and applied in a way which makes it incompatible with the UN Declaration and its concepts, this is seen as embarrassing.

2. As Islamic Sharī'a is more and more frequently seen and applied in this way, with enthusiasm or as a result of pressure from certain groups, there will be further conflicts between the UN Declaration's definition of "Human Rights" and an integristic "Islamic" definition of them.

We can also see from the reports on the Human Rights situation in several Muslim countries[12] that the topics mentioned above are the most problematic: The ḥudūd punishments and the qiṣāṣ, the legal status and the rights of women, discrimination of non-Muslims, especially the non Ahl al-Kitāb (e.g. the Bahā'īs in Iran), the limitations of the freedom of opinion, expression, and religion ("religion" in the sense given in the UN Declaration).

3. The main purpose of the Muslim debate on Human Rights is apologetic.[13] (This is perhaps the reason why it arouses almost no interest whatsoever outside the Muslim community.)

One of the main themes in the apologetic attitude is to show that in the cases where they do not agree the rules of the Sharī'a (=Law of God) are much more in accordance with inborn human nature (=God's creation) than the secular UN Declaration of Human Rights. This argument is used especially to justify the differences in the legal status of the sexes: differences in rights and duties presumed to correspond to the biological and psychological differences between the sexes. The main premise is that since God created the nature of man, and gave us the Law (Sharī'a), its strictures cannot, by definition, be human. They must be "Human Rights".

4. As there is a tendency in the discussion in the Muslim world today to attribute to the term "Human Rights" at least in parts a content other

than that of the UN Declaration, *based on altogether different premises*, it will be necessary to be more precise when criticizing phenomena in the Muslim countries as being against "Human Rights". We must indicate explicitly which article(s) in the Declaration the criticism alludes to, to show in what ways the phenomenon in question is not compatible with the Declaration, and with its implicit premises. There is no consensus today on the meaning and significance of the term "Human Rights".

Such precision in arguments could also be of value for those Muslim groups and individuals who do not agree with the interpretation of Islam and the religion's function in a society promoted by the "integristic" groups, and who repudiate their concept of the term "Human Rights". The conflict is not between "Islam" and the "West", but between different attitudes toward the function of "religion" in society.

3

THE SOCIO-POLITICAL ASPECTS
OF THE MODERN ISLAMIC MISSION

Gasym Mamed Ogly Kerimov

The modern Islamic movement is both a religious and a socio-political revival and the Islamic mission takes a special place in this movement.

Modern Muslim missionary activity comprises the following tasks: propaganda for Islamic cultural values, for the Muslim way of life, and for Islamic moral standards. It also involves the struggle against the penetration of Western ideas into Muslim countries and defence of the rights of the Palestinians. Depending on different circumstances and situations the tasks of the mission vary.

The specific tasks of the Muslim mission in Africa are the elimination of local pagan religious beliefs and syncretic Africanized Christianity; the struggle against the Israeli and Zionist penetration into the African countries, the struggle against the diffusion of Marxism and of a scientific-materialistic world view and of atheistic ideas throughout the continent.

The general political tasks of the Muslim mission are to contribute to the political unity of the Muslim countries and to increase the role and prestige of the World Islamic League (with its headquarters in Saudi Arabia) in the Middle East and throughout the world. The missionaries try to prove that the Muslim countries are an independent third political force, on equal terms with the so-called "Soviet bloc" and the USA and their allies. According to the Muslim missionaries, the Islamic countries must reject both capitalist or socialist orientation. The slogan of the Islamic missionaries is "Neither East nor West, but the Islamic way". The main task of the "third world theory" is to overcome socio-economic and technical backwardness and to gain political independence for the Muslim countries. The Muslim countries have organized economic, cultural, scientific, technical and other committees within the framework of the World Islamic League.

In order to study the possibilities for scientific and technical progress in the Islamic regions, a number of scientific conferences and symposia have been held, e.g. "The Islamic solidarity in science and technology" (Saudi Arabia, 1976), "Technical progress in the Muslim countries" (London, European Islamic Centre, 1979), "The History of Science and Technology by Turkish Moslems" (Turkey, 1981), "Science in the Islamic State: present, past, future" (Pakistan, 1983) etc.

The Muslim missionaries do not conceal the fact that the Muslim world is at present behind the West in technology and industry. However, Islamic missionaries assert that the pioneers of European science, technology and philosophy were Muslims (Al-Rāzī's and Ibn Sīnā's works in medicine and mathematics; Al-Khawārizmī's, Ibn al-Haitham's and Al-Ferghānī's on astronomy; Ibn Sīnā's, Ibn Rushd's and others' on philosophy).

Islamic centres, financed by international Islamic organizations and rich oil-extracting countries, conduct their work in Europe, the USA, Canada, Japan, Australia, and Latin America.

These centres originated during the last 10 – 15 years. In countries where Islam is not a state religion, they may function as a Muslim headquarters.

There are large Islamic centres in London, Paris, Bonn, Hamburg, Rome and other cities. Islamic centres outside the Muslim countries maintain contacts with Muslim countries by means of regional and international Islamic organizations.

The World Islamic League with its headquarters in Mecca (Saudi Arabia) has a special department for Muslim minorities. International Islamic organizations have special economic funds to help Muslim minorities. They finance Islamic centres and build mosques. The Islamic centres have Muslim schools, libraries, Islamic culture centres, cinemas, clinics, and free centres for conducting Islamic funerals, commemorative feasts, Muslim holidays and the like. Some Islamic centres have press offices. Almost every big Islamic centre has its own newspapers, magazines, and Muslim calendars. The Islamic centres organize seminars, lectures, discussions, Islamic culture months, and expositions. Prominent scientists, politicians and specialists on Islam and Middle Eastern problems often participate in these initiatives.

The Islamic centres regularly study publications from Western Europe, the USA, Canada, Japan and other countries. They quickly react to anti-Islamic materials and inform international Islamic organizations and Muslim countries about them.

The Islamic centres work actively to propagate Islam, carrying out various political activities. West European newspapers and magazines describe the Islamic centres' activity. One can obtain information about the Islamic centres from their own press and from the press of the Muslim countries. For instance, in 1980 the Egyptian newspaper *Al-*

Ahram published sensational news about a Greek musician, Stefance, from London. Stefance appeared in the London Islamic centre unexpectedly and declared his wish to become a Muslim.

The newspaper gave the following information about the reasons of Stefance's conversion: he was in love with a Turkish girl named Fovzia who lived in London. According to Islamic law a Muslim cannot marry a non-Muslim, so to marry his beloved Stefance had the only way out — conversion to Islam. It should be noted that cases of conversion to Islam from other religions are used by the Islamic centres and press of the Muslim countries in order to propagate Islam and missionary work. For example, a few years ago the Egyptian *Minbar al-Islam* magazine (Cairo), informed readers of the conversion to Islam of a Christian hermit, Hariladis Davis, who had belonged to the Greek-Orthodox Church. Davis had been travelling for a long time in order to solve his problems about Christianity and Judaism. He related that he spoke to Christian and Judaic theologians, but they could not solve his problems. He could find answers for his questions only by turning to Islam. In Kenya, Davis converted to Islam and took the "Islamic" name Muhammad Tāleb. He explains his repudiation of Christianity by the fact that three things are contrary to common sense: studies about the soul, the Holy Trinity, and the Immaculate Conception.

As M. Taleb says, Islam and Christianity admit duality of the human nature (body and soul). An eternal soul is in a temporal body. When a man dies the soul separates from the body and exists for some time between heaven and earth. According to Christianity, it is possible to bring the soul closer to God by praying and by giving alms.

The doctrine of the Trinity cannot be understood by the human mind because otherwise the boundaries between God and man, between spirit and matter disappear. According to the Christian doctrine, a man can easily become God. From the Islamic point of view it is "shirk", the negation of a single God.

According to Islam there is no intermediary between God and man, a soul cannot "hang" between heaven and earth. In the Qur'ān it is said that "There is no other God but Allah, he is alone". There is no place for the Holy Spirit and Son. A man is a servant of God and there is no intermediary between them.[1]

The preferred form of mission work for Muslim theologians is to employ newly-converted Muslims. The goal of such a mission is for the Islamic centres to find out people who have converted to Islam from Christianity, Judaism or pagan religions and on their behalf explain the reasons for their conversion to Islam. Thereby the inadequacies of the other religious doctrines are revealed. For example, the journal of Egypt's Supreme Council for Islamic Affairs *Minbar al-Islam* (the faculty of Islam) has a special section called "Why I became a Muslim" in which articles of such a kind are published.

In their missionary work, the Islamic organization cite R. Garaudy (ex-member of the Political Bureau of the French Communist Party, now director of the International Institute for the Dialogue between Civilizations in Paris). In 1982 R. Garaudy converted to Islam, his new Arabic name is Rejā Jarūdī.[2] Garaudy believes that modern civilization and scientific technical progress have led the world to the brink of catastrophe. Garaudy's solution is to spread Islam throughout the world. Travelling in Arabic countries, Garaudy "proves" in his speeches that Marxism and Leninism and scientific socialism do not suit Muslims, that they can build an "Islamic socialism" based on the Qur'ān, and Sharī'a and on the works of Arabic Muslim scientists like Ibn-Khaldūn and Ibn-Rushd.

Islamic centres in Western countries receive financial help from the rich Arabic countries. These funds are used to buy and build mosques and Muslim study centres. Recently the Washington Islamic Centre announced that it had received more than 100,000 dollars from Saudi Arabia and other Arab countries and had bought a church in the centre of Colorado City (New Jersey), converting it into a mosque. This fact surprised journalists and irritated churchmen, who accused Colorado municipality of disrespecting Christianity. It was discovered that the half-ruined church has been standing empty for a long time and the municipality had no money to repair it.

Islamic centres in West European countries have a common viewpoint, according to which Europeans know little about Islam and its traditions, culture and habits. Their source of information comes mainly from distorted stories, spread long ago by the Crusaders and later by modern colonizers. Discussions and lectures organized in the West European Islamic centres try to acquaint Europeans with the "real Islam".

An Iranian doctor, 'Alī Parvar, who was educated in England, writes about it. The London Islamic Centre tries hard to propagate Islamic cultural and moral values in order to acquaint Europeans with Muslim culture. 'Alī Parvar says that in London he once discussed Islam with Englishmen and found that the only thing they knew about Islam was that Islamic laws permit polygamy. 'Alī Parvar decided to organize a discussion on this theme in order to demonstrate the correctness of Islamic laws about the family.

Islamic political activity in the Middle and Near East, and the increasing role of the Muslim countries in the world economy have led to an increased activity by the Muslim minorities and Islamic centres in Western countries. Since the overwhelming majority of Muslims in the

European countries come from the Middle and Near East and are poor, much of their activity is directed against forms of ethnic and economic discrimination. For example, at the World Conference on "Men of Religion for the Salvation of the Sacred Gift of Life from the Nuclear Catastrophe" (Moscow, 10 – 14 May 1982) Abdurrahman Said, representing the Islamic centre in Andalusia (Spain) said that Spanish Muslims live under the oppression of the Roman Catholic Church. The authorities suppress the rights of Muslims and limit their activity.

Islamic centres in West European countries expose anti-Arab and anti-Islamic campaigns organized by Jewish circles and imperialist reaction. For example, the head of the Rome Islamic Centre, Muhammad 'Alī Sabrī, says that the Centre's Islamic News Agency exposes Jewish intrigues and plots in the Near East, and disseminates accurate information about Islam among Italians and Muslims. Employees of this Agency have often been attacked during assaults upon the Islamic centres.

Muslim missionaries and Islamic centres in Europe have recently tried to change Europeans' negative ideas about Islam. *Rabita al-Alam al-Islami*, the World Islamic League magazine published in Mecca, has published several articles on this subject.

The West European Islamic centres assert that governmental authorities restrict their activities and conduct discriminatory policies. Mass media in the Western countries — radio, TV, press — do not let representatives of the Islamic centres inform public opinion about the situation of Islamic minorities in the West.

The representative of the London Islamic Centre, Jahja Saed, said that "in spite of the fact that in England there live about one and a half million Muslims, they have been given not a single possibility to speak on radio or TV in order to tell about Islam. TV and Intervision very often give programmes about the Jewish religion, but I do not remember a single true and undistorted programme about Islam".

On his own, Jahja Saed has tried to clarify the political motives for the reluctance of the British government to allow true information about Islam and Muslims in order "to destroy the prejudice of Englishmen against Islam".

Jahja Saed thinks that Europeans cannot forgive the Muslims for their struggle against the Crusaders and for the fact that the Muslims "were the pioneers of European civilization". Besides, in the West Muslims want to popularize Islam among people who doubt or are sceptical about religion. They are afraid that if these people know the truth about Islam, they might follow it.

Such statements by representatives of the Muslim minority and Islamic centres concerning the policy of Western states towards

Muslims are a new phenomenon. The great increase of the Muslim population in Europe, the moral, financial and political support given by Muslim countries and international Islamic organizations have all strengthened the positions of the Islamic centres.

The foundation of "The Institute for Moslem Minority Affairs" in 1976 at the initiative of the University of King 'Abd-ul 'Azīz in Jeddah was the first attempt to solve systematically the problems of Muslim minorities as an integral part of the Muslim world and to intensify missionary activity.

The Islamic centres do not confine their activity solely to Islamic problems. Under the cloak of Islam, the centres popularize Arabic writing, culture and traditions. Arabic cultural centres are organized in Western and Eastern Africa, where Islam's position is weak. Unlike the European, Islamic centres in Africa organize work projects in order to make the African's life more like the Arab's. This is done simultaneously with the Islamization of the population. In Morocco, Tunis, Libya and Egypt culture-educational centres have developed extensively in this direction. Rich Arab countries have financed the construction of huge university centres in Sierra Leone, Nigeria, Ghana, Mali, Niger, Upper Volta and in other African countries.

Recently, the Islamic Centre in Japan has become more activated. As is known, Japan imports more than 80% of its oil from Muslim countries. The Islamic Centre and the Muslim community in Japan help to strengthen ties between Japan and Muslim countries. Representatives of the Japanese Muslim communities take an active part in international and regional Islamic forums. For instance, the Japanese Islamic Centre sent two representatives to the Muslim Conference, celebrating the anniversary of the hijra, which took place in September in 1980 in Tashkent. Doctor Abu-Bakr Marimoto, editor-in-chief of *The Islamic Cultural Forum*, a magazine published by the Islamic Centre in Japan, spoke to the Tashkent Conference on the "Place and Role of the Muslim Press in the Strengthening of Mutual Understanding and Respect". A. Marimoto said that the Islamic Centre in Tokyo has published its Muslim magazine since 1974 and distributes it free to Muslim organizations and individuals in 90 countries of the world.

A. Marimoto stated that more accurate information can make sincere friends of Muslims. On the other hand, false information inspires conflicts among Muslims.

The representative of the Islamic Centre in Finland also spoke about Islamic unity. The Finnish Muslim community is not large, and its members are mainly of Tatar origin.

It should be stressed that international Islamic organizations see Muslim minorities as inseparable from the Muslim world. In connection with this point, the USSR, India and China are considered as Muslim countries, while the USSR is considered as the fifth largest Muslim country. In official publications of the World Islamic League in Mecca it is pointed out that 50 million Muslims live in the USSR, 75 million in India, and 40 million in China.

As Muslim missionaries confirm, the expansion of sharī'at courts, and applying sharī'at norms of punishment — stoning, amputation, prohibition of alcohol, pornography, narcotics, pop-music, and sex-films — can be more effective in the struggle against crime, depravity and theft than secular laws. For instance, the late rector of the Muslim University Al-Azhar in Cairo, Shaykh 'Abd ul-Ḥalīm Maḥmud, openly stated that if we chop off a hand of only one thief, stealing would disappear completely.[3]

Muslim missionaries believe that religious fear is much more effective in Muslim countries, where private-property psychology and ancient traditions are dominant, than are liberal laws. They consider Islamic forms of punishment quite reasonable and effective means of defending social and private property and public order.

One of the most important aspects of the Islamic mission is its propaganda for the Islamic theory of the state. The rejection of both capitalism and socialism in the Islamic countries reveals the ideologist's strivings for a renewal of Islam and sharī'a embracing all the functions of a modern state system.

As is well known, from the very beginning Islam has served as an ideological base for the Muslim state. Ideas about state government, laws regulating economic life, moral and ethical norms, jurisprudence, a believer's behaviour and the whole mode of life of a Muslim community have been based on the principles of Islamic religion.

The sign of the Islamic state is the existence of a special system of organs and institutions which fulfil the functions of state power and law, and which consolidate a juridical system of norms, sanctioned by the state.

Islam also determines the territory, over which the Islamic state has jurisdiction — that is dār al-Islām (an Islamic country or state).

Islam's universality permits different historical types of state with different forms of government — absolute or constitutional monarchy, republican and so on.

The existence of different forms of government all with Islam as the recognized state religion, proves that Islamic norms are in conformity with any state system which recognizes Islam as a regulator of socio-political and private life. It justifies the state system in the Muslim world.

It would be interesting to know the Marxist point of view on the correlation between Islam and the state.

The role of religion is extremely great throughout the Near and Middle East, where Muslim states exist.

A Muslim state needs the Islamic religion in order to complete itself as a state. "The democratic state, the real state, does not need religion for its political completion. On the contrary, it can disregard religion because the human basis of religion is realised in a secular manner".[4] One of the main reasons for Islam's political activity in modern circumstances is that Muslim countries treat Islam from a political point of view, and policy-making from a religious one. For Islam it is necessary that a state recognize God as the supreme governor, at least on the surface. In practical terms, the spiritual aspects may be subordinated to the secular ones. An amīr, caliph, king, president or prime minister may remain "governor" by advantage in Muslim countries, without being sanctioned by Islam. At the same time he has in his hands all the power — both secular or Islamic.

As Islam is the dominant form of social consciousness in the countries of the Muslim Orient, socio-political movements there take a religious form under Islamic slogans.

It is known that when people demand liberty and social progress and nevertherless do not want to renounce Islamic traditions, Islam becomes politicized.

The classics of Marxism say that "it is by no means contrary to political emancipation to divide man into the non-religious citizen and the religious private individual, that just as the state emancipates itself from religion by emancipating itself from state religion and leaving religion to itself within civil society, so the individual emancipates himself politically from religion by regarding it no longer as a public matter but as a private matter".[5]

Islam as a religion has always been a political factor, and has always evoked great interest. Nevertheless, some problems have appeared that complicate the political situation in Muslim countries. In Muslim states, Islam is an integral part of the state system so that protest against Islamic traditions means attack on the present system and government.

Classics of Marxism assert that such situations can be resolved without transforming secular problems into ideological ones. On the contrary, it is necessary "to transform" theological problems into secular ones. "If we find that even in the country of complete political emancipation, religion not only exists, but displays a fresh and vigorous vitality, that is proof that the existence of religion is not in contradiction to the perfection of the state. Since, however, the existence of religion is the existence of a defect, the source of this defect can only be sought in the nature of the state itself. We no longer regard religion as the cause, but only as the manifestation of secular narrowness. Therefore we explain the religious limitations of the free citizens by their secular limitations. We do not assert that they must overcome their religious narrowness in order to get rid of their secular restrictions; we assert that they will overcome their religious narrowness once they get rid of their secular restrictions. We do not turn secular questions into theological questions. We turn theological questions into secular ones. History has been merged long enough in superstition, we now merge superstition in history".[6]

Recognition and observance of Islam as a state religion does not exclude the possibility of a sharpening of contradictions between the state and certain secular elements. The reasons for these contradictions lie in social life, not in religion; religion is simply a form of this contradiction.

Taking into consideration everything said above, it is necessary to stress that the Muslim world, with its great human and economic potential and its ancient civilization and culture, contributes to the economic and political reality of the modern world.

At present there live about one billion Muslims in the world. Among world religions, Islam occupies second place after Christianity in number of adherents. Islam has become an important political factor, and has influenced international politics and diplomacy.

Islam's contribution to improving modern ethical and political realities (an extremely important problem) is viewed as follows: millions of people confess Islam, and Muslim states and organizations can play an important role in normalization of modern ethical and political reality.

This problem is essentially a human one and we should not try to make it theological. When we speak about Islam contributing to the improvement of modern social and political life we assume that states, political and religious social organizations, and the millions of people in Muslim Oriental countries will act in this direction. The contribution of Islam to this important problem can be considered in two ways:

(1) to extract from Islam moral-ethical norms and political conceptions and to use them as secular arguments to improve modern ethical and political conditions.

(2) to use the Islamic interpretation of secular moral-ethical norms and political conceptions in order to improve existing ethical and political conditions.

The necessity of such an approach to Islamic values follows from the specific features of Islam. Islam is not only a religion reduced to a belief in God, but a basis for a mode of life, thought, a state system, laws, and civilization for dozens of nations. For believers Islamic monotheism is a unity of idea, purpose, mode of life, and balance between labour and property. The Prophet's words: "A white man is equal to a black man, an Arab — to a non-Arab", "All people are brothers and slaves of one God" are apprehended as a just moral code of equality understood by the masses. Theologians confirm that in the oneness of God there exists no domination by an individual, group or class, and that the Islamic thesis "all the people are brothers" is directed against racism and national discrimination.

The Islamic moral code condemns love of power and pursuit of enrichment. Ḥadīth such as "poor people will enter paradise 500 years sooner than the rich", "My God, make me poor, make me utterly poor, resurrect me with poor people", "Poverty is my pride", are aimed at improving moral-ethical conditions.

Muslim missionaries pay special attention to the problem of misinterpretations of the Islamic teachings about jihād. Some Western experts on Islam have wrongly interpeted jihād, seeing it as an appeal to war and violence.

An Egyptian theologian, Hasan Fatkh Al-Bab, says: "Jihād is an aspiration for God and there is no place for violence and hostility to liberty and religion in it".[7]

A Syrian theologian, Abdullah Ulvan, considers different forms of jihād under modern conditions. It can be:
1. support of jihād by property;
2. propagation of jihād;
3. teaching of jihād;
4. political jihād;
5. a holy war.[8]

Abdullah Ulvan interprets jihād as a form of defence and preservation of Islamic values, cultural heritage, individuality, and an adherence to Islam. He understands jihād as a form of mission and popularization of Islam. The theologian admits that not everybody can directly participate in the holy war, but that everybody must support the spirit of jihād by alms and speech. Here are the ḥadīth of the Prophet Muhammad: "One who has equipped a soldier on the way to Allah has already made ghazawāt", "One who has spent his property on the way to Allah would receive 700 times more". Concerning the necessity of financially supporting jihād, the Qur'ān says: ". . . fight by your property and your thoughts on the way to Allah!" (9.41). Political jihād demands that believers make efforts to organize a Muslim state on the basis of the teachings of Islam and on the principles of Muslim monotheism.

Many researchers have remarked that Islam has successfully replaced either Christianity or local religions in Africa. The reasons for the success of Muslim missionaries are the following:

1. Islamic missionaries are seen as not having compromised themselves by their connections with the colonizers. At the same time, Islamic slogans are used in national liberation movements and propagated as a religion and ideology of colonized people.

2. Islam penetrated Africa at the dawn of its existence. It means that the process of Islamization of the local populations has been going on for more than 1300 years.

3. The fact that Arab and Muslim traditions, rituals, moral-ethical norms, habits, and modes of life are both closer to and clearer for Africans contributes to the success of the Muslim missions in Africa. It had often happened that in some African countries Afro-Christian communities have resorted to Islamic prohibitions on alcohol, smoking, European dress, etc. in their struggle against colonial interests.

4. The influence of Islam on African paganism and other forms of religious life on the continent is extremely strong. It facilitates the advance of Muslim missionaries.

5. The World Islamic League, the Arab League and other Muslim organizations provide financial support to many African and Asian countries. This helps to increase the authority of Islam and Muslim missionaries.

6. Muslim missionaries study in many schools and universities of the Near and Middle East. Cairo's theological university, Al-Azhar, more than 1,000 years old, is one of the most influential in the Muslim world. Its graduates work in almost all the continents.

7. The programme of activity of Muslim missionaries in Africa includes four main tasks:

eradication of the local pagan religions,

competition against syncretic africanized Christianity,

struggle against the spreading of Western, Marxist and atheistic ideas,

struggle against Israel and Zionism.

8. The characteristic feature of the modern Islamic mission is to attract those who have medical, technical, economic and philosophical education into its activities. The opening of secular faculties in theological universities (for example engineering, medical and agricultural faculties were recently opened at the theological university, Al-Azhar, in Cairo) proves that the modern Islamic mission tries to adapt its activity by raising the level of culture and education among modern people. Several books about Islam, written by engineers, doctors and philosophers, have recently appeared. Two examples: a Turkish engineer, Mehmet Shukru, wrote two volumes entitled ''Mehmet Sükrü Sözet. Müsbet ilim metodlariyla Kuran-i Kerim. Ankara, 1963'' (Studies of the Qur'ān from the point of view of exact sciences), and an

Iranian doctor, 'Ali Parvar, also published two volumes entitled "Ali Parvar, Bar rasī dīn az rāh-e dānesh. Teherān 1974" (Studies of religion from the position of knowledge).

Muslim missionaries propagate Islam while presenting different interpretations of "Islamic socialism". They confirm that the ideas of socialism are included in the Qur'ān and hadīth. For instance, an Egyptian ideological doctor, Jamāl al-Dīn Muhammad Said, confirms that Muslim socialism is based upon five principles:

1. Limitation of property.
2. A socialist means of production.
3. A socialist way of distributing the necessities of life.
4. The desire to work.
5. A struggle against excessive wealth.[9]

In the Muslim countries, the left-wing political forces use the ideas of "Islamic socialism" to reach wider circles of the Muslim masses concerning certain aspects of scientific socialism and democracy. At the same time, the slogans of "Islamic socialism" serve as an ideological basis for the anti-imperialistic socio-economic transformations.

PART II
AUTHORITY AND THE STATE

4

THE CONCEPT OF AUTHORITY IN ISLAMIC THOUGHT
Lā hukma illā li-llāh

Mohammed Arkoun

My main concern in this essay is not to describe once again the historical genesis of different doctrinal developments on the concept of authority in Islam; this has been done in several books and articles.[1] However, the most recent studies are focused more on power in its political expression at the level of the state. The orientalist approach remains more narrative than critical, while the Islamic presentation is still dominated by the ideological need to legitimate the present regimes in Muslim societies. For these reasons, it becomes urgent to initiate a critical evaluation of authority in Islamic thought from the perspectives I had proposed in my *Critique de la Raison islamique* (Maisonneuve-Larose 1984).

Before we start our analysis, it is necessary to consider some basic facts. Are there authors, texts, periods which could be considered more relevant to a critical, decisive evaluation than others? Is it possible to discover a hierarchy or a solid articulation between levels of authority as represented in Islamic thought during its classical and contemporary periods? We shall try to answer these difficult questions and, beyond that, to propose some new conceptions of authority and power in Islam.

I Methodological Issues

The first obstacle to be identified is the vocabulary used by ancient as well as contemporary thinkers or writers to deal with religious phenomena. Enough has been said about authority, the sacred, rites, beliefs, faith . . . to build an ideal theology, or apply an ideological system of explanation! From this point of view, the theorization of al-Māwardī, or Ghazālī does not differ from E. Durkheim, or Marxist sociologists of religion.[2] The only way to clarify the situation is to reveal the ideological frame in which each text has been written. This we cannot do entirely here; we shall only point to those aspects which require new analysis so as to prepare a comprehensive and objective theory of authority. For this purpose, we do not need only to reconstruct the historical background of each text, or period; we must also have a philosophical scale for the modern evaluation of all problems related to authority. A philosohical reference is particularly important and relevant to our subject for the following reasons:

(1) It has been rejected by all the jurists who had contributed to the theory of authority in Islam; a competition has been evolved between opposing views and falsified until the triumph of so-called orthodoxy;

(2) The philosophical critique has also been eliminated by orientalists as irrelevant to their narrative and philological approach;

(3) Only a philosophical perspective gives the possibility of going beyond the purely technical description of doctrines and also the ideological assurance implicit to all Western scholars when they compare Islam with the West concerning the confusion or separation of religious and temporal authority. This point is particularly important in the debate opened some years ago regarding the revival of Islamic Law and modern legislative procedures.

The comparative method raises many objections. It is no help, for example, to say that Arabic has no word for the concept of authority as it has been developed in Roman Law, opposing *auctoritas* to *potestas*. But this remark becomes important if the historical process leading to Roman and Islamic conceptions is carefully presented. Let us go further in this critical search for a new approach using a text quoted in the introduction to *State and Government in Medieval Islam* by Ann K. S. Lambton (see pp. 2ff.)

From this excerpt we can draw the following observations:

(1) "Islam" is used here in the sense accorded it in its orientalist construction. It is a substantial, stable, defined area (*in* Islam) where all kinds of categorical definitions, answers, rules, and practices are to be found at any time and in any society; at the same time, "Islam" is a sovereign subject: It *knows*, it decides, it confuses morality and legality . . . In spite of all these confusions, this complex, obscure, active entity is, compared to Europe, a precisely known historical, social, cultural space. One would expect a comparison with the

Church, which was also identified with the whole of organized society in the Middle Ages; most comparisons made are related more to Europe after the sixteenth and even the eighteenth centuries than to the Middle Ages.

(2) "The clean-cut boundary between morality and legality", "the separation between the spiritual and the temporal" are, as usual, presented as ideal solution found very early in Europe, and ignored until today by Islam. It is undeniable that there is no formal doctrine of separation proposed by a Muslim thinker; but this fact is less important than the historical and cultural factors operating in both cases and their respective philosophical consequences. The social and political struggle between the bourgeoisie and the Church has been more decisive than the formal doctrine still used today to legitimate ideological positions such as we recently saw in France concerning public and private schools. The philosophical approach of *laïcité* has to be revived.

(3) The common anthropological issues, implicit to all the points touched on in comparisons between Islam and Europe, are not stressed as being basic and prior to any narration of events or doctrines developed in both historical experiences: here I mean the historicity, the societal, the polity, the state, the individual and the person, meaning, the rational, the imaginary, consciousness, unconsciousness, ideation, ideology, myth, etc. . . . Islam is given just as (A. K. S. Lambton avers) "the State is given": Then, one has only to read, to listen and to report formally the actual discourse of Muslims; showing the ideological roots and functions of such discourse produced by social groups in competition for power and, consequently the epistemological distance between ideation and ideology, and critical knowledge and controlled, offensive-defensive discourse. All this is beyond the "scientific" perspectives of the classical orientalist.

(4) If one aims at any objective, critical, comparative understanding of the concept of authority in the cultural space of "Book societies",[3] three models of historical development are to be considered: Islam, Christianity, and the West. The West is a new model which emerged in Europe opposed to the *vision du monde* derived from the revelation. The theological differences on revelation among Judaic, Christian and Islamic traditions must be seen as ideological productions of communities using different cultural material; on the other hand, revelation and secularism (I prefer the term *laïcité*) are axial,

basic, structural forces steering the human mind towards knowledge and the related conduct of social agents. *Laïcité* is an alternative more successfully developed in the West since the thirteenth and fourteenth centuries than in classical Islam (8th – 10th c. AD), for social, economic and cultural reasons that have not yet been studied comparatively, owing to the ideological pressure of each cultural tradition. The success — in different degrees in European countries — of the *laïcité* is more a *de facto* question of social forces (bourgeoisie and, where Marxist-Leninist revolutions have succeeded, proletariat against peasantry and religious communities) than a philosophical attitude unanimously accepted in all countries (just as a *de facto* separation between the spiritual and the temporal existed in Islam without any intellectual attempt to give it cognitive foundations).

These propositions are more a programme for a new exploration of our subject than definitive explanations. I want to put an end to the ethnographic approach to "Islam"; it is necessary to initiate an applied anthropology meeting the demands of our contemporary societies.[4] The interesting debate opened in France since the Left came to power is instructive for our study. The relation between authority deriving from Constitutional Law and political power, with its strategies and tactical trick, is currently illuminated by the policy measures of President Mitterand and the reactions of his opposition.

How should we approach, then, the concept of authority in Islamic thought? Would it be sufficient to start once again with the authority of sacred texts — the *Qur'ān* and the *Hadīth* and then continue with the "orthodox" sources claimed by each great tradition of Islam (Sunnī, Shī'ī, Khārijī)? Certainly we have to read these texts; but we must do so with a *progressive-regressive* method: We go back to the past not to project on fundamental texts the demands and the needs of the present Muslim societies — as the *iṣlaḥi 'ulamā'* do — but to discover the historical mechanisms and factors which produced these texts and assigned them such functions (= regressive procedure). At the same time we cannot forget that these texts are still alive, active as an ideological system of beliefs and knowledge shaping the future. We have, then, to examine the process of transformation of initial contents and functions into new ones (= progressive procedure). The role played in contemporary Islamic thought[5] by the substantive, essentialist, mythical "Islam" is so dominant that it forces all scholars to adopt the progressive-regressive method, with all the necessary references to traditional as well as modern knowledge.

Let us see how these methodological remarks could be applied.

II Authority in Classical Thought

We shall consider five points in this section:

(1) The emergence of the concept: the Qur'ān and the Medina Experience;
(2) Sultān, mulk/Khilāfa, Imāma, hukm, amr . . .; the formative period;
(3) 'Aqida and intellectual authority: the role of ijtihād;
(4) Tradition and authority;
(5) Ideologies and authority.

II-1. The Emergence of the Concept

According to our previous definition of the progressive-regressive method, we cannot read the Qur'ān and the historical experience of Muhammad with all the vocabulary used by Muslim tradition after the triumph of an Islamic state. At the stage of Muhammad's prediction and struggle, the authority of revelation itself had to be defined and explained; daily initiatives were required to overcome the opposition of both the Jāhilīyya (Pagan Arab society) and the people of the Book. I have examined the conditions of this opposition and the linguistic tools used in the Qur'ān to assert the authority of the Messenger through the constant intervention of God.[6]

The originality of the process lies in the exceptional combination of successful political, social, and cultural action and its sublimation into a specifically religious discourse using an organized system of metaphors. The followers of the Prophet were engaged in creative movements and uplifted by the rich symbolism describing the goals of every initiative. The impact of any civilization is proportional to its capacity to symbolize human existence; the Qur'ān achieved a great deal in this direction; its permanent influence on contemporaries as well as on later generations can be traced to its symbolic expression of the profane vicissitudes of history. In spite of all this, there were groups of Bedouins (a'rāb) who continued to refuse obedience to the Prophet, participation in the jihād and refusing to pay the sadaqa.[7]

This means that symbolized authority needs time, repetition, ritualization, and a long progress of literalization to be internalized as a system of transcendent norms by all members of the community produced by and producing this tradition. We must insist on this point. Originally, the authority of the Prophet was directly affirmed and perceived through his charismatic historical action and the semantic, syntactic, and rhetorical structure of the Qur'ānic discourse; after his death, this integrated representation of living authority broke up into two processes of development. The Qur'ān and the Ḥadīth were collected, transmitted, registered, interpreted, ending in a large corpus of scriptural tradition; the state, on the other hand, used this facet of authority to exercise a political and cultural power controlling more and more the first process and ending in the scriptural tradition. We shall come back to this dual mechanism unperceived by modern scholarship engrossed in the ideological versions of the authority residing in the caliphate-imāmate.

There is another significant point to be emphasized in the emergence of authority from the perspective of God's revealed word. We have paid much attention to the texts as material documents to be used by historians; but very few considerations have been given to the *aesthetics of reception*:[8] how a discourse — oral or written — is received by listeners or readers. This question refers to the conditions of perception of each culture, or, more precisely, each level of culture corresponding to each social group in every phase of historical development. The succession of diverse exegeses and interpretations of the Qur'ān provide a good example for studying the development of the aesthetics of reception of a religious discourse. One could say that these are very trivial remarks; everybody knows that it is almost impossible to read any text — especially symbolic religious texts — totally free from the specific postulates of the dominant culture. But even if this psychological linguistic mechanism is currently recognized, we have to confess that history of perception in a particular culture is still a neglected discipline. I tried to raise the problem when I studied the marvellous in Qur'ānic discourse. The respective dimensions and mechanism of mythical and historical knowledge in Islamic thought have not yet been considered either by Muslim scholarship or by orientalists, in spite of the fact that this historical chapter is fundamental to any attempt to explore the basic cognitive organization of a given culture.

These considerations will reveal their true significance when we shall deal with *ijtihād*: intellectual, methodical activity to transfer authority based on symbolic sublimation of history to the constraining legal power of the *Sharī'a*. The same discursive transformation affected the charistmatic authority of the Prophet as expressed and perceived by contemporaries, when it was narrated in the *Sīra* with the procedures and the ideological trends of all Muslim historiography. The psychological forces at work in the evolution from the early stage to a formal centralized state are social imagination and the search for pragmatic rationalization. Imagination and reason already appear interacting in the *Qur'ān*; the consolidation of the state after 661 favoured a specialization of the imaginary in all kinds of *akhbār, āthār* and literary productions of the rational mind in speculative disciplines. But the separation was never total and irreversible. The contents and functions of authority depend on this psychological and cultural evolution.

II-2. The Formative Period

W. M. Watt and J. van Ess have traced the main lines of this period. For our purpose, we need to concentrate on the new conditions of perception and thinking created by the Umayyad and 'Abbāsid state. The relevant point here is the inversion of the process described for the Qur'ān and the charismatic presence of Muhammad: priority was given to the definition, expansion and internalization of authority as coming from God, who both guided and legitimated the decisions and measures taken by the Prophet. Authority chronologically and ontologically preceded any exercise of power (the predication in Mecca was focused on authority of divine Commandments and teachings). In the period of the Right-guided *khulafā*, the collective memory of the *Sahāba* and the cultural climate of Medina could help to preserve — partly at least, the hierarchy of values which prevailed at the time of the Prophet. But the struggle between traditional conceptions and the mechanisms of Arabic society and the new vision set by the *Qur'ān* had already shown the power of profane history on the efforts to transcend human existence. The fact that 'Umar, 'Uthmān and 'Ali were assassinated is sufficient to demonstrate the radical violence prevailing in all societies and, consequently, of the true and limited function of authority as revealed religions have tried to impose it. The purpose is to control the natural violence of man by the ethical and spiritual sublimation of his desires. This means of controlling violence had some success, but ultimately proved inadequate since societies remain basically *systems of inequalities* imposed by bloody or structural violence.

The state established by the Umayyad, and after them by the 'Abbāsid was a result of bloody violence. It was the inversion of the hierarchy of ethical-spiritual authority/power using violence to impose a socio-political order fixed by the victorious group. The State, as a constraining and controlling power, will use authority as a necessary reference to legitimate a temporal power originally lacking any intrinsic authority of its own. Thus, we can speak of official ideology imposing an *image* of legitimate power by misrepresenting the actual genesis of the state. These are two main characteristics of the ideology: misrepresenting the true process of history to maintain the adhesion of people to an idealized image of legitimacy. We see now why ideological constructions differ from prophetic discourse seeking symbolization and rational discourse seeking objective knowledge; and we understand the responsibility of a violent state in transforming for its own advantage open symbols of a religion into a constraining system of *orthodox* religion. Orthodoxy — in its Sunnī or Shī'ī version — is no more than the official religion resulting from the collaboration of the majoriy of *'ulamā'* with the state. This is very obvious with the Umayyad and the 'Abbasīd; but we depend more on the historiography and the jurists who worked under the 'Abbasīd. That is why *mulūk* is applied to the Umayyad but not to the 'Abbasīd who developed the conception of the caliph as a sacred representative of divine authority.[9]

All the theories elaborated by the jurists to meet official demands must be described under the title of ideological activity in Islamic thought. Nevertheless, it is correct to detect in these theories the impact of the model of authority as it has been represented and internalized through the main corpus claimed by the tradition: *Qur'ān, Ḥadīth, Nahj al-Balāgha*, and various speeches collected in anthologies. All these texts are full of existential experiences expressed in a genuine, concise, lyric language; and we can see in this literature three faces of authority: (1) the ideological face used to strengthen the legitimate image of the official state, or to remind the princes of the ideal rules which must always be imitated; (2) the mythical and mythologizing face consisting of literary construction of ideal-typical figures of authority projecting all desirable virtues and abilities on historical personalities like Muḥammad, 'Alī, 'Umar I and 'Umar II, Abū Bakr[10]; (3) the original authority of the personality used to build an ideal type, like Muḥammad, 'Alī, Ja'far al-Ṣādiq. This third fact is the deepest in the stratified construction of the collective memory manipulated by historiographers, by *udabā'*, and by the *'ulamā'*; the modern historian can reach some aspects of this level after a critical evaluation of ideological and mythological elements which are needed in order to know all facets of authority.

In the formative period, we must look not only to the state and its evolution; before the state could control all fields of social and cultural activities, authority was emerging and expanding in the study of Arabic language, history (*akhbār, āthār*), poetry, exegesis, theological discussions and elaboration of the Law. In the seventh century, many lines of development were still possible; this has been clearly expressed by Ibn al-Muquaffa' when he wrote his famous *Risāla fil-Sahāba*;[11] but all the ideological movements fighting for power or independence from the new state had to refer to the same sources of authority: the Qur'ān and the Model represented by Muhammad, known through the *Hadīth* and the *Sīra*. To make explicit this authority, the technical authority of the *akhbārī*, the philologist, the grammarian, the theologian, and the jurist were needed. The virtues assembled under the concept of *'adala* were the common condition required from the transmitter, the *qādī*, the *Mujtahid*, the *imām* or the caliphate. Here we meet a significant convergence of qualities, behaviours and functions in the concept of authority: the ideal Muslim acting in the ideal city had to reproduce the perfect Model actualized by Muhammad (and 'Alī for the Shī'ī) who concentrated in his person all the attributes of authority. This Model will actually be imitated endlessly in many different ways. The Mahdī — like Ibn Tumert in the Maghreb — the Saints or *Murābitūn*, the *sūfī*, the *qādī*, the *'alīm*, the *walī* and the more humble believer all strive to reach some authority by walking in the steps of the Prophet, or 'Alī, or other Imams and Saints who represent more concretely and immediately the desired ideal.

This aspect of authority is collective and independent from the state seen, for this reason, as the manipulator of power especially when the sultanate and the emirate take the place of the caliphate. One could say that the popularized Model of authority as communicated through the sermons and the various narrations of the prophets, *sahāba* and *imām* by the popular story-tellers (*qussās*), authority as an articulated system of desired images of ethical-spiritual thinking and acting, circulated more widely and durably than the power reserved to the state and its servants. But we must add that this type of authority has been and still is internalized by the social image more than it is formulated by critical, theoretical thought. That is why in Islamic discourse today, the social image is so easily mobilized for an Islamic revolution restoring the central themes of the Model rooted for centuries in the collective soul, or the common Islamic image. The more authority is reduced to a combination of ideal Images, structuring the social imagination, the more it works as a powerful collective force which is easily involved in revolutionary movements by militant leaders (see the cases of the Mahdîs in Sudan, Senegal, Maghreb, and Ismā'īlī missionaries and Khomeini recently).

To complete these short observations, we must mention the authority of the poet and poetry, especially in the time of the Umayyad and the first 'Abbasīd! The new state needed the heip of the poet as much as it wanted the support of high religiously minded personalities like Ḥasan al-Baṣrī. We know the role played by great poets like Jarīr, Farazdaq, al-Akhtal, Kuthayyir, Bashshār, etc. The authority of literary aesthetics is used for ideological support, as well as the authority of religious texts and personalities; the pressure of official demands can help the creativity of the poet, and it did in some cases; but it can also transform the most talented into a vulgar propagandist. The significant point in all this is the historical dynamism introduced by the state at all levels of social and cultural life; authority and power, interacting continuously in all fields, came to reflect the whole movement of the societies penetrated by Islamic phenomena.

II-3. *'Aqīda and Intellectual Authority*

'Aqīda means all beliefs and propositions accepted without questioning as a matter of faith. Muslim *'aqīda* is basically the same for all Muslims in its main principles; when the core is accepted, each *mujtahid* can develop his *'aqīda* including or excluding some irrational beliefs.[12]

In the high intellectual context of Islamic cities during the classical age, Islamic thought had to rationalize many elements of the *'aqīda*. The most important exercise developed in this direction is represented by two disciplines: *Uṣūl al-dīn* and *Uṣūl al-fiqh*; the first corresponds to theology, the second to a methodology and to some extent epistemology of the Law. We shall pay more attention to *Uṣūl al-fiqh* because we can discuss the significance and the role of *ijtihād* as the intellectual foundation of authority.

Let us again point to the inadequacy of the orientalist method. Ann K. S. Lambton gives a simple description of the *Uṣūl* as they have been used by the representative Sunnī authors; nothing is said of the validity of the postulates used by this discipline, which claims precisely to practise a rigorous intellectual control. More than that: we know how several Islamic states today enforce the *Sharī'a* on the basis of the intellectual authority of the classical *mujtahidūn* who elaborated the *corpus juris* and the *Uṣūl*. This means that the authority of the *Uṣūl* is not merely an historical issue for learned scholars; it is a burning intellectual authoritarian issue for all contemporary Islamic societies. We must all be in the same movement of research, both learned historians and solid thinkers.

Uṣūl al-dīn and *Uṣūl al-fiqh* are interdependent; both are built on the following postulate: God has delivered his revelation to Muhammad in a clear Arabic language, understandable by all Arabic-speaking people;

Arabic has thus been transcendentalized and, at the same time, confirmed in its human dimension.

This postulate has many consequences which need to be explained.

(1) To be reliable, the *ijtihād* of the jurist must be based on a perfect knowledge of Arabic grammar, lexicography, semantics and rhetoric; that is why all treatises of *Usūl al-fiqh* open with comments on linguistic problems.

(2) Since *Usūl al fiqh* is accepted as authoritative, the authors have reached the perfect required knowledge of Arabic so that there is no need for any revision of their work.

(3) The methodology defined and used by jurists trained in Arabic is so reliable that all the *ahkām* correctly derived from the sacred texts express the authentic *hukm* of God Himself; that is why all the *Sharī'a* is the Law given by God, sacred and transcendant, and not revisable by any human legislator.

(4) *Ijmā'* and *qiyās* depend, for their correct use, on the *Qur'ān* and the *Hadīth*; they refer again to competency in reading Arabic texts.

In practice, *Ijmā'* and *qiyās* have always been subject to divergence; the *Qur'ān* and *Hadīth* are accepted as stable, objective sources of the Law; but, whereas the whole *Qur'ān* is received in one version by all Muslims, the *Hadīth* is presented in two very different corpus: the Sunnī (Bukhārī, Muslim and others) and the Shī'ī (Kulaynī, Ibn Bābūya). Add to this the fact that the divergent readings and interpretations make the *Usūl* less authoritative than it claims. If we raise problems of reading according to modern linguistics and semiotics — as I have — we can start a task never undertaken in Islamic thought: the critique of Islamic reason. Obviously, the *Shī'ī* theory of *ijtihād*, relying on the authority of the Imāms and *marja' al-taqlīd*, falls within the scope of the same critique.[13]

II-4. Tradition and Authority

We have alluded to tradition as a source of authority and a space for its expansion. We mean not only the technical concept of prophetic tradition or *sunna*; but all practical knowledge, beliefs, habits and values which assure the order, the security, the identity of a group, or a community. *Sunna* or *Hadīth* provide a selection of elements in wider and diversified traditions under the authority of the Prophet. We need not discuss here the problem of authenticity: the relevant point is that all traditions collected in a received corpus give authority to the ideas or behaviour of Muslims. Scriptural tradition, assuming valuable elements of local traditions, is the historical consciousness of the Community. The process of this concentration of history in tradition and control of history by tradition started with the death of the Prophet. In this process, there is a constant conflict between tradition and innovation (*bid'a*); through this conflict appears also the tension between the authority of internalized traditional values and the power of not yet integrated ideas, discoveries and events (which we now call modernity). Let us try to clarify this dialectic with some answers to three question:

(1) Which type of authority is perpetuated by tradition?
(2) What makes tradition authoritative?
(3) What is the value of authority expressed by tradition?

II-4-1. The authority of scriptural as well as oral tradition is related to the memory of the group as it is perpetuated by its wisest and most learned members. The difference between scriptural and oral tradition is linked to writing, which is a cultural phenomenon related to the triumph of a powerful, centralizing state. The linguistics of written and oral discourse shows significant differences in the processes of reason and articulated thoughts; but these differences do not necessarily refer to any intrinsic superiority of the written tradition. We have to pay special attention to the theological theory of tradition to discover the ideological biases imposed by the ruling class and its intellectual servants.[14] This is also a new intellectual task for "the people of the Book" who have developed, separately and in a constant polemic, three conflicting scriptural traditions on the basis of the same anthropological oppositions between authority and power: (1) plurality of power centres and a single centralizing state; (2) poetic and logocentrist expression; (3) paganism (as a philosphical attitude) and monotheism monopolized by theological speculation with the unavoidable trend towards orthodoxy.[15]

The authority of scriptural tradition is conditioned by the value of each testimony. Only the generation of the *Sahāba* has *seen* and *heard* the circumstances and the words which are reported as the *Qur'ān* on the *Hadīth* and the *Sīra*. Historically, it is difficult, if not impossible, to assert how each reporter saw and heard the object of his report. In spite of this, the so-called theological theory imposed the dogma that all the *Sahāba* were infallible (*ma'sūm*) in their testimony.[16]

It is recognized by the Tradition[17] that after the *Sahāba* there occurs a degradation of the information and of its authenticity; the transmitters more and more had to rely on the story made by memory, which means on a *literary*[18] narration of the original wording appraised in a unique existential situation. Many difficult problems arise through my formulation: historical, literary, psychological, sociological, linguistic, semiotic. A radical critique of the whole Tradition must be done on the lines traced, for example, by P. Ricoeur in *La narrativité* (CNRS 1980) and *Temps et récit* (Seuil 1982). Tradition — with or without T — is alive and authoritative as long as it protects itself from the changing scientific environment. I shall give below a very recent and significant example of this socio-cultural mechanism. This protection has been assured until now by the following postulates (*musallamāt*):

(1) The *Sahāba* are infallible and have carefully transmitted the total authentic texts and "historical" facts related to the mission of Muhammad.

(2) The following generations have continued the same transmission of the Tradition learned — with due control and critical mind — from the *Sahāba*.

(3) The results of this transmission are registered in the *Mushaf* and the authentic corpus of the *Hadīth*.

(4) All historiographical literature completes and consolidates this Tradition in so far as it is conceived and elaborated using the same critical criteria as for the sacred Tradition.

(5) The *'ulamā'-mujtahidūn* have added to the sacred corpus, the *corpus juris* — the sacred Law — elaborated according to the principles and methods given in the *Usūl al-fiqh*.

(6) The totality of reliable corpus thus constituted affords the possibility of producing a terrestrial history entirely integrated in and controlled by the Tradition: this history is then oriented to the eschatological end.

(7) The Caliph-Imām is legitimate as long as he protects and applies the Tradition which, in turn, is used to establish the legitimacy of a Muslim government.

II-4-2. We now see more clearly how tradition is authoritative: the group or community recognizes and respects in it what they selected in their own history and integrated into their mythical-historical memory. The secret of such authority lies in the process and criteria of the selection; it is also in variable combination, in all traditions, with mythical ways of knowledge and historical elements.

The concepts of selection and mythical-historical memory are totally excluded by the structure and ends sought by the tradition; they are unthinkable in the tradition itself because they lead to discover what the tradition has hidden. Here we understand why orientalist scholarship applied to the *Hadīth*, the *Sīra*, the *Qur'ān* is still rejected by Muslims. It disqualifies the mythical knowledge with the postulates of positivist historicism, without any intellectual attempt to explore anthropologically and philosophically the concept of mythical-historical memory, which is basic for Christian and Western traditions too. That is why we insist on the question: What makes tradition authoritative? It is necessary to know the right chronology, the genuine facts, the historical individuals; but it is misleading to cut off this positive history from the mythical support which is at work in all social-cultural traditions. This approach is a result of recent studies on history considered as the anthropology of the past.

The tension between historicism and myth reached a high point when the mu'tazilī movement imposed its rationalism as an official ideology. But neither the rationalism of the Mu'tazila nor the traditionalism of the religious opposition have been analysed from the perspective of the tension between *mythos* and *logos*, the rational and the social imagination. The issues lie not in the manifest arguments exchanged by the two parties, but are more essentially related to the cognitive systems represented by the *'ulūm 'aqliyya* (called *dakhīla* by the opponents) and *'ulūm Dīniyya*, or *naqliyya*.[19] Why and how has the authoritative tradition ultimately prevailed? The answer will be found in historical psychology and sociology.

II-4-3. What is the value, then, of authority expressed and exercised by tradition? In other words, what are the respective roles of rationality and imagination in the genesis and functioning of tradition? At which levels and to what degree did rationality emerge in a socio-cultural space all dominated by mythical knowledge? If we succeed in answering these questions *historically*, we shall have to face the philosphical problem of mythical and rational knowledge.

Even with respect to our modern societies, sociologists can still speak of their "imaginary institutions";[20] what is to be said, *a fortiori*, of the medieval societies? We use an inadequate vocabulary elaborated in the positivist climate of nineteenth century Europe to describe religions and especially the so-called "popular religion": the marvellous, the supernatural, the sacred, the profane, the secular, the miraculous, the charismatic, the superstitious, the survivals . . ., all this conceptual apparatus refers to a negative imagination opposed to a positive

rationality.[21] Imagination is structured by fables, illusory representations, popular tales, mythological beliefs, etc; reason is the critical,
analytical faculty, directing science towards true knowledge. Islamic
thought, highly influenced by Aristotelism, developed this wrong
opposition in spite of the impact of Platonism and neo-platonism.[22]

Historically, we must first underline the nonexistence in medieval
societies of the main media of our modern rationality: no paper, few
written documents, no generalized teaching in public schools (see the
later role of the official *madārīs* in reinforcing orthodoxy leading to a
narrowing, degrading use of rationality), no or few and weak technical
tools, weak and limited administration. On the contrary, oral cultural
tradition — with its code of honour, pragmatic ways of learning and
working (peasants, crafts), ''symbolic capital'',[23] collective consciousness merged in a common cosmic vision — was sociologically and
structurally dominant. Consequently, social imagination had to play a
positive, constant, determinant role at all levels of social and cultural
existence. Islamic tradition cannot be separated from this context; but,
since the *Qur'ān* itself,[24] it has sought a kind of rationalization,
integrating convictions, beliefs, representations considered as matters
of faith, but psychologically related to the social imagination. The
authority of this type of rationality is expressed in the so-called
''oriental wisdom'' (*ḥikma*) in the form of positivist reason. *Ḥikma* is a
psychological attitude, a behaviour, a style of knowledge, thought and
perception; it is a collective *ethos* integrated, enlarged and expanded by
the *Qur'ān* and by the tradition. With this ethical-spiritual *ethos*,
imagination and rationality are combined at a deeper level (see the
psychology defined by the *Qur'ān* through the concept of heart = *qalb*)
such that a typical harmony and internal distance are the characteristics
of the true wise man, representative of the living tradition.

This positive aspect of the authority of the living tradition cannot be
separated from the negative one represented by the dogmatic,
conservative control of emancipating history (scientific, economic,
social and political innovations). Wisdom is seen as marginal, reserved
to a minority; ideological use of tradition has a larger and stronger
impact on the society; we have to clarify, then the problem of
ideologies and authority.

II-5. Ideologies and Authority

The concept of ideology has been elaborated in modern critical thought;
it has been used in a very impressive way by Karl Marx who has

influenced the subsequent practice of social sciences. Islamic thought has not yet discovered the importance of this concept; it produced conquering ideologies misrepresenting even its own past and values, without free access to contemporary scientific research. The Islamic discourse claims to be scientific while at the same time human and social sciences are rejected as the product of Western societies and tools for cultural aggression (*al-ghazw al-fikrī*). It is difficult to explain to Muslim militants, or to *'ulamā'* trained in traditional sciences, that human and social sciences are the vital counterpart of the ideologies produced in industrialized as well as in developing countries.

Ideologies of developing countries are mostly negative and inadequate; they are obliged to accept Western models in political, social and economic organization to meet the massive needs of their growing populations; but they give the illusion of going back to tradition, to protect and restore the Islamic way of life and thought. Who is able to take over such an historical project? Official ideologies, people say; *min al'sha'b ilā-l-sha'b* (= from people to people) claims a well-known slogan written everywhere in many "revolutionary" countries. The implications of this sentence are diametrically opposed to the constant principles adopted by classical theology: the masses (*al-'awāmm*) must be kept away from any participation in *ijtihād* which means the exercise of authority (see *Iljām al'awāmm 'an 'ilm al kalām* by Ghazālī). Actually, the decision-makers in the new regimes are very few; they rely on the leader: king or general secretary of the sole party. The *'Ulamā'* have less independence than in the past; they are officers of the state and they have to maintain the fiction of spiritual authority illuminating and assuring legitimacy to the political power.

In the past, ideologies existed, but have been eliminated or criticized under the name of sects, heresies and religious error. The hard and suggestive polemic between Sunnī and Shī'ī is an excellent example of the ideological basis of theological reason. Only the modern critic of ideologies can show that each orthodoxy is ultimately founded on ideological postulates. We face, then, a general crisis of authority: not merely the authority of political institutions, of the established tradition, of the cultural legacy, but of reason as the source and instrument of any knowledge used by men. The problem of authority does not today depend on any religious or secular institution; in so far as reason has established its autonomy *vis-à-vis* outside authorities (revelation, church, *sharī'a*, state), it must constitute knowledge as a sphere of authority to be accepted and respected unanimously: a knowledge independent of ideologies, able to explain their formation and master their impact.

Let us enlarge these remarks by looking at authority and powers today.

III Authority and Powers Today

Under this title, we shall mainly consider two points:

(1) The problem of secularism (*laïcité*).
(2) The reappraisal of Islam.

III-1. Secularism Today

The commonly received view is that Islam did not allow any secularism. This is true if we accept the traditional definitions of the Law enforced by all governments in Islamic societies. But we have shown how ideological systems can be presented and accepted as the orthodox truth revealed by God. Accordingly, the concept of religion cannot be approached as a system of knowledge and beliefs manipulated by various social forces in order to transform initial spiritual aims into the ideological principles of a specific social and political order.

The French Revolution imposed secularism as a political and philosophical alternative to the regime controlled by the Church. Universal suffrage became the source of authority in the place of Revelation interpreted and applied by the authorized spiritual authorities. Louis XVI was executed to symbolize the death of the sacred monarchy and the rise of secular authority. In contrast, when Khomeini came to power, he wanted to judge and execute the Shah as a symbol of the death of the secular *Ṭāghūt* and the reappearance of the sacred Imām.

Secularism is much more than a simple distinction between spiritual and temporal affairs. Such a distinction exists *de facto* in all societies even when it is negated and hidden by a religious vocabulary. When it is recognized by law and enforced in several institutions, it does not lead to the division of each individual into religious and secular parts! These radical oppositions, expressed by political parties as in France, show the necessity of finding a new language going beyond the polemic definitions used in social and political competitions. The intellectual attitude underlying such a new language, already exists on both sides. Secularists are able to integrate a critical acceptance of traditional religions, while religious minds work to consolidate secularism as a decisive step towards the emancipation of human reason from all forms of wrong consciousness. But the appropriate concepts for expressing this new attitude of mind confronted with the problem of knowledge and its correct communication, do not yet exist.

How can we adequately discuss secularism when we do not have an adequate theory of the sacred, and how can we deal with the sacred, the spiritual, the transcendant, the ontology, when we are obliged to recognize that all this vocabulary which is supposed to refer to stable, immaterial values, is submitted to the impact of historicity? One could say that these values have been eliminated, or misinterpreted by triumphant material powers; but, on the other hand, who could object to the wrong consciousness, the religious dogmatism and fanatism developed over the centuries by religiously controlled states?

One could also speak of secular religions. The recent spread of dominant ideologies (communism/liberalism; socialism/capitalism) are legitimized as religions with their respective institutions, economic organizations, celebrations, rites, systems of knowledge and beliefs. It is evident that our so-called modern culture is not yet emancipated from the mythological and ideological constraints of traditional cultures.

In the light of these observations, we can revise our ideas concerning the place of secularism in Islam and the position of official Islam on secularism. Islamic societies are more involved than ever in a secular history; since the colonial impact, enlarged by the ideology of development, they have adopted all the attributes of material modernity; this total involvement is precisely the reason for the success of fundamentalist movements claiming a total application of Islamic Law and teachings. These movements are themselves secular in their daily life, their professions and their basic needs; the majority of the militants come from the lower classes, cut off from the traditional culture, unable to reach the modern urban culture; they rightly ask for more justice, less brutal oppression, possibilities to participate in the new history; but they express these basically secular hopes in a religious language, the only one at their disposal.

The future of secularism in Islam depends essentially on the large diffusion of what I have called intellectual modernity.[25] I do not minimize the importance of political and economic changes in creating new possibilities for the circulation of emancipating culture; but I maintain that intellectual modernity is a more necessary and more efficient means with which to undertake a whole reappraisal of Islam. This is seen in the attitude of the middle classes and new bourgeoisie concerning the issue of Islam and its role in the present phase of history. Those who enjoy all economic and social privileges are ready to share conformist and very conservative views on Islam, because they do not have access to intellectual modernity! We also know that many students in technical sciences adhere to the fundamentalist movements: they have no notion of the critical views developed in human and social sciences, especially history.

In such a context, dominated by a cultural vacuum, secularism cannot be developed as a positive virtue. There is no political and cultural possibility for a fruitful confrontation between secular and religious *vision du monde*: they are two ways of perception, thinking, acting, creating and knowing. Western thought has explored new fields through this confrontation since the sixteenth century. For the time being, secularism, in Muslim societies, is an ideological means to criticize the atheism and materialism of the West; a process of materialism in which machines, cars, and gadgets are imported from this same criticized West. Thus, all obstacles are accumulated to prevent any serious thinking to discover a secular dimension of thought, a way and a domain to constitute a new concept and a new subsequent practice of authority. This is not the place to develop this decisive point: it needs a special essay; but I can summarize the main lines of a deconstructive history of Islamic thought:[26]

(1) Secularism is included in the *Qur'ān* and Madinan Experience.
(2) The Umayyad-'Abbāsid state is secularist; the ideological theorizing by the jurists is a circumstantial product using conventional and credulous arguments to hide historical and political reality; this theorizing is built on an outdated theory of knowledge.
(3) Very early military power played a pre-eminent role in the caliphate, the sultanate and all later forms of Islamic government.
(4) Attempts to rationalize the *de facto* secularism and to develop a lay attitude have been made by the *falāsifa*; that is why a new history of Islamic thought has to devote a chapter to the *sociology of the failure* of philosophy: it is one of the requirements of reasserting a philosophical attitude in Islamic thought.
(5) Orthodox expressions of Islam (sunnī, shī'ī, khārijī all of which claim the monopoly of orthodoxy) arbitrarily select and ideologically use beliefs and practices conceived to be authentically religious.
(6) The whole status of the religious, the sacred, and the revelation has to be re-examined in the light of a modern theory of knowledge.

(7) All political regimes which have emerged in Islamic societies after their liberation from colonialism are *de facto* secular, dominated by Western models, based on the classical theory of authority and on intellectual modernity.

(8) From the point of view adopted in this essay, secularism, as a source and domain of intellectual freedom to initiate a new theory and practice of authority, must also be undertaken in Western societies today.

III-2. *The Reappraisal of Islam*

The eight points which have just been mentioned are an important part of a comprehensive programme for the reappraisal of Islam. I have developed many other points of this programme in my *Lectures du Coran* and *Pour une critique de la Raison islamique*: it is a work for future generations. But we can already see very clearly the lines and methods to be followed, the themes to be emphasized, the intellectual tasks to be fulfilled.

The reappraisal of Islam is not only a necessary solution to the demands of Islamic societies: this is certainly a vital task; but Islam has three other dimensions which are highly significant for two reasons: first, for pursuing a critical theory of knowledge, and second, for improving peaceful co-operation in the world. The three dimensions are:

(1) the religious perspective, its place in human existence and its vocation for the absolute;

(2) the historical perspective on the cultural domain specific to the societies of the Book, with special emphasis on the Mediterranean dimension;

(3) international co-operation for a new cultural, political and economic order based on a new theory and practice of Authority.

* * * * * * * * * *

With such enthusiastic perspectives, one can easily see how scholarship on Islam remains intellectually inadequate and absent from our burning history! Is it not disappointing to read cold, distant narratives or militant apologetic presentations of classical Muslim "theories" of authority? Scholars teaching and publishing at the highest level remain prisoners of the image of a provincial, ethnographic Islam, locked into its classcial formulations inadequately and poorly reformulated in contemporary ideological slogans. The living core of Islam in the perspectives mentioned is increasingly hidden by both the classical orientalist discourse and by the revolutionary Islamic discourse. A growing number of silent voices await the possibility to speak, to express a rich experience rooted in the core of Islam; when this political possibility comes about, will learned scholars start to write new views with a new spirit? But those scholars engaged in a continuous struggle to create new spheres of freedom, to give new intellectual articulations to the silent voices, are those who harmonize their thoughts with their concrete involvement and the involvement with their thought (*al-'ilm bi-l-'amal wal-'amal bil-'ilm*). This is the ultimate source of authority, as symbolized by the prophets; and with this Authority, we can actualize the philosophy of the person summarized in this sentence:

"La personne, tout en faisant partie de l'Etat, transcende l'Etat par le mystère inviolable de la liberté spirituelle et par sa vocation aux biens absolus" (J. Maritain, *Christianisme et Démocratie*, 1932).

5

THE ORIGINS OF THE ISLAMIC STATE

Hichem Djaït

The Prophet was born into the Qurayshī environment and it was there that he preached for thirty years. He was a direct descendant of Qusayy who was the founder of Mecca as an urban entity, the man who had founded the Quraysh and who had gathered together all religious, political and military functions in his own hands. More specifically the Prophet belonged to the clan of 'Abd Manāf named after the youngest son of Qusayy whose prestige had very quickly surpassed that of the elder son 'Abd ad-Dār.[1] Although the 'Abd Manāf clan had become subdivided into two sub-clans, that of Hāshim and that of 'Abd Shams, it had remained sufficiently cohesive for one to consider that the "close 'ashīra" that God commands the Prophet to warn about in the Qur'ān refers to the 'Abd Manāf as well as the Hāshim.[2] As a result of this the Prophet belonged to one of the two sacred clans of the Quraysh[3] which shared the care of pilgrims and military command. Although the expansion of commerce, which was a recent phenomenon, had created a social differentiation giving stature to clans which were not descendants of Qusayy such as the Makhzūm, or to the sub-clan of 'Abd Shams to the detriment of that of Hāshim, both descendants of 'Abd Manāf, nevertheless the 'Abd Manāf clan retained an institutionally privileged position and was the effective representative of the bayt of Quraysh, i.e. the House of Quraysh *par excellence*. This is of the greatest importance in understanding the rise of Muhammad as a prophet and his subsequent success at Medina and among the Arab tribes. Muhammad, in spite of his poverty and that of his uncle and protector Abū Tālib, was not a descendant of just anyone but of Qusayy and 'Abd Manāf and for this reason he was able to appear to the Arabs as eminently representative of the Quraysh. Also, without doubt it was thanks to this that he had at the outset a position of arbitration at Medina. It was this also that enabled him to make Medina a haram[4] — a sacred and inviolable enclave. To a certain extent the Islamic State he founded owed its existence and its status to the concept of haram[5] while on the other hand being a creation of the prophetic and Islamic dynamic. So there is here a large measure of continuity in relation to the

Qurayshī legacy. Muhammad was a product of the religious and ruling House of Quraysh, itself considered to be the pre-eminent religious tribe of the Arabs — a man more qualified than most to speak in matters of religion and politics. And the refusal of the Quraysh to recognize him must be attributed to the fact that this teaching threatened to destroy the Meccan religious, political and commercial system which was then at the height and functioning in its fullness.

The Islamic State was constructed in three stages: the first at the moment of Hegira when a prophetic power emerged; the second in the year 54, after the siege of Medina or Khandaq, when this power gradually acquired the principal attributes of State and when its geographical basis expanded throughout all Arabia; the third after the death of the Prophet and with Abū Bakr when the Islamic State demonstrated its ability to crush all dissidence by force. Certainly among the foundations of this State should be mentioned the supreme authority of God, the charisma of the Prophet, the constitution of community of solidarity or Umma, the founding of a system of law, the appearance of a unifying ritual. Here we have constructive State elements which gave the first nucleus its cohesion. But looked at from the perspective of all Arabia and from the point of view of its relations with the outside world, this State was built on warfare, on the establishment of a force of intervention which was to prove to be the real instrument of expansion of the Islamic State. Moreover, the constitution of Medina out of which was born the Islamic Umma under the eyes of God and of his Prophet, the second 'aqaba or agreement with the Muslims of Medina, on the eve of the Hegira, represents the moment of birth of the Islamic city. This was indeed a defensive pact with the aim of defending the Prophet against any aggression. But the idea of war and the martial intent were present. According to tradition[6] God had commanded his Prophet to go to war even though until that moment and for thirteen years the career of the Prophet had evolved as peaceful preaching. The emigration from the impious city and the break with the tribal surroundings coincided with a major turning point in the concept of prophecy henceforth converted into a policy of politics and warfare. Had there been a question of founding a self-sufficient and peaceful Islamic city, the establishment of Medina could have been considered as the act of foundation. But this was not the case. On the contrary, an aggressive initiative was very quickly to be revealed as the *raison d'être* of this city, and likewise the formation of a striking force which, starting off with a few hundred men, later expanded so as finally to comprise 30,000 warriors. It is therefore no accident that 'Umar later considered having taken part in the battle of Badr as the prerequisite for the awarding of pensions, nor that tradition described it in every detail.

Badr was in fact a determining phase, and first of all because there
came into play a movement of the original defensive pact (al-'aqaba)
towards the warrior state bent on plunder. It was elements among the
leaders at Medina personally loyal to the Prophet, in particular Sa'd b.
Mu'ādh, who helped to take this step, followed by some but not all.
Whence the tiny number of combattants at Badr — about three hundred
men[7] — in contrast to what the Prophet could muster later on. The battle
of Badr, the way in which the whole affair was organized, is clear proof
that from the second 'aqaba the Prophet intended declaring war on the
Quraysh and an uninterrupted war at that, and that in no way did he
envisage a defensive pact.[8] Of course, the Prophet sought to spread his
truth and his faith, but he undertook it through armed might and
warfare using the methods of his time and of the world in which he
lived. At Badr as well it can be noticed that plunder became a vital
factor in training his men. Finally, apart from the Muhājirūn or *émigrés*
and the Ansār or auxiliaries, the Prophet's forces at Badr contained
elements of the Juhayna tribe from near Medina which was associated
with the Ansār.

The battle of Badr resulted in the consolidation of the Prophet's
power of arbitration at Medina and enabled him to embark on a course
of decisive military action. It revealed him *vis-à-vis* the other Arabs as a
challenger of Qurayshī authority. Lastly, it allowed him to define his
policy towards the Jews: a policy of individualizing Islam as a religion
and making the Jews a target. On the occasion of every military crisis
(Badr, Uhud, Khandaq, Hudaybiyya) the Jews were to pay a heavy
price not only on account of being the living negative witness but also
as a source of plunder for those who followed the Prophet and the new
power that was being born. Whence came about the expulsion of the B.
Qaynuqā' followed by that of the B. Nadīr, then the massacre of the B.
Qurayza and finally the capture of Khaybar.

The battle of Uhud was simply a replay of the battle of Badr but with
the Qurayshīs taking their revenge. It demonstrated a remarkable
capacity for resistance on the part of the infant Islamic State. Further,
the Prophet was able to mobilize more men and extend his sphere of
influence. Together with the Juhayna and Muzayna tribes he succeeded
in making a satellite of the Khuzā'a tribe which had once been the
guardian of the Ka'ba before being removed by the Quraysh after
Qusayy but still living at Mecca. Without yet actually converting to
Islam except for a few individuals, this tribe was to display active
solidarity with the Prophet: it entered into his system of alliances and
played a part in diplomacy and espionage. This transitional phase
between Badr and the Khandaq is marked by embryonic expansionism
towards the Bedouin world of the Najd, diplomacy, the confiscation of

goods from the Jews of B. Nadīr, and the role of distributing the spoils of the State.

The Khandaq (5/626) marks a decisive stage in the progress towards the formation of a State. One might even say it was at this exact moment that the Prophet's authority assumed the aspect of a State, by means of military assertiveness. The Prophet faced a coalition comprising the Quraysh, the Aḥābīsh of Dināna, and the great qaysi tribe of Ghatafān represented by the clans of Fazāra, Ashja' and Murra.[9] The economic aspect of the struggle was transparent. The Ghatafān had their eyes on the Medina oasis and in order to appease them the Prophet offered them a third of its yield. It was even more notable in the seizure of the goods of the B. Qurayza and the inauguration of the division of the durable and non-durable *fay'* according to the rules which were to govern future Arab conquest. The fifth share obtained from such a prize considerably swelled the Prophet's coffers.[10] More than ever the Islamic State in its formative stage tended to become a pillaging state, bowing to the Peninsula's rules of warfare but having a determination and efficiency unusual in inter-tribal wars. Above all, the episode of the cold, calculating massacre of the B. Qurayza was to bring in a period of state and military violence absolutely new to Arabia which derived from the practices of the ancient Orient: massacre without exception of all the men and enslavement of women and children.[11] Bedouin violence did not have this systematic character, determination and organization and was never on such a scale. The state element was certainly a factor likewise the defence of religious ideology with the clear vision of a future to be ensured to which human lives must be sacrificed on a massive scale. The emergence of this kind of organized violence stupefied the Arabs in general and the Quraysh in particular. As a result there arose an impression of the insuperable power of the Prophet which was accentuated between Ḥudaybiyya and the capture of Mecca. Even in Medina clan loyalty disintegrated before the charismatic and personal power of the Prophet. The Islamic State rewarded itself by financial coercion of the converted tribes on instituting the ṣadaqa. The extraordinary thing is that these successes were not obtained by a clean victory over the main adversary — Quraysh — but by a victorious resistance accompanied by collective action which provide a picture of sustained action towards one aim, of organization, rationality, coherence, an image that has spread through the collective subconsciousness of the Arabs.

From the moment of Ḥudaybiyya this aim became clear: first of all unite the Arabs, then push them towards the conquest of the North. For this it was necessary by one means or another to go through with the capture of Mecca. How can one explain this extraordinarily sudden

change in that less than a year from the siege of Medina by the Quraysh
and its allies the Prophet was seriously contemplating leading his troops
on the little pilgrimage — 'Umra — around the Ka'ba? Definite
information is lacking, but it is noticeable that after the Khandaq and
even after the battle of Uḥud the Qurayshī chief and especially Abū
Sufyān were averse to exploiting thoroughly their advantage as if they
wished to give this Prophet from Quraysh a chance to pull himself
together. At any rate we know that during this period of two years from
the treaty of al-Ḥudaybiyya to the entry into Mecca (8/629) many
Qurayshīs were converted and joined the Prophet. Among them were
two highly prominent personalities: Khālid b. al-Walīd the victor of
Uḥud and 'Amr b. al-'Aṣ the negotiator at the Negus. There is no doubt
that at this critical phase both the two opposing parties, Quraysh and the
Prophet, were beginning to revise their previous positions towards a
reconciliation in depth which was to afford the Quraysh a dominant
place in the Prophet's system but would make it, by a bewildering
reversal of perspectives, the main defender of the Islamic State. One
sign of this change on the part of the Prophet lies in his admission and
recognition of the 'Umra, thus of the pre-eminence of the Ka'ba,
together with the *ḥajj* one of the two principal elements of the Meccan
religious system. The Prophet brought with him 70 sacrificial beasts,
all ritually prepared, and this could not fail to impress and to neutralize
the Aḥabish of Kināna[12] who had retained an attitude of devotion to the
sanctuary from their old role of guardians of the Ka'ba. The Prophet
took a step in a syncretic sense towards pagan religion until, shortly
before his death, he completely Islamized the integrated pilgrimage.
None of this could have been accomplished without the immense work
which brought forth the might of the Prophet as the chief power of the
Ḥijāz with a vocation to extend itself throughout Arabia.

Certainly not all the Qurayshīs changed their attitude towards the
Prophet. They refused him even a peaceful entry into Mecca.
Negotiations began which resulted in a ten-year truce. The Prophet
behaved as diplomat and statesman, convinced of the necessity of
handling the Quraysh cautiously for the moment while awaiting more
propitious circumstances and a strengthening of his potential, and this
against the advice of his counsellors and chief companions. It is
noteworthy that the opposing negotiator, a thanafite, was impressed by
the Prophet's royal demeanour, the extraordinary discipline of his
companions and his boundless power over them.[13] The notion of royalty
keeps returning as a *leitmotiv* and the Jews of Khaybar were shortly to
perceive him as King of the Ḥijāz.[14] Except perhaps among the hard
core of his partisans, the Muhājirūn and the Anṣār for whom he was
first and foremost God's Prophet, all the others — Arabs, Qurayshīs,

Jews — seized upon him as a force, as a power, as the power of the Hijāz.

The episode of the capture of Khaybar enhanced this state apparatus by giving it a stable agrarian base, overstepping the ordinary notion of plunder. The Prophet's army camped before Khaybar, besieged one after another of the forts where the Jews had shut themselves up, and obtained their surrender. The Prophet took possession of the lands and, keeping one fifth for himself, distributed the remainder among his Medina companions and certain Arabs who had taken part in the siege. The Jews offered to continue to work on these lands, no longer theirs, under a sharecropping contract which was revocable and indeed was revoked under the Caliphate of 'Umar. The combination of plunder and obtaining possession of the land cemented loyalties. As already stated, this power engaged in a dialectic of dealing with its enemies, dispossessing them, and then sustaining their loyalties once they had been dispossessed. It is in fact the dialectic of the organized warrior state, in this case justified by religion.

This enhanced economic power was attractive to the surrounding Bedouins such as the Aslam, who were wasted by famine.[15] Both Khuzā'a and Ghifār converted to Islam while the Ahābīsh proclaimed their neutrality and guaranteed not to oppose the Prophet any more. Bedouin elements increasingly swelled the ranks of his army so that in the year 8/629 when he was preparing to lay siege to Mecca he found himself leading 10,000 men thanks to the massive Bedouin support for the new religion and the Prophet's system. Beyond the central nucleus of the Muhājirūn and the Ansār there were tribes or fragments of tribes which were to provide an outer circle of loyal elements: Muzayna, Sulaym, Ghifār, Khuzā'a.[16] When, after the capture of Mecca, they were joined by the Kināna and the Quraysh and, after the surrender of Tā'if the Thaqīf, this whole group was to be the nucleus of the permanent loyal Muslim army devoted to the new order and prepared to resist any tribal apostasy.[17] In the Iraqi town-camps of the future this enormous mass of people was to be called the ahl al-'Aliya or men of Medina. Some of them emigrated to Medina and called themselves émigrés or Muhājirūn in an effort to be on a par with the earliest followers. These tribes were either those neighbouring Medina, allied of old to the Khazraj and the Aws or tribes from near Mecca allied to the Quraysh. The Prophet integrated them one by one into his circle of followers acting as both chief of the Medina community and heir to the Qurayshī authority. But it goes without saying that the inmost nucleus was formed by the original Muhājirūn and the Ansār.

When he laid siege to Mecca in the year 8/629, breaking the ten-year truce after only two years, the Prophet assumed the stature of a true

conquering warrior chief the like of which Arabia had not yet seen. In
his army, side by side with the troops from Medina and other loyal
neighbouring tribes, were various other Bedouin elements of Tamīm,
Qays and Asad.[18] Ten thousand torches were lit. A great impression
was made on the Quraysh: "your nephew's empire has become
important", said Abū Sufyān to al-'Abbās the Prophet's uncle. The
army was organized to perfection, with flanks and a centre.[19] So Mecca
surrendered without a shot and embraced Islam, twenty-one years after
the Prophet's first arising. An important event, which made the Prophet
master not only of the Ka'ba and of pilgrimage but also of Meccan
commerce, and made him generally heir to Qurayshī authority. Chief
of a power patiently built around the community of the Muhājirūn and
the Ansār, a power founded on belonging to a religion with its credo, its
rights, its taboos and its laws, and gradually spread to a large part of the
Bedouin world of the Hijāz, he was now in possession of the most
important centre in Arabia. The Quraysh embraced Islam. The
Prophet's army, shortly thereafter fighting against the 20,000 men of
the Hawazīn tribe, defeated them and took possession of an immense
booty distributed according to political calculations aimed at cementing
the new loyalty of the Qurayshī leaders, which created tensions with the
Ansār, the faithful basis of the system relegated to second place. The
Qurayshīs, mainly newcomers to Islam, prepared themselves to play
the leading role in the new State because they were the tribe of the
Prophet and blood ties took precedence over pure ideological loyalty.
Thus the new power was riddled with latent conflicts between diverging
loyalties and varying examples of fidelity: blood ties versus precedence
in the Prophet's struggle, townsmen versus tribesmen. The whole
future of Islam would be bound up around these tensions which can be
traced to two systems of values, one the residue (but a powerful
residue) of the Jāhiliyya, the other that of Islam as a renewing force and
a dymanic of struggle. In outlining a massive return to the Fatherland
and to blood ties the Prophet removed its aura of intransigence and
purity from the Islamic message but in doing so provided it with the
political conditions for success in this world.

The two years between the surrender of Mecca and the Prophet's
death were to see the extension of Islamic power throughout Arabia, a
certain return to religious rigidity through the islamization of the hajj,
consolidation of the vision of conquest in the North. According to
tradition, deputations from all the tribes were sent to Medina to make
an act of allegiance.[20] This did not mean actual conversion of all the
tribes but a political subjection which frankly smacks of the miraculous
and has never been explained. How indeed could one explain how a
number of proud warrior tribes that had never bowed to any authority
could suddenly offer their allegiance without even a fight?

One is tempted to believe that there was a need for unity, that the new power awakened hopes, that its religious structure with God as sole authority encouraged obedience and that indeed this power was endowed with sufficient strength for punishment and repression. We should remember also that these tribes, those from the Najd, the East and the Yemen were not as independent as at first appears since they had offered their allegiance to princes such as the Lakhmides of Ḥīra and the princes of Yemen among the Abna. This was the case with Bakr, Tamīm, Madhḥij and Hamdān. In fact the complete independence of the tribes is a myth except in certain cases like the Hawāzin whose resistance was broken by the Prophet at Ḥunayn and the tribes of the Yamāna which were urbanized around a ḥaram[21] and were to harbour their own prophet. Thus tribal Arabia had been prepared by its own experience to give its allegiance to a strong power. Now the Prophet's power had the following advantages: it was purely Arab, supported by the radiance of the ḥaram, organized human life without breaking any blood ties, and finally it offered the prospect of conquests. In the meantime the tribes would support him by agreeing to the payment of legal alms and accepting the Prophet's local agents.[22]

The Prophet's external aims are an element which became apparent in the early days. In the year 8/629 he sent an expedition of 3,000 men to Mu'ta which proved to be a fiasco. In 10/631 an army of 30,000, the mightiest ever assembled by Medina, moved towards Tabūk. It subdued various districts and demonstrated very clearly the Prophet's designs on the countryside and towns of the North which were emphasized by the Qur'ān as Arab towns stricken by the curse of God. The forgotten Arab tradition of the North is strongly integrated into the text of the Qur'ān and appears as the basis of its truly Arab memory and reflection. At the end of his life the Prophet clearly considered external conquest to be the alternative to commerce. The Qur'ān emphasizes that God's promises are better than commerce[23] and the necessity of obedience to God even if that endangers commerce through the ban on polytheists approaching a pilgrimage.[24] This was a new prohibition that arose as if from a moment of last-minute repentance. The commerce of Mecca was threatened with strangulation and it was in this context that the Qur'ān offers in exchange the promises of God, new ways of living and new perspectives. It was a question of the conquest of the already Arabized North which anyhow seemed to be the natural extension of Arabia. So even in its early stages the Prophet's power contained within itself the germ of the idea of external conquest. The disorganization of trade, the impossibility of offering the prospects of booty in a peaceful Arabia, the fact that it was essential for this power to be propped up by tangible material successes — all this continued to make the Islamic State one that was oriented towards conquest. In view of the fact that from the moment of its birth at the time of the Hegira this was a warrior state, conquest was by no means accidental, it was part of its very nature. The only way to federate the tribes was by offering them a familiar objective, that of the ever-renewed pursuit of booty. From Badr to Ḥunayn and to Tabūk, taking in the successive seizures of the Jewish oases, the Prophet's State pursued the one goal: that of transplanting the customs of the nomadic world into a settled habitat with more adequate means and a regular aim in life, subordinating this uninterrupted martial progress to the transcendence of God.

6

ADMINISTRATION IN THE ISLAMIC STATE:
AN INTERPRETATION OF THE TERMS
"DHIMMA" AND "JIZYA"

Jørgen Bæk Simonsen

Anyone who has been working with Arabic sources for the early history of the Arabian Middle Ages in order to comprehend the developments that fostered the creation of the Islamic State in Medina in A.D. 622 will agree that historical traditions are adapted to serve an ideology.[1] Ideology regards historical events as proof of a religious truth. This view of history is not specific to the Arabic-Islamic tradition. We know it from Europe too, in fact, we still use a fragment of it in our chronological framework. We place persons and events before Christ and after. We know it also from the Jewish tradition. Here it still forms a very active ideological force — think of the situation on the West Bank, which is always referred to as Judea and Samaria by Israeli radio and television.

In the West, however, we have generally given up this religiously flavoured view on history. We now work with a theory of cause and effect. All historical events are results of specific human activity. This is true at least as far as our own history is concerned. In our approach to medieval Arabic-Islamic history, this scientific attitude unfortunately is not always present. It is not surprising that religion and history still blend together in many works by Arab-Muslim historians of our own age, but it is surprising to see how often ideological beliefs are taken over by non-Muslim scholars, thus limiting any deeper understanding. These dogmas tend to obstruct any analysis of the historical structure that formed the background of the establishment of the Islamic State; they also obstruct a more scientific interpretation of *what* type of state Medina actually was.

To take the fundamentalist tradition, the Islamic State in Medina is the great example to turn to if one is to resolve the various problems of the modern Islamic world. According to this view, the Islamic State in Medina was governed pursuant to the divine precepts of Muhammad. Take, as an example, to the following quotation from Imām Khomeinī:

"The most noble Messenger (peace and blessings be upon him) headed the executive and administrative institutions of Muslim society. In addition to conveying the revelation and expounding and interpreting the articles of faith and the ordinances and institutions of Islam, he undertook the implementation of law and the establishment of the ordinances of Islam, thereby bringing into being the Islamic state. He did not content himself with the promulgation of law; rather, he implemented it at the same time, cutting off hands and administering lashings and stonings. After the most noble Messenger, his successor had the same duty and function".[2]

In traditional circles one can also find examples of how the Islamic State in Medina and the Golden Age during the first four rightly-guided caliphs are used as models to follow by modern Muslim nations. But while the fundamentalist interpretation argues that the rules according to which the Islamic State must be governed are eternal, the more traditional groups accept that even Islam has changed from time to time, although the central religious dogmas are, of course, considered unchangeable.

One of the events interpreted as an example of "Heilsgeschichte" is the hijra in the autumn of 622. In the classical Arabic literature, this event is but one of several examples of how Allāh intervened directly in history. In this way the tradition makes a virtue of necessity. When Muhammad and his first Aṣḥāb went off to Medina in 622, the prospects for a future stay in Mecca were totally lost. In order to understand this, it is necessary to say a few words about Mecca.

Mecca lies on the western part of the Arabian peninsula. Agriculture in Mecca was impossible due to insufficient water supplies[3] and the city was dependent on food imported from its neighbouring town Ṭā'if.[4] In the late sixth century and in the early seventh century Mecca had nevertheless secured itself the position as the leading caravan city on the peninsula. This position was achieved only as a result of long and difficult negotiations with the surrounding world — and by good contacts with leading circles in Byzantium and Yemen. Mecca had also made agreements with various tribes on the peninsula and was thus able to commence its monopoly on trade between Arabia Felix and East Africa to the south and the Byzantine Empire to the north.[5] Other cities,[6] tribes and tribal groups[7] had had the same position earlier, but at the beginning of the seventh century no one outside Mecca could pose a threat to Mecca's hegemony.

The position of Mecca was further supported by a skilful use of the markets held yearly at the Ka'ba. The markets were held during holy months and every Arab tribe coming to these markets could be sure that no one would attack. This institution gave further advantages to the

Quraysh and greatly supported their hold on the caravan trade of the Arab peninsula. Indeed, Mecca at the birth of the Prophet was the caravan city *par excellence*.

The position of Mecca could, however, be threatened from within Meccan society itself. As far as we know, all leading tribes were involved directly in the management of the city. Various privileges linked to its status as a local holy city were also divided between the largest tribes. But some tribes had no part in this system, and as pointed out by Montgomery Watt, Maxime Rodinson and others,[8] the prosperous situation some tribes found themselves in was criticized by other tribes. Social conditions were very different from one tribe to the other, and there are many signs of a profound crisis in the values and the moral beliefs of the Meccan society. Not only was Muḥammad critical, but perhaps better than anyone else he was able to describe the situation.[9]

Muḥammad was a sincere and honest person. He was about 40 years old when he first realized that he had received revelations from Allāh.[10] There is nothing fanatic about his revelations — they are honest thoughts and wise sayings. But once in motion he had to carry on. As soon as others accepted his religion he had to behave as their leader and had to take care of their interests. In this respect he had to face the power-structure of his own time. Possibilities for survival in Mecca were contingent upon an active participation in the caravan trade. But the Quraysh had no intention of giving up their own privileged position, and they perceived the religious message of Muḥammad as a fundamental threat to both the religious ideas forming the basis of the holy markets at the Ka'ba, and to their monopoly of the caravan trade. This threat had to be removed, and therefore the Quraysh decided to strike where it would hurt the most. They arranged a total boycott of all commerce with Muḥammad and his Aṣḥāb.[11] The Muslims were now forced to reassess their position — but instead of giving up the fight, they tried to establish contacts with groups outside Mecca. This was not an easy task. It is written in the Sīra how Muḥammad again and again made contact with different tribes coming to Mecca's markets, but although some individual persons were impressed by his religious message, no one dared offer him and his Muslims shelter on their own territory.[12] When he finally succeeded, it was due to specific problems inside the Oasis of Yathrib itself.[13] The Oasis of Yathrib had for several years been involved in inter-tribal fights and wanted an outsider to step in and serve as arbitrator. The inhabitants therefore decided to talk to Muḥammad and invite him to come to Yathrib to help them to resolve the situation. It was their need for an arbitrator and his own desperate situation in Mecca that formed the background to the hijra in 622. He was not a person with any special political or economic position when he arrived in Medina in the summer of 622. The best proof of this is the so-called Constitution of Medina.[14] He ended up as such — but no one had any possible way of perceiving this in 622. The only thing he knew for certain was that he had to fight Mecca and the Quraysh — and he knew how to do this.

In order to survive in Medina, the Muslims engaged in trade from the very first day of their arrival. One of the first things Muhammad did was to establish a new market.[15] This aroused opposition within Medina, but Muhammad successfully silenced the opposition. The battle of Badr[16] was a big political victory, but a victory without visible economic gains. The Muslims went out to catch a rich caravan returning to Mecca from Ghaza,[17] but the caravan returned safely to Mecca. Instead, the Muslims won a victory in the battle with the Meccan army and Muhammad immediately used this victory to topple the Jewish Banū Qainuqā'a. This is very important, because the Banū Qainuqā'a had no land at all. But they had something else — they were in charge of all the trade in Medina.[18] However, trade had to be effected with the outside world and therefore Muhammad had to carry on his long-term policy against Mecca. In order to win the outside world for his trade he had to fight Mecca. One of the means used in this fight were the ghazāwāt. If one looks at the long lists of ghazāwāt done by the Muslims, one sees that not very many resulted in actual fighting between the two parties. Fighting is not necessary. Caravan trade depends on security; when there is no security it stops. Huge sums of money were invested in each caravan — and no serious trader wanted to lose his invested capital because the route was not secure.

While Medina was fighting Mecca in order to gain control of the caravan trade, it slowly built up its own trade system. This Muslim trade system rested upon "dhimma". Dhimma is mentioned twice in the Quran:

Sura 9,8:   Kaifa wa-in yatharū 'alaikum lā yarqubū fīkum illan wa la
            dhimmatan yardūnakum bi-afwāhihim wa ta'bā qulūbuhum wa
            aktharuhum fāsiqūn.
Bell: How? if they get the upper hand of you they will not regard bond
            or agreement, they will satisfy you with their mouths, but their
            hearts will refuse; the most of them are reprobates.

Sura 9,10: la yarqubūna fi mu'minim illan wa lā dhimmatan wa ulā'ika hum
            al-mu'tadūn.
Bell: In respect of a believer they will not regard bond or agreement;
            they are ill-disposed.

The Constitution of Medina stresses "Dhimmatu Allāhi wāhida" with the important addition "yujīru 'alaihim adnāhum'.[19] An analysis of the old layer of traditions indicates that this practice was used by Medina from 622 onwards. Medina gave dhimmā security to any tribe or any community that would adhere to their new trade system. As time went by and as more tribes and more communities approached Medina, this dhimmâ had to be paid in different ways. By the dual means of ghazāwāt and dhimma Medina was able to gain the upper hand in the struggle with Mecca and finally in 630 to win the fight.

The practice of dhimmâ was not an Islamic invention. Mecca had used the same policy in the sixth century,[20] and the same practice had been used by other caravan cities before.[21] Only the terms were different.

Jizya is another central institution and, like dhimma, a concept belonging to the early Islamic State in Medina. Jizya is also mentioned in the Qur'ān:

Sura 9,29: qātilū alladhīna la yu'minūna bil-lahi wa la bil-yaumi al-ākhiri wa lā huharrimūna mā harrama Allāhu wa rasūluhu wa lā yadīnūna dīna al-haqqi min alladhīna ūtū al-kitāba hatta yu'ṭū al-jizyata 'an yadin wa hum sāghirūn.

Bell: Fight against those who do not believe in Allāh nor in the Last Day, and do not make forbidden what Allāh and His messenger have made forbidden, and do not practise the religion of truth, of those who have been given the Book, until they pay jizya off-hand, being subdued.

The composition of the Sura is very difficult.[22] In this verse there seems also to be a later insertion, namely the words "min alladhīna utū al-kitāba".[13] This is very important — and Bell's view is supported by the fact that it was not until later that the main opponents of the Islamic State were Christians. Apart from a few scattered Jewish settlements and the Christians in Najrān, the main enemy of Muhammad and the Islamic State in Medina were Arabs. The main part of Arabia had surrendered to Medina at the time of the revelation of Sura 9, but there were still some tribes that had not entered Pax Islamica. These were the ones meant by this verse. They, too, were to acknowledge the supremacy of Medina — and pay "jizya 'an yadin" in order to be allowed to enter the new Islamic power-structure.

In the later caliphate taxation system, jizya becomes a central institution. In the final Islamic fiqh jizya is a tax paid by Jews and Christians for protection.[24] But this is a later development and has nothing to do with the way dhimma and jizya were used in the early

Islamic State. Muḥammad did not create the Islamic State in order to gain control of what today is known as the Islamic world. The Muslim hijra was necessary in order to fight the Quraysh, and all he wanted was to create a new caravan city. He was aware that his religious sayings had a possible universal message, but as a politician he had no intention of going beyond the Arab peninsula.

7

STATE AND POLITICS IN THE
PHILOSOPHY OF SHĀH WALĪY ALLĀH

Mahmood A. Ghazi

Shāh Walīy Allāh (1703 – 1762) is undoubtedly one of the greatest leaders of thought produced by Muslim India during the course of its long history. He is considered to be the bridge betweeen the medieval and the modern in the religio-intellectual history of the Muslim subcontinent. His deep impact on the subsequent development of Muslim thought in India (and Pakistan of course) finds its parallel only in the impact left by his great and illustrious contemporary, Muḥammad ibn 'Abd al-Wahhāb. In the following pages an effort had been made to extract his ideas on state and politics from his voluminous writings.

It is the religio-philosophical thought of Shāh Walīy Allāh in which lies his real greatness. It provides a comprehensive metaphysico-theoretical framework for his entire thinking and its study should precede any inquiry into his political ideas. But unfortunately, the philosophical aspect of his thought cannot be expatiated upon in detail in this brief article for that does not come within our purview.[1]

Here we confine ourselves to the socio-political thought of Shāh Walīy Allāh which is based on the basic framework of his religio-philosophical thought and is closely linked with a well-knit ideological system. Hence it is somewhat difficult to understand his ideas in a purely analytical way. His approach to social and political problems is different from those of most modern sociologists and political scientists who see these problems from a non-metaphysical point of view. It is on the basis of this theoretical framework that Shāh Walīy Allāh was able to make a successful effort to find out the relationship between social, political, economic and even ethical aspects of Islamic thought.

Shāh Walīy Allāh first of all expounds his ideas about God and Universe and the creation of Man. Then he discusses death and the life in the Hereafter. The position of man in the Universe and his relation to the Creator form part of his religio-philosophical thought, while his characteristics, his nature and his relations with other members of his species form part of his socio-political thought.

Man, according to Shāh Walīy Allāh, is distinguished from other Creatures by his 'Perfect Signs' or (*Āthār Tāmma*), such as the faculty of forming "generalizations" and "comprehensive opinions" about his works and activities, faculty of speech, writing and *esprit*. Such signs are innumerable and cannot be reduced to a limited number but these are based on three basic principles.

Firstly, in his action and behaviour man is governed by generalizations or "comprehensive opinions" (*Al-Ray, al-Kulliyy*) he forms. On the other hand, for example, beast (*bahīma*: animals other than man) is moved and sometimes becomes motivated only to repel the immediate danger and to acquire the immediate benefit and good; in effect it is impelled towards a perceptible or imaginary goal. On the other hand, man is sometimes motivated in order to create a perfect system in the city. Man sometimes takes the trouble in order to realize an object which has no relation to his bodily appetites. He takes the trouble in endeavouring to materialize an object in the Hereafter or to realize a worldly social benefit for the people.

Secondly, it is the *Zarāfa* or *esprit* which has the meaning and connotation of aesthetic attitude according to Shāh Walīy Allāh. The need for food and shelter is common to man and beast to allay hunger and to ward off heat and cold. The beast is satisfied if it fulfils these two ends but man is never satisfied with this stage of the realization of his basic ends. He requires them to be achieved in an aesthetic and most accomplished way. This urge is termed by Shāh Walīy Allāh as *Zarāfa* i.e. *esprit*.

Thirdly, the beastly arts and "sciences" are designed only to meet economic and subsistence needs while the human sciences are sometimes directed towards the attainment of spiritual perfection and psychic accomplishment. These are the three fundamental principles on which all the signs of mankind are based.[2]

It is a blessing of God on mankind that He has deposited in mankind moral excellences and social temptations. Had these excellences not been so deposited no one would have performed acts conducive to moral excellences and no one would follow people possessing these excellences. In such a case no moral excellence could have been established and men would have been categorized with beasts. But, instead, God has fashioned the intellects of people like mirrors in which ideas and images are reflected on each other, and thus goes on the process of adopting and learning from each other the manners and decorums based on moral excellences. If a survey is made in this regard it will be revealed that many acts and practices of cultural and civilizational importance are communicated through imitation. However, apart from this natural motive there should be some outward support to bind people to these manners.[3]

Thus, Shāh Walīy Allāh develops the socio-anthropological basis for the emergence and formation of society. After a society takes birth it passes, according to Shāh Walīy Allāh, through four stages until it reaches its perfection. These stages are termed by Shāh Walīy Allāh as *Irtifāq*.

The urges of food and sex are basic human urges which ensure the continuation of human existence on earth. Food keeps man's body intact while the sex-urge perpetuates the human race and regulates procreation. God has also inspired mankind to build shelters to live in and to defend himself against the weather. These needs are common to all men who have an innate desire to excel in the modes of acquiring them. For this purpose different ways and means are adopted which include the use of agricultural methods, co-operating with each other, adopting civilized styles of speech, cuisine, and monogamy.[4] When society achieves these requirements of social development it acquires the first degree of its perfection, i.e. *al-Irtifāq al-Awwal*.

When these requirements are met in a more refined and sophisticated way they need five sciences to usher in the second degree of social perfection. These requirements and the five sciences, embraced together, constitute the second degree of perfection, i.e. *al-Irtifāq al-Thānī*. The five sciences are:

1. Economic Wisdom (*al-Hikma al-Ma'āshiyya*).
2. Earning Wisdom (*al-Hikma al-Iktisābiyya*).
3. Household Wisdom (*al-Hikma al-Manziliyya*).
4. Business Wisdom (*al-Hikma al-Ta'āmuliyya*).
5. Co-operative Wisdom (*al-Hikma al-Ta'āwuniyya*).

Economic wisdom, as enunciated by Shāh Walīy Allāh, includes the adoption and utilization of edifying manners, new experiments and modes of eating, drinking, dress, domestic habits, sitting, walking, speaking and travelling. When those requirements are met in the proper manner and in the light of past experience it gives rise to economic wisdom. Wisdom of earning means that every individual should adopt a distinct and separate activity befitting his energies and faculties, such as agriculture, trade etc. Household wisdom includes marriage, procreation, the rights of close relatives etc. Business wisdom includes such matters as selling, making gifts, renting, hiring, lending, incurring debts, loans, or mortgages, and so on. Co-operative wisdom embraces surety, bail, guarantees, partnerships, agencies, etc.[5] All these five social wisdoms have a great bearing on the economic life and activity of a society. This shows the extent to which Shāh Walīy Allāh gives importance to the economic dimensions of the social development. The second *Irtifāq* is the most important in the process of the perfection of a society; its role is more fundamental. If the second *Irtifāq* duly achieves its perfection the remaining degrees are easily attainable. If these five wisdoms are practised in a sound and suitable way they give birth to innumerable developments in culture and civilization.[6]

When these five wisdoms interact with the moral human excellences they give rise to the third degree of social development. This *Irtifāq* is mostly based on the co-operation of men so as to achieve the results of the five wisdoms. Without co-operation these sciences can neither be put into practice nor produce the required results. Co-operation is essential because men are not equal. An average group of people includes fools, the wise., the wealthy, the poor, the one who is capable of earning, and the one who is not, the one who disdains practising small and ordinary professions and the one who does not, the one who has several types of commercial undertakings and the one who is unemployed. If these people do not co-operate with each other in realizing their socio-economic objectives their socio-economic life will be of no effect. The socio-economic institutions of a developed society are only forms of co-operation; *Muzāra'a, Muḍāraba* and other such institutions are based on co-operation.[7]

The interaction of the five wisdoms with each other and with the moral excellences and mutual co-operation naturally leads to the emergence of a socio-political organization — *Madīna* or state. *Madīna* is not merely a city; if the citizens of a group of cities and towns have this interaction and co-operation their group will also be termed as *Madīna*. Every *Madīna* or state has a unity which must be preserved in its original and perfect form and its benefits should also be accomplished. The medium through which this perfection can be preserved and accomplished is, in fact, *Imām*. By *Imām*, Shāh Walīy Allāh does not mean any particular individuals;[8] *Imām* seems to be the equivalent of government or the ruling group in Shāh Walīy Allāh's terminology. This, however, will be discussed at length later.

The state is not confined to its boundaries, its bazaars and its edifices. The state, in fact, means a special kind of relationship among various groups. This relationship is imperative and is necessitated by the five principles of the second *Irtifāq*. When these groups co-operate with each other for the realization of the five wisdoms and carry on transactions and intercourse with each other they resemble a single individual having a spiritual entity. This ''corporate'' individual undergoes health or illness arising from outward and inward causes. To cure this corporate individual, i.e. the state, from its illness and to preserve its health there should be a competent state physician. This physician is *Imām* and those who adhere to it. This stage of social development is called the third *Irtifāq*,[9] the first stage of political organization — the state. The first *Irtifāq* represents the most primitive societies or to be more correct the pre-social human existence. The second *Irtifāq* represents the pre-political stage of social organization. The third and the fourth *Irtifāqs* are the stages of political organization of society.

When several states (*Mudun Kathīrah*) exist at a time, dissensions arise and illnesses infect the body-politic of the states. Then a superior physican (*Tabīb al-Atibbā*) is required to cure these inter-state diseases; he may also be called *Imam al-A'immah*.[10] Elsewhere the *Imām al-A'immah* has been termed as *Khalifa*.[11] This is the fourth *Irtifāq* which is, in fact an elementary form of international politics. Defining the fourth *Irtifāq*, Shāh Walīy Allāh says, "it is the science (*hikma*) which discusses the policy of the rulers and kings of the states and the ways and means of the preservation of co-ordination and relationship existing among the peoples of various countries."[12] This seems to be the social ideal of Shāh Walīy Allāh, and it is only after achieving this stage of socio-political development that the system of *Khilāfa* can be properly established. After this brief introduction to his social philosophy we shall now discuss the political thought of Shāh Walīy Allāh

Shāh Walīy Allāh has written extensively on politics. His works *Hujjat Allāh al-Bāligha* and *Al-Budūr al-Bāzigha* contain useful and comprehensive discussions on political problems, and his *Isalat al-Khafā'*, an encyclopaedic work on the history and philosphy of *Khilāfa Rāshidah*, gives thought-provoking ideas about the concept of *Khilāfa* and its development as the supreme political institution of Muslim polity. Our discussion is based mainly on these three sources.

It has already been pointed out that the need for a political organization is initially felt in a given society in its second degree towards perfection while a definite political organism takes place in the third degree — *al-Irtifāq al-Thālith*. Defining politics (or *siyāsat al-Mudun*), Shāh Walīy Allāh asserts that it is the science which discusses the ways and means of preserving the relationship existing among the citizens of the state; and by "state" he means a community of closely related people having mutual transactions and relationships but of different families and houses.[13] From the point of view of its size and population the state is of two kinds, according to Shāh Walīy Allāh.

1. The perfect state or *al-Madīna al-Tāmma* and
2. The imperfect state or *al-Madina al-Naqisa*.

If a state can produce four thousand warriors in times of emergency and has sufficient number of peasants and artisans, it is a perfect state; by sufficient number he means that which can meet the requirements of the second *Irtifāq*. The Imām (leader) of this state shall be a Perfect *Imām*. But a state which is smaller than this should be called an imperfect state. States are of various degrees even in respect of their perfection.[14]

A *Madina* or state generally has a large population. It is not possible for all its inhabitants and citizens to agree on the maintenance of just and equitable behaviour. None of them can admonish the other without the force of authority, for that would lead to widespread dissention. Therefore, Shāh Walīy Allāh maintains, the affairs of the state can never be organized and properly regulated unless the majority of *Ahl al-Hall wa 'l'Aql* agree upon obedience to certain lieutenants endowed with power and prestige (*Shawkah*).[15] Such an individual is named by Shāh Walīy Allāh as either *Imām* (leader) or *Malik* (king). It seems that he conceives of an elected king as enjoying the confidence of the people in "Loosing and Binding".

The Imām, according to Shāh Walīy Allāh, should possess seven Major Virtues; otherwise he will be a burden on the state and the state will be a burden on him and both will degenerate.[16] These Seven Virtues are *Shajā'a* (bravery), *Samahah* (magnanimity and tolerance), *Hikma* (wisdom), *'Iffa* (moral integrity), *Faṣāha* (eloquence, *Diyāna* (piety) and *al-Samt al-Ṣalih* (good manners). The absence of one or more of these virtues will create difficulties in the execution of his office. The absence of *Shajā'a* will render the ruler incapable of defending the state from outside aggression and preserving it from internal disturbance; this applies also to the other virtues.[17] Furthermore, he should be wise and of sound mind, of major age, free, male, and having perfect faculties of understanding, hearing, seeing and speaking. He should be one whose dignity and respect and that of his family is recognized by the people. In view of the praiseworthy achievements of his forefathers people are assured that he will exert himself for the betterment of the state.[18] As to the authority and source of these virtues, Shāh Walīy Allāh says that all these details have been inspired by reason, and since the people of various geographical, ethnic, cultural and ideological backgrounds have reached similar conclusions it can readily be concluded that these qualifications of a king are based on reason and *Maslaha*.[19]

Another important quality which Shāh Walīy Allāh considers inevitable for a king is *Ja*, or dignity and prestige.[20] A king should always try to create *Ja* in the minds and hearts of his people and should take all possible steps to maintain and preserve it. *Jā*, according to Shāh Walīy Allāh, can be achieved by adopting such moral excellences as may endear the king to the subjects.[21] *Jā* is conducive to love, respect and veneration for the *Imām* which is the basis of every leadership — perfect or imperfect.[22]

Shāh Walīy Allāh has also extensively dwelt upon the need and the qualifications of the associates and lieutenants of the *Imām*. The *Imām* cannot execute all his duties himself and cannot attend in person to every problem and difficulty. He is always in need of a lieutenant (*'Awn*) to look after any important specific field. Thus, several lieutenants will be required to look after different matters. A lieutenant should be just (*'Adl*) and should execute his duties with perfection and minuteness. He should be obedient to the king and should not disobey him either in private or in public. If a lieutenant does not fulfil these conditions he deserves dismissal; and if the *Imām* does not dismiss him it will lead to the disruption of the *Irtifāq*, i.e. the respective degree of socio-political development. Wisdom requires that the *Imām* should not appoint his lieutenant from among those who cannot be easily dismissed.[23] Moreover, a lieutenant should not be appointed from amongst the relatives of the king because if he has to be dismissed it might prove shameful to the king.[24]

Shāh Walīy Allāh considers seven types of lieutenants necessary for the *Imām*:

1. The *Wazīr* (or prime minister). He will be the supreme authority for all the government functionaries; he will also be responsible for the collection of taxes and their distribution and expenditure.

2. *Amīr al-Ghuzā* (or commander of the warriors). He will raise armies and study their affairs; he will also keep himself informed about their ranks and rates of pay.

3. *Amīr al-Ḥirs* (or chief of police). He will attend to misdeeds and will admonish those responsible.

4. The *Qāḍi*, who will adjudicate in legal affairs and in disputes between the litigants.

5. *Shaykh al-Islām.* He will look after the establishment of the *Dīn* and the organization of religious guidance. His lieutenants will look after the institution of *Amr bi'l Ma'ruf* and *Nahy'an al-Munkar*.

6. *Ḥakīm* (probably minister of secular education). He will organize the teaching of medicine, literature, astronomy, history, arithmetic and the art of writing. The *Imām* and the government have need of these arts and sciences in the conduct of the state.

7. *Wakīl* (or private secretary). He will ensure the proper organization and management of the ruler's personal income and expenses.[25]

After elaborating on the duties and functions of these seven lieutenants of the ruler, Shāh Walīy Allāh gives advice to the ruler on how to control his lieutenants. Such forms of advice are of practical and strategic significance rather than theoretical and philosophical.[26]

These discussions on *Madīna* (or state) and the *Imām* (leader or king) are general and can be applied to any kind of state which has reached the third stage of development. They are based on philosophical speculation and have no reference to the Holy Qur'ān or the Sunna. The Islamic concept of the state is international and extraterritorial. It belongs to the fourth and the last *Irtifāq* because it is a perfect and mature concept of both state and society. The fourth *Irtifāq* and international polity seem to be identical according to Shāh Walīy Allāh. It is only in the course of discussions on the fourth *Irtifāq* in *Ḥujjat Allāh al-Bālighah* that we come across references derived from the Holy Qur'ān.[27] It shows that according to Shāh Walīy Allāh, the ideal of the Islamic state or the *Khilāfa* can only be realized in a perfect and developed society.

Shāh Walīy Allāh discusses the institution of the *Khilāfa* from two different angles: rational and classical in the Islamic context. When he discusses the concept of the *Khilāfa* as a continuation of his theory of socio-political development of a society (*Irtifāqāt*) he visualizes the *Khalīfa* as an emperor or potentate. To him, a *Khalīfa* is required when several kings quarrel with each other and become jealous of each other's power. Thus, a *Khalīfa* is one who has acquired superior armies and armaments such as to render him indomitable and unable to be deposed.[28] Elsewhere, Shāh Walīy Allāh defines the magnitude of these armies. If an *Imām* has a standing army of twelve thousand men and the state can afford their subsistence, the wisdom requires that such an Imām be termed a *Khalīfa*.[29] Like the *Imāms*, the *Khulafā'* also have different degrees of power and status. If a *Khalīfa* can afford one hundred thousand warriors and the state is able to pay them he shall be the "greatest *Khalīfa* second to none."[30]

Consideration should be given to the superior degree of this "greatest *Khalīfa*" or *al-Khalīfa al-A'ẓam* who has also been termed as *Khalīfa al-Khulāfā'*. The concept of *Khalifa al-Khulafā'* seems to be something like the head of a confederation of several states or of a commonwealth of states. Discussing the need for *Khalīfa al-Khalafā'*, Shāh Walīy Allāh says[31] that when every *Imām* becomes independent and established with his state or group of small states, and he regularly collects taxes and levies, and acquires the services and affiliation of skilled soldiers who love their *Imām* and who are enthusiastic in their support to him, then avarice, greed, and enmity ensue. This leads to disputes and wars among the *Imāms*; in consequence there is violence and death, and every *Irtifāq* is annulled. This situation, whenever it arises, must be corrected and the solution is to establish a *Khalīfa al-Khulafā'*. The definition of *Khalīfa al-Khulafā'* is that he is one who acquires power, prestige, enthusiastic support and the affiliation of skilled military manpower to such a high degree that it is almost impossible for him to be overthrown. If one tries to dethrone him it would not be possible without giving rise to disorder, vast expense and anarchy. Persons, habits and customs will differ. If the *Khalīfa* is disputed and armed conflicts prove of no avail, then there is no solution other than a divinely appointed conqueror, armed with anger, who will gather to himself armies obedient to him. Only an avenger of this stature can vanquish the forces of disruption. Nevertheless, since such occasions are infrequent, people would do well to adhere to the fourth *Irtifāq* and implications.[32]

Such was the exposition of *Khilāfa* on a scientific and historical basis. The other aspect is classical which Shāh Walīy Allāh discusses from a purely juristic point of view. The establishment of a *Khalīfa* among the Muslims is necessary for achieving innumerable objectives which can be classified into two categories:[33]

1. Those which come within the purview of political science (*Siyāsat al-Madīna*), e.g., national defence, administration of justice, etc. which have been discussed earlier.[34]

2. Those which come within the purview of the *Milla*. This is because the exaltation of the Islamic *Dīn* over the entire genus of religion cannot be possible without a *Khalīfa* who must enforce Islamic injunctions. We shall later discuss this second aspect.

According to Shāh Walīy Allāh, it is collectively incumbent (*Fard Kifāya*) upon Muslims at all times to elect and install a *Khalīfa* possessing the requisite qualifications and preconditions. To support this contention he gives several arguments that can be summed up here.[35] First of all, the collective reason of mankind requires that a *Khalīfa* should be there to look after interests which otherwise cannot be protected. Secondly, the *Khalīfa* is appointed to achieve the two categories of objectives. The Holy Prophet was also sent to achieve them. Therefore, after the Prophet passed away, a *Khalīfa* or *Imam* was needed to succeed him and implement his injunctions and commandments. That is why obedience to the *Imam* is equal to obedience to the Prophet of God and his disobedience amounts to disobedience to God. This fact has also been stated in a few *Ahādith* quoted by Shāh Walīy Allāh in this context:

Whosoever obeys the *Amīr* (Commander of the Faithful) verily he has obeyed me; and whosoever disobeyed the *Amīr*, verily he disobeyed me.[36]

The *Imam* is a shield from the back of which one fights and protects oneself; if the *Imam* commands to fear God and guides (to the right path) his will be a big reward for this; if he orders other than this he will bear (the burden) of it.[37]

Whosoever sees in his *Amīr* something unpleasant he should take patience: because there is no single person who parts with the community even a single inch and dies who does not die a *Jāhilī* (anti-Islamic) death.[38]

Commenting on this last *Hadīth*, Shāh Walīy Allāh says that it is the distinction of Islam that it provides two categories of objectives for the achievement of which the *Khalīfa* is appointed as the successor of the Holy Prophet; otherwise the system would resemble the *Jāhiliyya*.[39]

In *Izālat al-Khafā'* he has also mentioned another *Hadīth* which he considers to tbe the clear textual commandment (*al-Nass*) in this regard. It is this:

> Whosoever dies and there is no oath of allegiance (*Bay'a*) in his neck he dies a *Jāhilī* (anti-Islamic) death.[40]

Apart from these *Ahādīth*, Shāh Walīy Allāh maintains, the Sahāba precipitated the establishment of *Khilāfa* immediately after the death of the Prophet and even deferred the funeral of the Holy Prophet. Upon the *Khilāfa* devolves the following: the *Jihād*, the administration of justice, the revival of Islamic sciences, the establishment of the pillars of Islam, the defence of the *Dār al-Islām*, and such other things which have been collectively enjoined upon the Muslim *Umma*. These are the arguments advanced by Shāh Walīy Allāh, to justify the institution of the *Khilāfa*.[41]

Unlike the early political thinkers of Islam, Shāh Walīy Allāh makes a distinction between *Khilāfa Zāhiriyya* (succession to the Holy Prophet in mundane matters) and *Khilāfa Bātiniyya* (succession to the Holy Prophet in spiritual matters). This distinction is absent in political discussion of even Ibn Khaldūn. Shāh Walīy Allāh is, perhaps, the first Muslim political scientist who has dwelt so elaborately upon a distinction between the two kinds of Khilāfas. In this respect he says,

> In the life of the Holy Prophet there is a noble model for all his followers. For those who are his successors in the affairs of state there these duties: the enforcement of Islamic Law; making arrangements for *Jihād*; the fortification and security of frontiers; granting gifts; sending embassies; the recovery and allocation of *Sadaqat*; taxes and revenues; the adjudication of disputes; the protection of orphans; the supervision of *Waqf* properties of the Muslims; the construction of roads, mosques and other buildings and similar matters. Those who are engaged in these services and occupations are successors of the Holy Prophet in matters of this world.
>
> The successors in spiritual matters and those entrusted with the teaching of Islamic law, the Holy Quran, and the traditions, or with enjoining what is lawful and forbidden; those whose words strengthen the true religion, either through polemics and discussions as was done by the *Kutakallimūn* or through preaching and advice as is done by Muslim preachers; those who through their company and spiritual guidance and training serve Islam and

Muslims as is the case with the Sufi saints; or those who arrange for prayers or pilgrimage or guide the people towards piety. These we call the spiritual successors of the Holy Prophet.[42]

We shall confine ourselves here to the terrestrial *Khilāfa* (*Khilāfa-Zāhira*) leaving the other or celestial *Khilāfa* to form the subject of another enquiry.

Shāh Walīy Allāh defines the *Khilāfa* in these words:

It is the general authority exercised on behalf of the Holy Prophet for the establishment of the *Dīn* through the revival of religious sciences, establishment of the pillars of Islam, carrying out the *Jihād* and what pertains to it of organizing the armies and paying the soldiers and allocating to them the *Fay'*, administration of justice, implementation of *Hudūd* (or capital punishments), elimination of injustices, enjoining the good and forbidding the evil.[43]

This *Khilāfa* is established by one of four means:

1. By the *Bay'a* (oath of allegiance) by the people, of loosing and binding by the *'Ulamā'*, leaders, and army commanders in the interests of Muslims in accordance with the *Khilāfa* of Abū Bakr.

2. By the will of the preceding *Khalīfa* in accordance with the *Khilāfa* of 'Umar.

3. By a decision by *Shūrā* (mutual consultation) of a certain group in accordance with the *Khilāfa* of 'Uthmān and also of 'Alī.

4. By the successful assumption of power by a man possessing the requisite qualities and qualifications as applicable to the Caliphs succeeding the Prophet.[44]

However, it seems that Shāh Walīy Allāh does not consider these four ways as being inflexible and the method of electing a *Khalīfa* is not confined, to these four methods. He argues that the most important consideration is the acceptance of the caliph by the people who by their consensus accord him all honour and respect. If he enjoys the confidence of the masses, establishes the *Hudūd*, defends the *Milla* and implements the commandments of Islam he is the *Khalīfa* irrespective of the means whereby he became a *Khalīfa*.[45]

Shāh Walīy Allāh has dwelt extensively upon the requisite conditions and qualifications of the person to be elected to the caliphal office. The most important is that the *Khalīfa* should be a Muslim because a non-Muslim cannot justly attain the objectives and ideals of the *Khilāfa*; moreover, the Qur'ān unequivocally declares that "God shall never grant to Unbelievers any form of supremacy over the Muslims."[46] He argues, first that if the *Khalīfa* apostatizes, his dethronement by force will be incumbent upon Muslims according to the teachings of Islam, therefore a non-Muslim cannot be elected a Caliph.[47] Secondly, a *Khalīfa* should be in full possession of his mental faculties and should have reached the age of majority.[48] In the absence of mental faculties and majority the ideals of the *Khilāfa* cannot be realized; moreover, mental defectives and minors are, by Qur'ānic injunction, unable to manage or dispose of their property.[49] It follows that such persons cannot be entrusted with the management and disposal of state resources.[50] Thirdly, he should be male[51] because womenfolk are considered to be generally less proficient in mental and physical faculties than men. There is also a *Hadīth* of the Holy Prophet which states, ''Success shall never attend a nation which has assigned its affairs to a women.''[52] Fourthly, he should be a free man and not a slave,[53] because a slave is unable to give a legal evidence and is generally despised; moreover, he is obliged to busy himself in the service of his master and therefore would be unable to discharge the heavy responsibilities of a Caliph.[54] Fifthly, he would be brave, courageous and gallant.[55] Sixthly, he should be of sound judgement and opinion,[56] having the capability and insight to reach the right decision at the right time.[57] Seventhly, he should not be lethargic nor inexperienced.[58] His reputation should be beyond reproach.[59] Eighthly, he should be *'Adl*; by this, Shāh Walīy means one who abstains from major sins (*Kabā'ir*) and refrains from minor sins (*Saghā'ir*).[60] This condition is important because the interests of the *Milla* (*al-Maṣālih al-Milliyya*) cannot be accomplished without it.[61] Ninthly, he should be a scholar,[62] having reached the status of a *Mujtahid*,[63] since the revival of religious sciences, enjoining Good and forbidding Evil, cannot be undertaken by a non-*Mujtahid*. It is not, however, necessary that the *Khalīfa* should be an independent *Mujtahid* (*Mujtahid Mustaqill*), like Abū Hanīfa and Shāf'ī; rather, it will be sufficient if he is an associate *Mujtahid* (*Mujtahid Muntasib*), having access to the researches of the early doctors of Islam (*Salaf*) and being able to understand their arguments and conclusions.[64] Finally, he should be a Qurayshī by his paternal descent.[65] In this connection Shāh Walīy Allāh refers to the well-known *Hadīth*: the *Imāms* (leaders) are from the Quraysh.[66] This will be discussed later.

These conditions would seem to be difficult to fulfil, but there is a close relationship between the qualifications of a functionary and his duties. The greater and more important the duties, the more difficult the conditions and qualifications. The duties and functions of the *Khalīfa*, says Shāh Walīy Allāh, are so significant that they cannot be performed without the conditions mentioned earlier.[67] A *Khalīfa* cannot revive the religious sciences, establish the pillars of Islam, enjoin Good, forbid Evil, organize the *Jihād*, administer justice and enforce the *Ḥudūd* (capital punishment) without these qualifications.[68]

Shāh Walīy Allāh further states that a *Mujtahid* in our time is one who is endowed with the following five knowledges:

1. Knowledge of the Book of God, literally and in content, commentary and interpretation.

2. Knowledge of *Aḥādīth* with an understanding of the chain of narrators, and the ability to distinguish between weak and sound *Aḥādīth*.

3. Knowledge of the opinions of the early doctors of Islam so that he will not transgress the established consenses (*Ijmā'*) of early Muslim scholars and might not venture a third opinion in presence of two already conflicting opinions.

4. Knowledge of Arabic language, grammar, etymology and lexicon.

5. Knowledge of the means of resolving problems and of effecting conformity between two apparently conflicting texts.

After acquiring these five knowledges he should have discovered the reason (*'illa*) of every commandment after reflecting upon particular problems.[69]

Concerning the stipulation that the *Khalīfa* be a Qurayshī, Shāh Walīy Allāh states that this was included in consequence of the Hadīth mentioned above, but it does not appear to have permanent effect. It was probably a temporary provision; the men possessing all these attributes belonged only to the Quraysh in the years following soon after the death of the Holy Prophet.[70]

If the office of the *Khalīfa* is assumed by a man who does not combine these qualifications, Shāh Walīy Allāh recommends that opposition should not be raised in haste, since his dethronement would be followed by confusion, disorder and wars.[71] He goes on to quote a *Ḥadīth*:

The Holy Prophet was asked about such self-appointed rulers and the question was, "should we not try to overthrow them?" The Holy Prophet replied, "No! as long as they perform the prayers among you. But if you see an Open Disbelief about which you have the Divine Proof (that is an open disbelief) only then can you overthrow them.[72]

If the *Khalīfa* becomes an apostate by renouncing one or more of the essentials of Islam, then the taking of arms against him becomes obligatory, since the objectives of the *Khilāfa* cannot be realized, while

the consequences of his apostasy would have to be borne by the people.
To wage war against such a person is an act of *Jihād* in the cause of
Allāh. Here Shāh Walīy Allāh quotes another *Ḥadīth* in which the
Prophet said:

> Listening and obedience (to the leader) is the duty of the Muslim in all
> matters whether the leader is personally liked or disliked so long as he is not
> ordered to commit a sinful act; if he is so ordered then he is not enjoined to
> listen and obey.[73]

These were the salient features of Shāh Walīy Allāh's political ideas.
In this connection he also discusses the "factors of decay and disorder"
in a state. After mentioning the social and moral evils that contribute to
disorder in a state, he proceeds to establish the need for the main organs
of the state, such as the judiciary, police, army, *Muḥtasib*, religious
instruction etc. These organs are meant to check social and moral
evils.[74]

PART III
SECULARIZATION:
NATION-STATE AND MODERNIZATION

8

ISLAM AND CIVIL SOCIETY

Mehdī Mozaffari

1. Toward a Secularization of Power

Secularization is not a recent phenomenon in Muslim societies. It has a long history going back to the first periods of Islam. The *Khārijīs* under the fourth Caliph 'Ali replaced in theory the Caliphate by the *Umma*, which, indeed, was a major step on the way toward the secularization of the seat of power. Later, the Mu'tazilīs, under the influence of Hellenism, would go even further, and extend secularization beyond the seat of power to the seat of authority itself. Thus it was that the sacred was replaced by Reason. Still later, the sacred nature of Islamic power would be challenged by the sociological approach of Ibn Khaldūn.

Then, after a long period of intellectual stagnation attendant upon the general decline of the Muslim world, secularizing efforts would begin again in a quite new international setting both to emulate the colonizer and to combat him. Men such as Al-Afghānī (1837 – 1897) and 'Abduh (1849 – 1905) 'Alī 'Abd al-Rāziq, the author of *Islam and the foundations of Power* (1925) or Mu'ammar Gadhāfī and 'Alī Sharī'atī (1933 – 1977) multiplied the efforts.

Secularization, however, is not a linear process; its path has been erratic and its forms diverse. Each society has its own way and its own style of secularization. Recent events in the Muslim world have fuelled the illusion that all secularizing efforts are doomed to failure, but this is at variance with both the facts of history and with present realities. It is obviously true that Muslim societies have encountered obstacles in their secularizing efforts, and sometimes have even been forced to shift their course. And secularization has also known its discontinuities and *caesurae*, such as ended with the establishment of the Islamic regime in Iran, and there will probably be others in the future. But the general fact remains. Though sporadic reversals may take place at the surface, the workings of secularization churn onward in society's depths. Contemporary models, even many of those that explicitly proclaim themselves Islamic, are striking examples of this deep-running process.

To be clear, let us distinguish between secularization from internal sources, and that which is initiated from without. By the former we mean all secularizing efforts undertaken by Muslim groups, which, while remaining part of the Muslim Community, and still invoking authentic Islam as their authority, have tried variously to divest the seats of authority and power of their sacred quality. Put differently, these Muslims do not reject Islam, but endeavour to use it with a view toward establishing a non-Islamic regime, often in the name of Islam. Examples are, in addition to the traditional movements mentioned earlier on (*Khārijī, Mu'tazilī* and others), all the modernist and secularizing movements that have spread throughout the various Muslim countries, especially the Ottoman Empire, Egypt and Persia, since the end of the nineteenth century. Whereas the Ottoman Caliph-Sulṭān was induced to accept the *Tanzimāt* under the intense pressure of secularizing movements, Egypt for its part experienced an extraordinary intellectual effervescence under the combined effects of the reformist (*Salafiyya*) and lay movements. The same occurred in Persia where aspirations of a similar sort were to move toward a constitutional revolution. The process of secularization was completed in the Ottoman Empire when the latter was replaced by modern Turkey. Egypt and Persia were only partly successful in this regard. In the 1906 Persian Constitution Allāh was very much present in the seat of authority, although he was no longer the sole occupant and had henceforth to share it with the Nation. This was the first of the dualist models of national essence.

The second wave of secularizing movements, still within Islam, brought new contemporary models, in particular fusionist models. Whereas the dualists undertook to separate Allāh and the nation, the fusionists — doubtless in consideration of the unsuccessful dualistic experiment — opted for another path toward what was ultimately the same destination. It would not be misleading to say that in submerging Allāh in the nation, the fusionists, put practically, nationalized Allāh.

Another aspect of institutional secularization is illustrated by the efforts of men such as Riḍā Shah (1925 – 1941) in Iran and Amanullāh (1919 – 1929) and Muḥammad Ẓāhir Shah (1933 – 1973) in Afghanistan. But a secularization of this type fits the more Kemalist model. It would be more exact to place these last efforts at the margin of or outside the Islamic framework. Let us go on then to an examination of some secularizing efforts of external origin. The most notable example is unquestionably that of Turkey. The Turkish experience is unique in its kind to the extent that it was a total secularization that affected power, institutions, and life-style all at once. Other undertakings, falling roughly into two categories, were later directly or indirectly inspired by the Kemal model. The first comprised projects attempted by the laity, thought remaining within an Islamic constitutional framework. Since any radical alteration of this framework was difficult, if not impossible, the tendency here was toward a gradual secularization of institutions (public education, implementation of a civil code, civic courts, etc.). Parallel efforts to alter the life-style (restrictions on wearing of the *chādor* and turban, liberalization of private life, etc.) were undertaken. Such on the whole was the policy pursued by Pahlavi in Iran, and to a certain extent by the Afghan kings as well.

The second group comprised projects which earlier on we classified as semi-monist models. Although these models are in theory more secular than the models of Pahlavi and the Afghan kings, their actual attitudes did not always follow their secular convictions. Pragmatism generally determined their politics, which could change quite brusquely depending on the general situation, with a flexibility that was sometimes mistaken for want of firmness. These models nevertheless remained basically lay models tending toward monist models that were national or confederate in essence. The Algerian, Tunisian, Syro-Iraqian and to a certain extent the Nasser model belong here.

Despite differences, secularization, whether of internal or external origin, was identical on one point: It always sought to eliminate the sacred from the system of government. The obstacles to secularization were of course many. Hence the slowness of secularizing movements, and hence also the ambiguity of some and the incertitude of others. Christian societies had taken whole centuries to separate the state and religion, and the work still remains incomplete. Surely it is asking too much therefore to expect Muslim society to do the same over a period of a few decades, or even years and, moreover, in their present situation at that, where differently from the Christian societies of Europe, they are still suffering from the weighty effects of domination and dependence.

2. Civil Society and the Nation-State

The secularization of power is a precondition for the establishment of civil society and the nation-state. A study of the contemporary models of power in Muslim society reveals that the great majority of them opted for processes of secularization as a means of achieving civil society and the establishment of the nation-state. There are several reasons for this, but we shall here focus on two before we go on to discuss the obstacles encountered by these secularizing efforts.

First, the idea of a nation-state was adopted to provide a propitious general framework for ensuring the success of modernization. Since modernity came from societies in which the nation-state was the dominant form, Muslim societies have tended to adopt this form as well as a guarantee of success in their modernization policies.

Later, the idea arose that the nation-state would facilitate the union, if but temporary, of the various disparate forces struggling to liberate their "fatherland" from the colonial yoke. Thus nationalism was able to go beyond the tribal, ethnic, linguistic, confessional and social parochialism to give substance to a rudimentary motive force. However, in Muslim societies this nationalism, forceful as it was, had to vie with another motive force which seemed to be more powerful and more entrenched than itself, namely Islam. Thus for more than a century and a half these two motive elements competed with and fuelled one another at one and the same time. As a result, most of the progress of the Muslim national movement (the two terms "national" and "Muslim" are already inherently contradictory) has been blurred and ambiguous. The nation-state as well has been marked by this original ambiguity, of which, it must be added, enlightened Muslims were well aware from the outset, and hence lost no time in setting about extricating nationalism from Islamism.

The theoretical efforts to this end were especially conspicuous in Egypt and Persia. In Egypt, in the *Nahda* movement, a theoretician of the stature of Ṭahṭāwī (1801 – 1873) devoted himself wholly and entirely to acquainting his compatriots with the culture, literature, philosophy and political system of European societies. Translations and publications thrived. To be sure, the end in mind was that of arousing Eygptian society from its slumbers and to open it to new ideas. But did not this call for a "new culture" also contain the implicit objective of establishing a counterweight to the traditional culture, religious in essence? The evidence seems to indicate that this indeed was also one of the ends envisioned. In their theories, Ṭahṭāwī and his disciples drew a basic distinction between the notion of *Umma*, Islamic at root, and the notion of *Waṭan*, literally, *fatherland*. The word *sha'b* (nation) had not yet come into use[1] since this was only the first stage of a national awakening, that of acquiring 'a self-centred autonomy within an empire of purely formal ties";[2] in other words, a *territorial* autonomy (the fatherland), with fully-fledged independence as the later and ultimate goal. The use of *Waṭan* in place of *sha'b* entailed other advantages as well. The fatherland, the earth, took the lead over Islam, the faith. Indeed, those who proposed to give priority to Islam found themselves utterly disarmed by the use of a term as neutral as fatherland, which, in fact, the Prophet himself had bid them to love as a *hadīth*, (*hūbb ul-waṭan min al-Imām*).

The theoretical disengagement of nationalism had been preceded by attempts of Muhammad 'Alī to establish an economy of national scope in place of the local economy. The works of Muhammad 'Alī are clearly entirely in the spirit of erecting a national state at some future date. However, such efforts remained unsuccessful and the young

Egyptian economy was very quickly brought back into the fold and absorbed into the system of world domination. Anwar 'Abdal Malek sums up this process of integration as follows:

> Thanks to Muhammad 'Alī, Egypt was given a national and not merely a local economy, an economy that was both statist and autarkic at one and the same time. The great works that had been accomplished under Isma'il structured the internal market. Loans, then cotton as a single crop culture — all these things initiated and deepened by colonial penetration and imperialist occupation, achieved Egypt's integration into the world market over the course of the last third of the nineteenth century.
>
> The distortions created in the Egyptian economy ran deep and their consequences were lasting: incorporation into the world market under European hegemony on terms imposed by imperialism; the essential dismantling of state monopolies in industry, and then the forced link to sterling, a horizontal division of the country between a Lower Egypt open to modern technology and an Upper Egypt, which remained relatively apart, and lines of transport and communication having the sole end of accelerating the funnelling of harvests to Mediterranean ports.[3]

During this same period, Persia underwent an evolution almost identical to that of Egypt. Although unlike Egypt it enjoyed a formal independence, it too was hardly immune to the effects of domination and the interventions of foreign powers in its internal affairs. Again as in Egypt, a commercial bourgeoisie began to develop in the second half of the nineteenth century and endeavoured to cement the foundations of a new national economy in its own interests.[4] Thus it was that the various Iranian trading companies were created, and the land, which traditionally had belonged to the King, began to be invested as private property. The commercial bourgeoisie profited roundly from the sale of lands and public domains. It began to organize itself. A Chamber of Commerce was established, first at Tehran (in the 1880s) and then in the major cities and the provinces. With the rise of the commercial bourgeoisie — and indeed to no mean extent because of it — rebellions began to take place against the economic concessions (tobacco, railroads, oil, communications) accorded to foreigners, ultimately to end in the constitutionalist revolution of 1906. With the establishment of a constitutional regime, a state, tribal in essence (the Qājārs), was replaced — at least in theory — by the nation state.

Parallel to the development of economic autonomy, the Iranians, following precisely the same course traced out by the Egyptians, attempted to steer their country down the path of political modernization. The word *mellat* (nation) began to appear in Iranian political literature for the first time: *mellat* — counterposed to the despotic prince, but also to Islam. Reality of course was more complicated. For example, *mellat*,[5] at the time represented by the commercial bourgeoisie, was, in its conflict with the authoritarian regime of the Shah, driven into an alliance with a number of the *'Ulamā'* who were also in opposition, although for other reasons (financial, influence, prestige). The ultimate consequence of this tactical alliance was a confusion in basic terms, of which the 1906 Constitution, with its dual source of legitimacy (Allāh and *Mellat*), is elegant written testimony. But that would not be the end of the matter: the confusion had grave consequences later on as well for the political life of the country. The fall of Moṣaddeq (nationalist — *melli* leader) in 1953 was due in part to the conflict which opposed him to his former ally, i.e. Ayatollāh Kāshānī (religious-*Madhhabī* leader and mentor of Ayatollāh Khomeinī).

The fall of the Moṣaddeq government was followed by an imperial regime which lasted 26 years, i.e. down to the fall of Pahlavi. The project of the nation-state set forth in the 1906 Constitution was discredited in praxis, thereby leaving a not inconsiderable opening for the spread of religious discourse. The commercial bourgeoisie (the *bazar*) tended toward traditionalist sources (the *'Ulamā'*) with a view to blocking the rise of the new oil bourgeoisie which was beyond the pale of influence of the bazar. Iranian political life became polarized between the supporters of the imperial regime and the supporters of an Islamic regime. Once established, the latter would pursue a policy toward the partisans of the nation-state that was far more severe and cruel than that of the Shah's regime. Nationalists were persecuted, imprisoned and executed.

3. Islam's Relationship to the Nation-State and Civil Society

After having reviewed the reasons for the option for a civil society and nation-state and the various obstacles that this option encountered along the way toward its fulfilment, we will now turn to the fundamental question of Islam's relationship to civil society and the nation-state in an effort to determine at what level and to what extent Islam is in contradiction with them. This question has occasioned impassioned debates both within Muslim society and beyond it. Indeed there are many who believe that Islam, by virtue of its singularity, is the antipode of civil society and the nation-state. This "singularity thesis" has the weakness that it regards Islam as a unified bloc, a completed system, an indivisible totality. Clearly such an approach, which is basically culturist, can only produce sweeping irrevocable judgements about Islam and Muslim societies. The conclusion was thus reached that, because of the presence of Islam, Muslim societies could never build civil society. Such a conclusion is possible only if one wholly disregards the impact of external factors on Muslim societies. Moreover, the anti-evolutionary bias of this approach impels it to set up the "law of the status quo" as a law eternal.[6]

A more plausible and realistic approach would seem to be to regard Islam as a human construction and, like all other constructions, subject to change and evolution. Islam too will undergo changes and modifications if the conditions are ripe for them. The Islam of today is not the Islam of yesterday, and the Islam of tomorrow will probably be even more different. The existence of a legion of Islams today, each of which holds itself to be the one and only authentic Islam, is sufficient evidence that Islam is neither a unified bloc, nor an edifice that will weather all eternity without change. To arrive at some understanding, however incomplete, of Islam's relationship to civil society and the nation-state, it is first necessary, we would suggest, to draw a distinction between the *conception* and the *reality* of Islam. At the conceptual level Islam does indeed contain a number of notions that could be construed as obstacles to the establishment of civil society. In the Qur'ānic system, for example, there is no place for the *status of citizen*. The Community is made up of believers, not citizens. Another example is the symbiosis between the temporal and the spiritual. It matters little if this symbiosis is genuinely of Qur'ānic origin, or if it has been fashioned over the course of history. What is essential is that it is one of the ABCs of Muslim consciousness that between Allāh and the prince in Islam there is no distinction. Furthermore, this idea can influence people's political choices. The notion of Allāh itself can serve as a barrier to the construction of civil society. As history will abundantly testify, the caliphs, the kings, the emirs, the sheikhs, and the ayatollahs have always been able to invoke Allāh as a pretext for refusing to recognize the civil rights of individuals.[7]

These examples — and others like them — demonstrate that Islam does indeed have concepts capable of obstructing the evolution of Muslim society toward civil society. But it would be mistaken to think that these concepts have in themselves been determining factors in the failure to achieve the civil society envisaged. The establishment of the Islamic regime in Iran has often been cited as the example *par excellence* of the conceptual powers of Islam. Since this example is currently the trump card of the "culturalists" for validating their own arguments, it will be useful perhaps to dwell a bit on this aspect of the Islamic revolution in Iran. My purpose here is to demonstrate that, contrary to what is generally thought, Islam at its conceptual level, or if you wish, as an ideology, has not played the role mistakenly attributed to it by some in this revolution. I shall limit myself to the most concrete and most verifiable examples.

Those who believe in the autonomous powers of Islamic concepts overlook (or pretend to overlook) two things. First as Amilcar Cabral put it, "people do not struggle for ideas or abstract notions; people struggle and accept sacrifices to obtain material advantages so as to be able to live in peace and prosperity. People want to see their lives progress and the future of their children assured."[8] Finally, referring to a specifically Iranian context, I wish to stress that Islam is not a religion that has recently been introduced in Iran. The country has been Muslim for fourteen centuries. It has been officially Shī'ī since the Safavids (1570 – 1747). Consequently, if Islamic concepts were efficacious in their own right, Persians would have been living for a long time already under a regime comparable to that of *Khomeinī's*

Even if we assume that, for one reason or another, these concepts had for fourteen centuries been unable to act and acquire concrete form in an autonomous Islamic political regime, and that they first acquired this possibility quite recently — even assuming this, the study of the remote, recent, and immediate origins of the "Islamic" revolution shows that the ideology of Islam was scarcely one of its fundamental causes. However, it not being my purpose here to analyse the revolution, let me merely enumerate some of the real causes of it. I shall concentrate on internal causes, leaving the external ones for the moment aside.

Among the deep-lying causes there was the fundamental question of the *system of property*. Traditionally, the large part of the land, water and pastures, the three essential elements of the economy, belonged in the main to the prince.[9] Privatization of the land goes back no further than the nineteenth century. This change played a major role in the formation of the new class that would later be the driving force of the constitutionalist revolution, but it would also give rise to a social ambiguity. The new class was not an autonomous class. In Western terminology it would be somewhere between a feudal class and the bourgeoisie. But with the appearance of oil as a new and essential element in the national economy, the situation reverted very quickly to that of the preconstitutional period. With the fall of the Mosaddeq government, the nationalized oil was effectively restored to the international cartels. Through the "second nationalization" under the Shah's regime, followed by a substantial rise in the price of oil, the Shah, strengthened by his new oil resources, was, like the preconstitutional Iranian kings, able to intervene unrestrained in all spheres of social, economic, and political life. Of course this was in clear contradiction to the Constitution. In 1973, the Shah, Chief of State, became the Leader, and above all the great Employer. Thus the path of civil society was blocked once again, this time, however, not by Islamic concepts but by an imperial regime.

As for the near-lying causes of the revolution, there were quite a number of them, but one would seem to be the most important: the disparity between economic development and political development. While oil had put some considerable financial means in the hands of various social groups, the Shah's authoritarianism not only did nothing to facilitate the political participation of these groups, but he made every effort to deprive them of all means of political expression. The inevitable result was a broad disjunction between economic and political life. Hence the "unexpected" and wide-spread discontent in all social layers, even the most privileged.

Disregarding various other factors (corruption, over-centralization, a single-party system, arbitrary imprisonment, torture, foreign intervention, etc.), we come finally to the immediate causes, likewise manifold. One of these was the power failure. To include such a factor, at the surface more technical than political, among the causes of a revolution so vast in scope might seem fanciful, if not misplaced. How, it may be asked, could a power failure contribute so amply to the triggering of a revolution so original and so vast that its advent astonished the entire world? The answer is simple enough: because the power failure in the summer of 1977 not only spread discontent even into the privileged layers who were particularly outraged by the fact that they were much more dependent on electricity than the less privileged layers, but also because this failure brought to light the weakness, fragility, and vulnerability of a regime until then reputed to be a powerful and cohesive force.

Let us take a closer look. The Shah boasted of having built a mass consumption society. This was true. The Iranians had never consumed as many things and in such a variety as during the last ten years of the Shah's regime. They consumed without thinking and spent without counting. All went well until the system was plunged into serious economic and financial difficulties, in the midst of which occurred the long power failure in the summer of 1977. For reasons as yet unknown, the central power station which the Shah's regime had constructed in conformity with his policy of centralization began having troubles, and consumers suddenly found themselves with electricity for only 2 or 3 hours per day, and very erratically at that. With temperatures between 35°C and over 50°C, life became unbearable, particularly for those who had become used to electric articles and electric home appliances. Fans, elevators, refrigerators, televisions and other similar articles on which the Shah had built his regime suddenly became superfluous and their mere presence in homes and public places was enough to inflame the tempers of anonymous consumers to the boiling point. Meat, imported at great cost from Australia and New Zealand, spoiled as the situation deteriorated. No freedom and no consumption — that makes for rebellions if not revolutions, especially when a suffocating heat stokes spirits. Everyone, from the Shah down, began looking for scapegoats. A committee of imperial inspection was even created to this end. Heads fell (dismissal and then imprisonment of the Prime Minister, other ministers, generals, businessmen), but this hardly improved the situation. Then it was the turn of the Shah's own family; his relatives discreetly left the country one by one. No progress. Finally, and ineluctably, as has happened so many times before in history, it was the turn of the Shah himself. His head too fell as a symbol of all the ills and misfortunes of his 37 years of reign.

I would, of course, not go so far as to say that the 1979 revolution was caused by a power failure, but its example does demonstrate how an outwardly commonplace event can lay bare an extremely powerful and cruel regime, and even bring it to its knees. In the event, it should be clear that the power failure had a much greater impact in the first phases of the revolutionary upsurge than any religious discourse. Similarly, it should be clear that the Iranians did not make their revolution because they were unable fully to perform their religious duties (which as a matter of fact they were able to do undisturbed) or even because the Shah's regime did not bear the characteristics of an Islamic regime. The deep-lying causes of the revolution must be sought elsewhere, as we observed earlier on. In the situation which the Shah found himself in 1978, the regime was doomed in any case, with or without Islam, with or without Khomeinī, or some other popular leader.[10]

Why then, we may likewise ask, did a rhetoric couched in religious terms, rather than some other, gain the upper hand? The reasons for this are basically two. First, the Iranians, weary of the Shah's regime, had their minds set much more on its departure from the scene than on the nature of the regime that should follow it. No political group, and no leader, had worked out a programme for change. Actions were ill defined and haphazard. Khomeinī alone had a blueprint for government and a plan of action. While others permitted themselves to be cast about hither and yon by the vicissitudes and unfolding of events, Khomeinī had a programme he had worked out beforehand, and he followed it. If he won, it was because he quite simply knew where he was going. There should be nothing mysterious about this. To be persuaded one need only restudy the positions adopted by the Iranian political groups and leaders from 1977 – 1978 onward and to compare them with Khomeinī's. It is an incontestable fact that Khomeinī was able to give an historical dimension to a specific political struggle. Moreover, he managed to reconcile the different social classes, if not permanently, at least long enough to forge an alliance among them against the regime in power. Thirdly, he showed himself to be courageous both physically (he arrived in Tehran in a situation that was more than uncertain) and morally. These are the characteristics Machiavelli called the virtues of a leader.

The second reason why the religious rhetoric prevailed over the others (socialist, nationalist, modernist) was because it managed to become the most impelling rhetoric within the overall context of the revolutionary movement. Thus, the great majority of Iranians believed at some given moment that the various other "mini" rhetorics, so to speak, could be integrated without clash or conflict into the great religious rhetoric. In the general confusion, each tendency couched its own rhetoric in the same terms of rhetoric as the one being propagated in the name of Islam. It was at about this time that the rumour began to circulate that Khomeinī's visage could be seen in the moon. Thus the Iranians, abandoning their non-religious rhetoric to oblivion, in the belief that they had finally found the one universal Rhetoric, found themselves suddenly on the moon. Each construed Khomeinī's rhetoric as he wished, and as we know, it did indeed contain something for everyone, at least for the moment.

From all this, it should be clear that Islam is not such an omnipotent force as can impose itself or obstruct the evolution of the structures of Muslim society by the irresistible power of its concepts alone. Yet it is equally true, that in the world of actual fact, of the social structures and institutions erected in the name of Islam, Islam is indeed quite able to erect obstacles to this evolution. But the structures of the society are, if they are anything at all, the products of society itself. There is no evidence that Islam *qua* faith is capable of producing these structures in society's stead.

Any real debate, therefore, must be centred on the *realities* of Islam, i.e. the basic structures of Muslim societies, and their possibilities for change and improvement, and many indeed are the efforts in this regard. But if these efforts have met with obstacles, it has not always been because of Islam's presence. All societies in the third world, whether Muslim or not, have similar tales to tell in this respect. The external factor must bear a quite large part of the responsibility for the backwardness of these societies.

The fact is that every time Muslim societies have attempted to free themselves from domination, every time they have begun to build an autonomous national economy and to take control of their own natural riches, and every time they have attempted to initiate a process of democratization to the end of establishing a Western-style political regime, external forces have lost no time in mobilizing every possible means to ensure that these efforts would fail. Examples abound in both Muslim and non-Muslim societies — the military *coups d'état* against the democratic governments of Mosaddeq in Iran and Allende in Chile, to name but two. Were these governments overthrown and replaced by dictatorial regimes because traditional structures could not accommodate democratization, or was it simply by order of the successors of President Wilson, who had the honour of having invented the noble phrase "the right of nations to self-determination"? It is gratuitious, one would think, to place the blame for the failure of the grand schemes of democratization solely on the societies themselves and the structures inherent to them. To say that these structures are resistant to all change is to belabour the obvious; but the real problem lies elsewhere, in the fact that efforts undertaken in Muslim societies to establish a nation-state, civil society, and a democratic regime have almost invariably been rudely crossed by the intrusions of foreign powers.

Indeed it is precisely because of these repeated interruptions that Islamism is today being reborn from its own ashes as a new alternative.

Note: This chapter forms part of the author's book: *Authority in Islam: from Muhammad to Khomeini*, published by M. E. Sharpe Inc., New York and London, 1987.

9

NATION-STATE BUILDING IN SYRIA: BA'TH AND ISLAM — CONFLICT OR ACCOMMODATION?

Annika Rabo

Many Westerners as well as people from Islamic societies have asserted that Islam is fundamental to the politics of the Middle East. The emergence of fundamentalist revival movements in many of these countries, and the developments in Iran after the overthrow of the Shah, have created a fresh interest in, and concern about the political impact of Islam. Yet until today we have had very few empirical means of determining the influence of Islam in the political processes of the Middle East. It is possible to make comparative studies of Islamic influences on legal codes, ideas of political authority and legitimacy, or expressions of political rhetoric. But for several reasons these approaches are of limited value if conducted alone. First, they tell us very little about political action on the part of the citizens. Second, the nation-states of the Middle East are highly diversified in how they use Islam as a vehicle of state. Third, we gain little information with prognostic value on how Islam may be used by hostile forces.

The following is an attempt to create a model for determining Islamic influence in the political life of Syria. The model is based on the assumption that the state is crucial in the development of Middle Eastern nations[1] and that state policies and official rhetoric are at the centre of political controversies. These controversies can be better understood by delineating the class structure of those groups contending for power. Yet it is equally important to study the indigenous societal analyses. Through these we can gain access to the symbols used in political discourse and discover the political myths which are fundamental for the expression of popular political goals. The conflicts between "secular" and "religious" politics is in this model regarded as part of the ideological aspect of the struggle for power. The severe civil disturbances in Syria in 1980 can serve as an example of the use of this model.

Civil disturbances in Syria

For the Syrian state, Islam — expressed in terms of *Sharī'a* — is vital only in the civil legal code. Political authority and legitimacy rest, not on Islam, but on a notion of a welfare state where all citizens have equal rights and obligations respecting the nation. Arab nationalism and Arab unity are also basic ingredients in the rhetoric of the powerholders. However, the state's claim to legitimacy has been disputed. In the winter of 1980, militants from the Syrian Muslim Brotherhood increased their hit-and-run actions. Strikes by shopkeepers in Aleppo closed down trade and spread to other cities. Professional unions demanded political reforms and a branch of the Syrian Communist Party joined the Brotherhood in condemning the regime. Special forces were placed in Aleppo forcibly to open the market. Sniping from Brotherhood activists was common and considerable blood was shed when the army retaliated and cleaned up the city. The revolt also became open and very fierce in Hama; a traditional anti-government and Muslim Brotherhood base. By the summer of 1980 the strikes and revolts were temporarily crushed. Was this a popular movement instigated by religiously oriented activists dissatisfied with the secular nature of the Syrian state? Why was this movement unable to overthrow the Ba'th regime? Was the ultimate goal of the revolt really the establishment of an Islamic Syrian state? In order to answer these questions we must first examine the nature of the Syrian state and the development of post-independence Syria.

Syria during the Ba'th period

For those in power, the history of modern Syria is said to have begun, not with independence in 1946, but rather with the Ba'th coup (revolution) of 1963. Since the Ba'th take-over, the scope, scale and ambition of the Syrian state's involvement in the lives of the citizens have increased dramatically. With the Ba'th coup the relation between state and party has also become strongly interlocked.

In spite of its aspiration to move the whole nation, Ba'th was a very small party when it came to power. The Party's core members were officers and intellectuals with a rural and often minority background. During the French mandate and early independence, joining the military or going into teaching were about the only upwardly mobile careers open to young men — especially those from minority groups — from the countryside and from small towns. These young men constituted the Ba'th party's main recruits. While the party was and remains non-sectarian, the 1963 coup brought minorities into important positions in the state-apparatus. The Ba'th take-over can, in fact, "be considered as a kind of national emancipation" (Van Dam 1978:205).

In its first two years of rule the leadership was struggling against enemies outside and inside Syria, and policy priorities were still unclear. Finally in 1966 the radicals of the party were strong enough to implement the land reform which curtailed the power of the big landowners. They also began nationalizations and state-planned development projects. However, the policies of the radicals alienated a large portion of Syrian society. The urban bourgeoisie and petty bourgeoisie were natural opponents to a state-controlled economy. Even in the rural areas peasants suffered from the general isolation, the lack of capital and lack of resources with which to develop the co-operatives instituted after the land reform. Defeat in the June war of 1967 also built up popular discontent. In 1970 there was an internal Ba'th coup in which General Hafiz al-Assad took power in what is termed the Correction Movement. The leftist and Ba'th revolutionary policies inside and outside Syria were abandoned, and instead the new regime began a period of accommodation to non-party groups (Hinnebusch 1983:184). Since 1963 popular organizations had been built up by the party, but the Correction Movement began a mass-enrollment campaign to strengthen the base of the party. New, more liberal measures stimulated private initiative in the economy, and a National Front was formed with the Ba'th and other parties to act on all political levels. The influx of oil-money in the early 1970s also made Syria's economy boom. The party grew larger and even the bourgeoisie was allowed greater room for manoeuvre. After the 1973 war President Assad achieved great popular support, but the inbuilt contradictions in the new liberal policies soon surfaced. The whole state-apparatus came, in spite of the National Front, under Ba'th dominance. Entrance to many positions in the public sector came to depend on party membership. It was soon forbiden for teachers and army employees — the two fundamental spheres of Ba'th power—base to be a member of other than the Ba'th party. Ba'th ideology, never very clear, became "ossified and bankrupt, as well as at variance with the regime's behaviour" (Alasdair 1982:4). The discrepancy between Ba'th ideals and Ba'th practice alienated leftist support for the party. Mass-enrolment had been at the expense of cadre training. The weakening economy after 1976 created discontent among the bourgeoisie and petty bourgeoisie. The Syrian invasion into the Lebanon in 1976 drew criticism both from leftists and from the Muslim Brotherhood who from time to time made violent attacks on the regime. The invasion into the

Lebanon also compounded the economic difficulties. All through the late 1970s and early 1980s discontent with the Ba'th intensified in Syrian society. The bourgeoisie felt threatened by the state's expansion and control of the economy. The Leftist and Muslim Brotherhood critique was centred on the growing power monopoly of the party leadership, which had rendered the National Front virtually defunct. The real centre of power was commonly felt to be vested in the Regional Command of the Syrian Ba'th party, or even more narrowly concentrated in the clique around the president.

The state: mediator between the dominant classes

The involvement of officers in Syria's post-mandate political life, and the numerous *coups d'état* before the take-over by General Assad, have led many outside analysts (cf. Vatikiotis 1972:228 & 238) to see Syrian politics as a struggle between factional élites, where sectarian links are more important than the class representations of the power-holders. By focusing on sectarian, ethnic and regional affiliations in the context of Middle Eastern politics it is implied that religion and ethnicity play a more fundamentally different role in the region than they do in the West. The "state" is then viewed to be in the hands of a clique whose relation to the rest of society is ignored. The state in "developed" societies is predominantly regarded as an integrator of social groups; as a force standing above group interests, and instead serving the nation as a whole. But this view is seldom applied to developing societies. I contend that the state, both in the bourgeois democratic societies, and in the Third World "is an essential means of class domination" (Miliband 1977:67). A lack of open class struggle or of class consciousness does not mean that it is impossible to analyse the condition of the Syrian state in a class context. Following Turner (1978) and Alavi (1982) I see the state in Syria as an instrument,[2] not of one class, but as the mediator between dominant classes: the landlords, the comprador bourgeoisie, the small indigenous capitalists and the metropolitan bourgeoisie. The governing class in control of the state-apparatus is best termed as an intermediate class.[3] The fact that dominant classes in Syria do not "rule" in a direct sense gives the custodians of the state special importance. While the dominant classes compete, the class in control of the state-apparatus is in a position to mediate between them and it can act with relative automony.[4] It may take action against the interests of the dominant classes, through heavy investment in the army, or in development projects. Losing part of the surplus is the price the dominant classes pay for the state's guarantee of their continued existence.

Seen in this way, the Syrian political economy and the political crises in the Ba'th period become more intelligible. The state rests on a new intermediate class: the army and a stratum of salaried public employees with roots mainly in the petty bourgeoisie and the independent peasantry. Through land reform and nationalizations, the power of the landowning and indigenous capitalist classes has been dramatically curtailed, but not totally broken. Metropolitan capital in the form of development aid, and Arab oil money, as well as direct commercial relations, all play a fundamental role in the economy. It is to a great extent through credit relations that the state finances its development projects. But the immediate effects of the land reform and the nationalizations threatened not only the landlords and the bourgeoisie, but also the ''rulers'' of the state. This economic crisis in the 1960s had repercussions for all classes in Syria and made the regime very unpopular. The liberalizing measures in the 1970s, both economical and political, broadened the support for the ruling class and spread welfare to all regions and classes in Syria. The growth of the comprador bourgeoisie was very important in this period. Many former landlords and industrial capitalists invested in the profitable sectors of trading, import-export and building. The relative autonomy of the class in control of the state made it possible for the Ba'th party — the vehicle of the state-apparatus — to dominate all aspects of civil life. The renewed economic crisis of the 1980s is partly a result of the Syrian involvement in the Lebanon and its ensuing political isolation in the Arab world, and partly a result of the world economic crisis. This has meant that factions of the dominant classes have withdrawn their support of the state and are in open conflict with it. There are also more elements in the state-apparatus — army officers, party cadres, high echelon bureaucrats — who compete with the comprador class for trade profits. Those who have withdrawn their support to the state have used another group — young Muslim Brotherhood activists — as their tool for militant activities against the state. These factions of the dominant classes, in particular the comprador bourgeoisie, probably never intended the revolt of 1980 to be the starting-point for an Islamic revolution, no matter how sincere the Brotherhood activists were.[5] Instead the Brotherhood's supporters wanted to tip the balance of power in their favour and end the competition from other elements in the state-apparatus. However, it should also be stressed that many Syrians from the subordinate classes — workers, peasantry and low echelon employees — in whose name the rulers rule, are critical of state policies, despite the Party's dominant position.

The critique openly or covertly formulated against the state is neither accepted nor acknowledged by the power-holders. The inability of the Syrian state to resolve the contradictions it has created is quite typical of the Third World. In order to keep power and the relative autonomy of the state, state authorities cannot accept democratic political institutions (Alavi 1982:304). The intermediate class itself tries to formulate policies which might partially satisfy all classes, or at least minimize active discontent. When a crisis becomes acute, demands for reforms — from the dominant or subjugated classes — are met with repression (Ahmad 1983:358). The ideology of the power-holders, the Ba'th perceptions of the Arab nation — vague and often contradictory — is rooted in the position of the intermediate class which formulated it. The Ba'th ideology is based on an anti-imperialist stand while trying to find an all-Arab solution. It is also against so-called "traditional" Syrian loyalties, whether ethnic, tribal or urban-merchant affiliations. But since the party was weak at the take-over and constantly threatened by external and internal enemies it was "forced" to revert to, or manipulate these loyalites (Van Dam 1978:201). This afforded a short-term stability to Syria in the 1970s At the same time, corrupt officials became very powerful, since ideological motivation among party cadres came to an end in the general "national unity" and liberalization period. The ensuing popular discontent with corruption and power monopoly, and the dominant classes' discontent with the economic policies, clearly show the internal contradictions of the Syrian political economy. The weakness of the state is hidden by the use of brute force. As in many Third World countries, the popular base of the regime is weak and the ruling class is itself divided. The state is weak because it is not the instrument of the dominant classes. At the same time the state is strong because it commands *not only* the tools of repression but *also* the avenues to careers, economic prosperity and welfare for a great many Syrians. Through this whole complex of contradictions and ambiguities, Syrian politics are acted out.

Syrian Perceptions

We turn now to an analysis of the development and functioning of the Syrian state, though this tells us little about how Syrians themselves analyse their political economy. It is equally essential to bring native analyses into the model of political action. An analysis stressing the class-interests of the custodians of the state is, of course, rejected out of hand by the ideologists of the *Ba'th party*. Ba'th ideology emphasizes the ideal classless society where the Ba'th represents the *nation* — a secular *umma* — against reactionary elements. For the Ba'th leadership the Muslim Brotherhood constitutes no more than henchmen for these reactionary elements and agents of foreign enemies of the secular Syrian *umma*.

The *Muslim Brotherhood* also rejects this anlysis of the Syrian state and political economy. It is rejected because the Brotherhood depicts the rulers, not as a class, but as a group of irresponsible, illegitimate, corrupt, unjust — in the Islamic sense — non-*sunni* opportunists out to destroy the country and who wish only to enrich themselves. The Muslim Brotherhood activists also naturally reject any analysis which stresses links between themselves and the big merchants, claiming that the latter — contrary to their own proclamations — do not serve the interests of the *umma* but those of the dominant classes.

The *leftists*, who aligned themselves with the Muslim Brotherhood in the 1980 crisis, issued pamphlets analysing the state much in the same vein as above. Their tactical alliance with the Brotherhood was apparently based on a strategic consideration whereby they hoped the revolt would spread to the subordinate classes. This consideration proved totally wrong. Most other leftists, including the majority of the Syrian Communist Party, felt the level of class consciousness of the masses to be too low to spark off a revolt. Most leftists saw an alliance with the Brotherhood as more profane than the National Front alliance with the Ba'th party.

Other Syrians outside the camps of the leftists and the Muslim Brotherhood make an "instinctive" class analysis where the rich, the poor and the middle class are the basic divisions. People frequently link the rich with the political leaders and point out that intimate relationships often emerge. The rich merchants have personal links with important individual politicians; the merchants gain contracts in exchange for bribes, people say. However, these relations are mostly analysed as individual conspiracies, or as symptoms of corrupt rulers, rather than as manifestations of class alliances.

Political myths in Syria

It is important to delineate not only a class-analysis of Syrian society but also to study various indigenous Syrian societal analyses. It is only through the latter that we can gain insight into the symbolic language in politics where both Islamic and secular rhetoric are used.[6] In Syria it is difficult to discern a clear line between "secular" and "religious" politics. Even the Muslim Brotherhood often discuss the evils of the regime in non-religious terms and they have presented a programme which is based on secular as well as "Islamic" ideology. The Ba'th leaders, while naturally basing their claims to legitimacy on their secular politics, often invoke the "Islamic heritage" in the building of a perfect society. Thus, instead of analysing the crisis in Syrian politics as one between opposing poles of secularity and religiosity, we gain more by seeing the conflicts as a struggle for power. The symbols in the political language lean between different kinds of *political myths*. There is the future-oriented myth of a just welfare state where the state caters for the needs of the citizens. There is also the myth — emerging from the past but to be realized again in the future — of the just Caliphate where the *umma* fulfils the aspirations of each and all Muslims. These two basic myths[7] are used and manipulated by both the Ba'th leadership and the dissident Muslim Brotherhood. Ordinary Syrians are moved and influenced by both.

The myth of the just welfare state is known and accepted literally as a political goal not only in a great part of the West, but also in much of the Middle East. In Syria today most people have, through the precepts as well as the practice of the state, come to expect and demand — though usually not violently — social welfare distributed to all citizens. People want social services from the state. They want free education for all, hospitals publicly paid for and better communications financed by the state. They also feel, in general, that in the Ba'th period, relatively speaking, welfare has been better distributed. The Ba'th has expanded public spending, employment opportunities and employment security, and given increased opportunities to people from poor or oppressed minority backgrounds. Today the Syrian state, with its welfare aspirations, reaches out and affects practically all citizens. The political leaders naturally utilize people's newly-created appetite for state services and state responsibility. Political rhetoric alludes to future progress, made possible by the Ba'th, and through investment in development projects. But this public appetite works two ways. While rendering services provides legitimacy for the rulers, the new welfare expectations also make people demand more and question the size and quality of expenditure (e.g., the military).

The Muslim Brotherhood cannot ignore the new well-entrenched welfare myth; its political rhetoric also promises to take care of the needs of its constituency. But while the Ba'th claims that its leadership alone can realize the aspirations of the Syrians, the Muslim Brotherhood asserts that this is impossible because of the corruption — spiritual and worldly — of the leadership. The Brotherhood stresses the injustices of the present political leaders and claims that in spite of welfare advances made, a truly just state can never be established by the Ba'th leaders. According to Muslim Brotherhood rhetoric, only truly Muslim rulers can accomplish this. Here the second myth merges into the first. The Brotherhood obtains the essence of its goals from what it refers to as *the period of the early, pious, orthodox caliphs*. From this period it gains spiritual insight also into how a future welfare, but *Muslim* state should be governed. Every literate Muslim in Syria is familiar with this myth and a great many sincerely believe in its historical truth. The just rule of the righteous — the one and only truly Muslim rule — of this period serves as a constant reminder and point of comparison to other unjust rulers; Muslim or non-Muslim, professedly religious or secular. In Syria many Muslims seem to feel that the re-emergence of this past is unrealistic, at least under the aegis of the Muslim Brotherhood. But the myth itself is very powerful and serves to underline the injustice among the custodians of the state. The political leaders, with an essentially weak power-base, are sensitive to attacks where their *unjust, non-sunni*, anti-golden-caliphate-period myth is underlined. The president goes to great lengths in trying to establish the Ba'th as being neither anti-Islamic nor anti-*sunni*, but on the contrary as close to what is called "the true open spirit of Islam". He frequently meets the official religious leaders and tries to portray himself, if not pious, at least as a reasonable and respectful man. This image appears to be accepted by many Syrian Muslims, even by those who laugh at his televised praying on religious feasts. During their mass-media campaign against the Muslim Brotherhood in the summer of 1980, Ba'th leaders turned the personal verbal attacks made on them to their own advantage. Where the Brotherhood made individual accusations against the political leaders — perhaps feeling this was a reflection of a popular opinon — the regime instead turned this ploy against the Muslim Brotherhood. By sinking to such vituperation, it was claimed in the mass-media campaign that the Brotherhood was showing its *un-Islamic* face. No true Muslim would ever sink so low in thought or deed. No true Syrian Muslim would co-operate with reactionary elements inside the nation and with hostile foreign regimes in order to undermine the legitimate national struggle of his fellow Muslims and fellow citizens. This official rhetoric probably convinced nobody of the virtues of the Ba'th, but it was quite effective in discrediting the Muslim Brotherhood. Many people with spontaneous sympathy for the Brotherhood's struggle found that they had lost faith in the Brotherhood's cause.

Model for studies of political action

Thus, there exists a sort of accommodation between the two basic myths. This is only natural since the Ba'th originated and developed in the context of an Islamic culture, and since the Syrian Muslim Brotherhood exists in the context of a state with welfare aspirations. When voicing their opinions about political goals, Syrians draw from both mythical sources. Both are accepted, available and vague enough to be used as symbols for various types of political struggles. As long as contestants in the power struggle use these myths and as long as people are motivated by them they will stay forceful. But in order to study if the myths are changing, we must again study the nature of the Syrian state and the relation between the dominant ruling classes and their subordinates. It is in these interrelations that the basic structure of the Syrian political struggle is formed and reformed. The two modes of analysis — a delineation of the class structure and a search for central political symbols and myths among power-holders and dissidents as well as various popular responses to these symbols — together make up a viable model for the understanding of politics in Syria.

This type of model — outlined here in a rather schematic way — could also be useful for the study of political action and political culture in other Middle Eastern countries. We need abstract models like that of class-analysis to condense many variables without reducing all nation-states to the same level, or of treating each one as too unique to compare with any other. But we still need a model which incorporates the people's own use of the available political culture. Through this type of model we can better analyse the oft-stated contradiction in the Middle East between modern secular politics and vestiges or re-emergences of Islam in politics. Secular and religious symbols are — at least in Syria — ideological expressions used by all contestants in the struggle for power, where the underlying contradiction reflects class-interests and not the goal of rebuilding an Islamic state.

10

ISLAM: WHAT IS ITS POLITICAL SIGNIFICANCE? THE CASES OF EGYPT AND SAUDI ARABIA

Gorm Rye Olsen

1. Introduction

In recent years new phrases like "Islamic resurgence" and "Islamic revival" have entered into the jargon of the international press and into the discourse of the international academic world. As a non-specialist on Islam, I have the impression that Islam is the Alpha and Omega in explaining numerous developments in the Muslim countries of the Third World. This is particularly the case in respect to the so-called Islamic revolution of Iran. The influence of Islam is also asserted to be decisive in Pakistan, Saudi Arabia and the Sudan — not to mention the Iran-Iraq war.

As a political scientist, I find it necessary to challenge this popular perception of the impact of Islam on societal developments in Muslim countries. Therefore, the hypothesis of this paper is more or less the opposite of the popular views on Islam. The hypothesis is as follows: Islam has had no signficance for the fundamental changes of Muslim countries, i.e. it has had no impact on either the development of the economic structures of capitalism or on the corresponding changes in the class structures of these countries. Its significance is limited to the sphere of ideology. Here Islam is significant in legitimizing the political (and economic) power of that class or élite which happens to be in control.[1]

In sections 3 and 4 below, I will attempt to test this hypothesis by looking briefly into the societal developments of Egypt and Saudi Arabia.

For a start (section 2), however, I have found it necessary to make a few comments on the theoretical framework of this paper. Section 2 also contains a brief overview of the possible functions of Islam. Section 3 deals with the Egyptian development after 1952, describing the economic changes over the past 30 years and the role of Islam in legitimizing the different Egyptian regimes, plus the role of the 'Ulamā'. Brief mention is also made of the Islamic resurgence in Egypt. Section

4 treats the development of Saudi Arabia, on similar lines. Section 5 forms the conclusion.

2. Islam and Societal Development

Implicit in the hypothesis presented above is that some elements of societal development are more "important" than others. According to my perception of societal development, the economic development and the accompanying changes in the class structure are the basic or most important.[2] Of course, these phenomena cannot be analysed and understood in isolation from the complex question of class domination and class rule. To explain how a ruling class in a specific country rules, it is necessary to include analyses of the political and ideological structures. In this context, I will restrict myself to a few words concerning the role of ideology in general and in developing countries in particular.

According to Antonio Gramsci, the dominance (and hegemony) of a social class does not and cannot rest solely on physical coercion.[3] Partly, and maybe most important, class dominance rests on ideological consensus or general acceptance of the prevailing societal conditions. That is to say, ideology is claimed to have a very important function in preserving the existing economic and political relations of power and dominance.

Concerning the developing countries of the Third World, I will go as far as claiming that ideology is of peculiar importance in these countries. Because developing countries are very often heterogeneous economically, socially, regionally, ethnically, religiously and nationally ideology obtains a special significiance as a means of integration or "cement" in such countries.[4] To sum up, ideology in developing countries has a dual function. On the one hand, it is used as a means of legitimizing existing societal conditions. On the other hand ideology serves as an integrating device in hetereogeneous societies. Hence, in relation to the prime function of the capitalist state, which according to Nicos Poulantzas is "cohesion of the unity of a social formation",[5] ideology is of invaluable significance.

I believe that it is especially fruitful to conceive Islam as an ideology within a general Third World framework.[6] To my mind, ideologies in the Third World are fundamentally nationalist in their function, disregarding their different forms; Islam is also fundamentally nationalist.[7] Even though Islam, in principle, is a transnational ideology which is not tied to a specific nation-state, I think P. J. Vatikiotis is right in saying: "The fact remains that all of these expressions of Islam(ic) . . . occur under the aegis of a modern institution, the nation-state, not in the name of a wider or single Islamic domination or authority".[8]

The question of integration and legitimation is somewhat more complicated in Muslim societies. Islam, as a political ideology, has at least two functions. Depending on the situation, Islam can function as a stabilizing force, serving to maintain the status quo, or it may serve as an agent of change and revolution.[9] According to Ali Dessouki, it is therefore fundamental to distinguish between Islam employed "from above" and Islam employed "from below". If Islam is employed by governments or ruling classes it acquires a legitimizing function: "At the level of practice, Islam functions as an ideology. It is used, in most cases consciously, by a ruling class to legitimize its position, justify policies, create consensus, generate mass support and discredit opponents. In these endeavours, the ruling class is usually supported, to varying degrees, by official Ulama, by sheikhs and imams . . .".[10] The prime example of this function should be Egypt, but I assert that Saudi Arabia can also be included in this category.[11] Therefore, the following empirical investigation includes Egypt and Saudi Arabia, as mentioned previously.

As indicated, Islam can also be applied "from below", i.e. as an instrument of opposition and change. Islam from below is used by many of the militant Islamic groups. They legitimize their opposition to the existing state of things with reference to Islam. This part of the Islamic revival can be interpreted as a response to a crisis of legitimacy of the ruling élites in many Muslim countries. In this interpretation, the revival of the Islamic opposition of the 1970s is a reaction to the failure of the élites in substituting secular ideologies of legitimization for traditional Islamic legitimacy.[12] To this crisis of legitimacy come the crises caused by the immense social changes in the Middle East during the past decade or so. It has led to a number of problems still unsolved. Rapid urbanization and rising unemployment are cases in point.[13] Therefore, in the past decade Arab socialism has been gradually overtaken by Islam as the dominating ideology in Arab Muslim societies. Part of the following empirical test examines these questions in more detail.

3. Egypt

3.1. Islam and Economic Development

We start with a brief look at the extension of capitalism in Egyptian social formation in 1952, when the Free Officers seized political power. A qualified estimate suggests that the capitalist economic reproduction processes represented something like 20 or 30 per cent of the GDP in 1952/53.[14] Because of a fairly developed and partly nationally controlled industry, the capitalist economic structures of Egypt in 1952/53 can be characterized as relatively self-centred.[15] The fact that the capitalist reproduction processes were relatively internally oriented meant that Egypt had a comparatively strong national bourgeoisie at that time. That is, the Egyptian national bourgeoisie had fairly strong economic power positions vis-à-vis the centre-based bourgeoisies, especially the British bourgeoisie.

Although the Free Officers did not even have the most general ideas about their future economic policy, they soon started a massive economic reform programme.[16] The first economic intervention was the famous land reform law No. 178 of 9 September 1952. Later, this intervention was followed by other interventions in the agricultural sector. A heavy public involvement in Egypt's economic development came with the nationalization of the Suez Canal Company in 1956. It was soon accompanied by nationalization of all foreign property in the country. In 1960/62, the Egyptian state finally took over all the modern or capitalist sectors of the economy. In this context, it was of distinct importance that the state gained control of the Egyptian manufacturing industry. As a result, the share of manufacture in GNP grew from 13.4 per cent in 1955/56 to 25.6 per cent in 1979. Further, the extension of capitalism in the Egyptian society increased from some 20 – 30 per cent to not less than 50 per cent in the same period.[17] This pattern of development reflected a corresponding strengthening of the economic power positions of the national bourgeoisie.[18]

Has Islam had any influence on the economic development of Egypt and on the strengthening of the national bourgeoisie over the past 30 years? Vatikiotis stresses that "the Free Officers' leadership understood from the beginning the importance of Islam as a link between their movement and the majority of a tradition-bound public".[19] This comprehension does not seem to have had any significance in relation to the introduction of land reform. One of the primary aims of the reform was clearly to destroy the economic basis of the landed aristocracy.[20] I have not been able to find sources indicating that either implementation or introduction of land reform was motivated or influenced by Islam. The military regime did not even need to legitimize this rather far-reaching reform with reference to Islam.

It is a bit more complicated with the other reforms. Starting from 1955, an Arab nationalist propaganda was intensified. The Arab nationalism was obviously functional in legitimizing the Egyptian take-over of the Suez Canal Company and the other foreign-owned companies. It is, however, worth noting that this brand of nationalism can be interpreted as a "nationalist interpretation of Islam".[21] That is to say, the military regime obviously felt it had to legitimize its still more radical nationalist economic policy with well-known ideological elements. I will maintain, however, that Islam played a minor role in relation to ('pure' or secular) nationalism in the 1950s.

The picture becomes more clear with the extensive nationalizations in the 1960s. At that time, Arab nationalism was replaced by Arab socialism. Obviously the nationalizations made it imperative for the military rulers to make a distinction between Arab socialism and atheist communism.[22] The specific thing about Arab socialism was the fact that it was not atheist. On the contrary, it was fully in accordance with the fundamental doctrines of Islam.[23] It is worth noting that Nasser asserted that socialism was derived directly from Islam. According to him, Islam was a socialist religion *par excellence.* Finally, the Muftī was to issue a Fatwā declaring that the socialist decrees of 1961 were in accord with Islamic jurisprudence.[24]

Only a few years after the introduction of Arab socialism, a new and more religiously inspired era came to Egypt. In his first speech after the 1967 defeat, President Nasser declared that in the future religion should play a more important role in society.[25] It seems obvious that Islam came to take up a more important position in the official Egyptian ideology after 1967. Under President Sadat, this was most conspicuous in the political struggles. Nevertheless, Islam was used as a "mask" by the late President Sadat to disguise the rather offensive manifestations of the "open-door" economic policy and the growing corruption of the 1970s, Nazih Ayubi claims.[26] On the other hand, Sadat made some effort to show that the new liberal economic policy was compatible with Arab socialism. It was not until 1979 that he openly proclaimed that capitalism was no longer a crime in Egypt. But in general, Sadat was much less interested in ideological legitimization of his economic policy than Nasser had been.[27] Sadat used Islam primarily in the political struggles with political opponents.

Islam has therefore played a changing role in relation to the last 30 years of Egypt's economic development, but it has had very little impact on the basic changes of the Egyptian society. That is to say, the expansion of capitalism and the strengthening of the national Egyptian bourgeoisie has been brought about irrespective of Egypt being a Muslim society or not. Depending on the need for ideological legitimization, Islam or other ideological elements have been brought into public life. I think Ali Dessuouki is very right in saying "(In Egypt) ideas have been used to justify decisions, to prepare public opinion for one, to suit a particular circumstance or simply to consolidate power. Ideology followed, rather than inspired and determined, events".[28] This is another way of expressing the basic point of this paper: It is the economic forces and the power of the social classes which have determined the fundamental developments and changes of Egyptian society. Ideology, for instance Islam, has an important function in legitimizing the economic developments that have taken place or will take place.

3.2. Islam and the Legitimization of Power

No doubt, religious questions were also important under Nasser's military regime. Shortly after the coup in 1952, the military leaders sought to increase their power over the religious institutions by tightening their control over the religious leaders and transferring their functions, specifically education and justice, to secular authorities.[29] Thus, the most important religious institution in Egypt, al-Azhar, became completely dependent upon the government financially and in general policy. The Egyptian 'Ulamā' became salaried employees of the state. Also the appointment of Shaikh al-Azhar, the paramount Egyptian religious leader, became the sole prerogative of the President of the Republic. The placing of al-Azhar under direct supervision of the President's Office enforced al-Azhar's role as a major channel of communication between Egypt and the Muslim world. It also stressed al-Azhar as the leading interpreter and legitimizer of Nasser's revolution. The total submissiveness of the Egyptian 'Ulamā' was most clearly shown by the acquiescence in the nationalizations of the 1960s plus the official expression in the National Charter of 1962.[30]

Furthermore, the military government solicited from the 'Ulamā' formal legal acceptance of its politics in the form of the so-called fatwās. They included a wide range of topics, like birth control, land reform, nationalization, scientific research, foreign policy and social affairs. There is no doubt that Nasser's revolutionary regime was well aware of the importance of Islam in Egyptian society. The regime, however, was very clever in curtailing the influence of the religious establishment and in turning Islam into an instrument of the government's policy. In the words of Gabriel Warburg, it can be concluded from the developments of the 1950s and 1960s that "Muslim leaders as Shaikh al-Azhar . . . provided in effect the Islamic legitimization for every Nasserist policy".[31]

With the new President, Anwar el-Sadat, an explicit resort to religious symbolism became a characteristic feature of the Egypt of the

1970s. As early as 1971, there was an extensive debate on the proper role of Islam in the new Constitution. From the outset, all parties agreed that the new Constitution must name Islam as the state religion. Likewise, there was broad consensus that the Sharī'a should be in some sense the basis of legislation.[32] Sadat further sought to cultivate his personal image as a devoted Muslim. He was seen frequently and in well-published Friday expeditions to mosques. In his speeches he always quoted the Qur'ān, he was keen to stress that his first name was Muhammad, and more in the same strain.

Sadat also cultivated his relations with the Islamic establishment in allocating large funds to al-Azhar and to mosques. Several of the leading spokesmen of the religious establishment found their way into government business and financial ventures, sectors which under Nasser were reserved for secular-inclined officers and technocrats.[33] In return for this, Sadat received general support from the religious establishment. Occasionally, it intervened under specific circumstances when Sadat found himself in political difficulties. The examples of this are numerous. The Shaikh al-Azhar supported his trip to Jerusalem in 1977. Al-Azhar issued a communique approving the Camp David accords. Sadat was also aided by al-Azhar in the debate over the new divorce law reform in 1979.[34]

Before concluding this section, I find it worth mentioning one more example. It relates to the much debated issue of economic liberalization in the 1970s. In 1976 a former Shaikh al-Azhar published a book dealing with Islam and economics. Among other subjects, it stated that private property was sanctioned by Islam and that Islam smoothes the path to wealth and property. Islam also clears the way for competition and incentives, and so corresponds to the true bases of human nature. Fouad Ajami stresses that the time of publication of the book was "neither accidental nor irrelevant. The open-door economy was in full face and the debate about inequalities was an intense one".[35]

To my mind, there is no doubt that Islam in Egypt has been used to legitimize the different policies of the changing governments over the past 30 years. This has been closely connected to the 'Ulamā's compliance to the ruling élite. Let me end this section with a few citations supporting my point of view. Ali Dessouki, for instance, stresses that "Islam functions as an ideology. It is used in most cases, consciously, by a ruling class to legitimise its position, justify policies, create consensus, generate mass support . . . In this endeavour, the ruling class is usually supported to varying degrees by official Ulama . . .".[36] Fouad Ajami claims that "al-Azhar has (always) been willing to repeat the utterances of the state and to give the deeds of rulers religious sanction and cover. The men of al-Azhar have always been ready to quote scripture and use it against rebels . . . As always, the opinions of the Ulama of al-Azhar are the opinions of Islam itself. Islam is what they will it and pronounce it to be''.[37]

3.3. The Islamic Revival: A Political Protest

Most observers agree that the rise of militant religious movements in Egypt dates back to the aftermath of the Arab defeat of 1967.[38] The characteristics of the years following 1967 were the combination of a national defeat followed by an increasing foreign presence (Russian, then American). That is to say, external forces made an immense impact on the Egyptian development in the 1970s. The external influence became apparent with the introduction of Sadat's open-door (infitāh) economic policy of 1974. This liberalization of the economic policy was accompanied by high inflation, indulgent consumerism plus increasing and open corruption.

These are, briefly, the "objective" circumstances surrounding Egypt's Islamic revival. To these can be added more subjective factors such as the lack of jobs for a great many of the urban educated youth. In the 1970s the possibilities of political participation were still restricted, which added to the strongly diminished possibilities of upward mobility for young individuals. What I am trying to suggest is that the Islamic revival of Egypt is basically a social phenomenon. Therefore the rise of the Islamic groups is, in a sense, a political statement.[39]

This assertion seems to be confirmed by the composition of the members of the militant Islamic groups. They share a number of common characteristics. First, leaders and members tend to be young, i.e. in their late teens to early thirties. Second, they are mostly university graduates or students, specializing in scientific subjects. Third, they normally come from a middle-class background. And, finally, the majority are urban, i.e. they live in cities, though they are mostly of rural or small-town origin.[40]

From this, it seems clear that the age factor is important. To a large extent, the Islamic revival is a typical youth revolt reflecting a real generation gap. Further, the educational and social background of the members seems to reflect anxiety over career prospects, especially as unemployment of the educated (and here especially science graduates) had become a very serious problem under the economic liberalization in the 1970s.[41] It is at least noteworthy that, in spite of the passionate dedication to their religion, many members of the Islamic movements seem to be poorly informed about many doctrinal matters in Islam. The data presented seem to confirm my basic point of view, that in the mood of national crisis after 1967, class factors interacting adversely with personal aspirations form the background to the rise of the militant Islamic groups in Egypt.[42]

If I am right in the jargon being theological and the symbolism being religious while the real worries of the militant groups are in essence social and economic, why then don't the young militants join left-wing groups and parties, whether Marxist or secular? It is of course, a difficult question to answer. But, to my mind, it is possible to propose some elements of an answer. Firstly, secular ideologies have suffered severe setbacks due to the Egyptian quasi-socialist experiment of the 1950s and 1960s.[43] Further, the secular ideologies appear alien and imported, and the Sadat regime was clever in dismissing especially the leftist opposition as atheists or agents of foreign powers. Thirdly, under Sadat non-Islamic outlets for open political expression and action were very difficult, not to say impossible to find. Fourthly, and probably most important, there is a positive socio-cultural sanction of being religious in Egypt.[44] To the leaders of the militant groups it is, so to speak, merely a question of politicizing the consciousness of the youth and of disciplining them organizationally.

In the 1980s, the militant groups seem to be losing ground in Egypt. Though there are still strong religious passions in Egypt, they seem to have stabilized. Islam is hardly to be considered a very important political ideology in the 1980s, and its significance may even be declining.[45] I think Hanafi is right in saying that "Islamic groups look more powerful than they really are. Their voices are loud, but they have no impact on the masses".[46] Islam has therefore had some impact on the political opposition of Egypt since 1967. Its real societal significance, however, has consisted in legitimizing the rule of Sadat. And in that respect, Islam is of consequence to the development of Egypt. In other spheres of society, and as a means of opposition, it has been of minor influence.

4. Saudi Arabia

4.1. Islam and the Development of Capitalism

Let us briefly consider the economic development of the Saudi Kingdom over the past 15 years. Even though the transnational oil-corporations had been operating in the country since the beginning of the 1930s, it had no perceptible economic, social or, for that matter, political consequences until the 1960s.[47] In this context, it is important to estimate the extension of capitalist economic structures in Saudi Arabia about 1970. Capitalist reproduction processes represented between 56 and 80 per cent of the GNP at that time.[48] Compared to other peripheral countries, it means that the capitalist economic structures were relatively widespread in the Saudi social formation. Furthermore, it can be concluded that the capitalist economic structures were extremely externally oriented. That is to say, the foreign or centre bourgeoisies had correspondingly strong economic power positions in Saudi society. Parallel to this, a weak national bourgeoisie can be identified.

The aims of the Saudi Arabian economic development policy have been laid down in three development plans. The general objectives of all the plans have been to maintain the religious and moral values of the Kingdom. But apart from this kind of proclamation, it seems impossible to demonstrate the impact of Islam on the economic development processes of the country.

The Saudi development policy is based on the principle of economic freedom and open competition.[49] The Saudi authorities seek to encourage foreign capital and technology so as to participate in developing the economy. Foreign assistance is especially welcome in relation to establishing and expanding export-oriented industries. The role of the Saudi state is limited to providing the right conditions for expanding capitalism; hence the state participates in expanding the material infrastructure (e.g. roads and harbours) and the social infrastructures (e.g. health and education systems).

A brief look at the Kingdom's economy in the early 1980s conjures up the following picture.[50] The capitalist economic structures have expanded further and have consolidated themselves. Further, the capitalist economic structures are still extremely externally oriented. This external dependency means that foreign bourgeoisies still hold strong economic power positions in Saudi society. That is, the effect of the development policy has neither been an obstacle to capitalist economic expansion nor has it resulted in a strengthening of the national bourgeoisie. To put it another way, it is impossible to show that Islam or the 'Ulamā' have had any influence on the economic development and the changes of the class structure of the Kingdom. That is to say that Islam has had no provable impact on the expansion of capitalism and so on the strengthening of the economic power of the foreign bourgeoisies *vis-à-vis* the national Saudi bourgeoisie.

This conclusion is in accordance with W. B. Quant when he says that the 'Ulamā' is not a powerful force in "influencing Saudi foreign policy, in determining strategies of development and oil production, or even in the direction of Saudi aid to Islamic countries'.[51] There is some disagreement, though, concerning this Saudi aid to Islamic countries.

On the one hand, Daniel Pipes claims that Saudi Arabian aid is given with strings attached to it, urging the recipient to apply the Sharī'a.[52] On the other hand, Ronald MacIntyre maintains that Saudi economic aid policy has generally been pragmatic and mainly concerned with social and economic development.[53] There is no doubt, that most of the Kingdom's foreign aid goes to Islamic countries. But that does not necessarily mean that Pipes is right. Personally, I am convinced that MacIntyre is right in saying, "Saudi Arabia's Islamic resurgence . . . tends in the direction of maximum national co-operation between Muslim states, while tolerating a wide diversity of social and political systems within the Islamic world".[54]

4.2. Islam and the Legitimization of Power

In the introduction, I mentioned the immense importance of ideology in peripheral societies. Saudi Arabia is no exception from this. Islam has played and still plays a decisive role in legitimizing the power of the House of Saud. Since the establishment of the Kingdom, the House of Saud has used Islam to legitimize its claim to govern the Kingdom. The need for legitimization has been met by "a revival of Wahhabism and in giving the Ulama a feeling of participation and influence in public policy. Hence, since the beginning of the Kingdom, Islam and the Ulama provided a continuing source of legitimation of the Saudi regime"[55]

This feeling of influence has been limited to areas such as the administration and application of part of the judicial and educational systems, likewise in the field of strictly religious matters.[56] Further the 'Ulamā' is supposed to have a marked influence in relation to the question of public order and foreign policy. But even within these areas, the importance of the 'Ulamā' and Islam seems to have been lessened over the past 20 years or so.

Let us start by looking at the judicial field. In 1962 King Faisal introduced his ten-point programme of reform. Although the programme reaffirmed the Kingdom's adherence to the basic principles of Islam, it also introduced important innovations. Prominent among these was the pledge to establish a Ministry of Justice and a semi-secular Judicial Supreme Council. The Ministry of Justice was eventually established in 1971 and the Secular Supreme Council in 1975.[57] A large number of important laws and regulations have further been issued since the 1960s. Thus, since that time a large number of important and non-religiously inspired laws have been issued to create a corpus of laws that will enhance the economic progress and development of Saudi Arabia, as described in the preceding section. Hence, the general position of the 'Ulamā' in the judicial field has been weakened due to the process of modernization.[58]

The same can be said of the rapidly expanding educational system. A great and increasing number of Saudis get a secular education. For example, in 1948 a primary-school student spent 78.5 per cent of his school hours on religious education, while in the 1960s this had dropped to 26.5 per cent. In comparison, the time allotted to social studies and other subjects rose from 7.2 to 44.2 per cent over the same period.[59] Moreover, a rising number of Saudi females receive an education which is far from solely religiously inspired. Finally, it is worth mentioning the great number of Saudis studying abroad, especially in the USA.

To my mind, the segregation of the sexes in the education system is of minor importance compared to the secular influences the students receive. The enormous expansion of the educational system in the Kingdom, and thus of its secular parts, is a reflection of the weakened position of the 'Ulamā' vis-à-vis the demands of modernization. To put it another way, the needs of expanding Saudi capitalism for a well-educated workforce are far stronger than the influence of the 'Ulamā'. This is not to say that the religious establishment is without influence. I think MacIntyre is right in characterizing the Saudi educational system in the following way: "The Saudis have proven themselves to be skilful in adapting traditional values and institutions to the requirements of a modernising state . . .".[60]

There is no doubt that the influence of Islam and the 'Ulamā' is most conspicuous in strictly religious matters and in regulating public order. It is hard to evaluate the importance of the 'Ulamā' in these fields. However, James Piscatori gives this evaluation to the situation: "It is clear that they (the Ulama, GRO) have become less active as they became more embarrassing to the Saudi government, which is worried about its reputation abroad. Nevertheless, because there has been a recent upsurge of conservative feeling throughout the country . . . the religious police are likely not to be abolished altogether".[61] The fact that the 'Ulamā' have become dependent on the government for their salaries and positions also serves to limit the influence of the 'Ulamā'. In that respect, "they (the 'Ulamā') have become agents of the state".[62] Piscatori makes an interesting point concerning the Saudi government's worries about its reputation abroad. I am not sure at all that Piscatori is right about this point. But if he is, the implications seem to support my general view, that one should be careful not to overestimate the influence of Islam. That is to say, if the present conservative feeling in the Muslim world is ever to disappear, it will most probably be followed by an additional reduction in the influence of the 'Ulamā' and the religious police.

Finally, we have the question of Islam in Saudi foreign policy. It is, of course, a complex field. Therefore, I will limit myself to a simple point, supporting my general assertion that Islam is usually applied in a very pragmatic way. For instance, the foreign policy of the late King Feisal is in general considered to have been led by Islamic principles. That goes also for his adherence to pan-Islamic co-operation. It is, however, interesting to consider the timing of his launching this policy. It was launched exactly at a time when Saudi Arabia was under severe ideological attack from Abdel Nasser. It suggests that Faisal saw pan-Islamic co-operation as a way to counter Nasserism and pan-Arabism. Islamic co-operation was thus introduced for very pragmatic consider-ations relating to the legitimacy of the Saudi regime.[63] I think it is possible to interpret the recent Saudi efforts to promote Islamic co-operation in the same way.

As mentioned at the beginning of this section, Islam is no doubt important in legitimizing the Saudi regime. Apart from this very important ideological function, one should be careful not to overesti-mate the influence of Islam in the political development of the Kingdom. In this section, I have tried to illustrate the point. I therefore agree with Sankari when he says, "The Ulama, although influential in their spheres, have little independent political power, they must work through the King to achieve their objectives".[64]

"But what about the transfer of power from King Saud to King Faisal in the early 1960s?" somebody may ask. Didn't the 'Ulamā' show their political influence on that occasion? To my mind, the answer is no. To a very high degree, the shift of power in 1964 was an expression of the strength and flexibility of the Royal Family itself. The Family, at that incident, simply kept power away from an incapable person.[65] In fact, all that the 'Ulamā' did was to legitimize this politically necessary transfer of power. The same interpretation can be put forward to the attempt of King Khaled and Crown Prince Fahd to secure a fatwā (religious opinion) to legitimize their actions in ending the Great Mosque take-over in 1979. "They certainly could have acted without a fatwa, but asking for one cost them nothing and probably gained them something important in the long run — a reaffirmation of the Sauds' special role as protectors of the holy places and thus of their primary claim to govern."[66]

4.3. The Islamic Revival and the Insurrection at Mecca

No matter how the Saudi authorities handled the seizure of the Great Mosque in Mecca, the incident showed that the Kingdom had its religious opponents as well. The take-over of the Mosque by some hundred Islamic fundamentalists was a deliberate challenge to the Royal

Family as a symbol of Wahhābī consensus and as the guardian of the Holy places of Islam. The militants demanded, among other things, a strict adherence to the Sharī'a, a ban on television, football, movies and the like, plus a prohibition against women working in public places. Further, they assailed the ruling regime as being corrupt and inept.[67] The western media gave the impression that the House of Saud was seriously threatened by the seizure, which showed only a minor part of an opposition movement in the Kingdom. However, the suddenness and violence of the incidents might have tended to exaggerate the immediate significance of the Mecca incident. It is, on the other hand, still interesting to look further into the incident. Nazih Ayubi sees the neo-fundamentalist groups in Saudi Arabia, like the militants in Mecca, as an expression of socio-political protest. They very often relate to socio-economic contradictions, cultural alienation and generation differences, he claims.[68] The Mosque intruders were actually expressing social criticism of, and political protest against, what they regarded as the false and opportunistic utilization of Islam to hide corruption, decadence and oppression, as well as subservience to the "for-eigner".[69] The composition of the Mecca group seems to support Ayubi's point of view. This group was chiefly made up of persons from the relatively deprived tribes, such as the Otaiba, Harb and the Qahtani, along with a number of immigrant Arab workers.[70] As in Egypt, a great number were urban and well-educated youth.

The insurrection at Mecca is clearly a manifestation of the dilemma in which Saudi Arabia finds itself. A regime based on traditional symbols, like Islam, is of course vulnerable to challenges of religious orthodoxy.[71] In this last respect, Islam legitimizes opposition even to the most orthodox Islamic regime in the Muslim world.

Politically, one questions whether a neo-fundamentalist movement will ever grow sufficiently strong to threaten the House of Saud. Personally I don't think this will ever happen.[72] The ruling class(es) and the important social categories have a mutual interest in maintaining the present politico-economic system in the Kingdom. In that respect, Islam "from above" is most important in its legitimization of the existing social order. To put it another way, neo-fundamentalists in Saudi Arabia have to challenge classes (and social categories) having both economic power and ideological hegemony as local economic and political élites. This task is far more difficult than that faced by the Iranian rebels in the late 1970s.

5. Concluding Remarks

In this paper, I have attempted to test a hypothesis concerning the role of Islam in Muslim societies. I have chosen Egypt and Saudi Arabia as test cases. From the empirical analysis I think it is possible to draw the following conclusions. First, it has not been possible to prove the decisive influence of Islam on the economic development of the two countries. Put differently, the expansion of capitalist economic structures has not been impeded by Islam.[73] Neither the changes in the class structure nor the power positions of the dominating classes of the two countries have been influenced by the fact that we are concerned with Muslim societies. In the case of Egypt, we observed a strengthening of the economic power positions of the national bourgeoisie and a simultaneous weakening of the foreign bourgeoisies. In Saudi Arabia, on the other hand, it was impossible to show a similar strengthening of the national bourgeoisie. Here the foreign bourgeoisies kept their strong economic power positions. That is to say, the "basic changes" of Egypt and Saudi Arabia have taken place regardless of the existence of Islam. Similarly, there is no preordained path of development for these countries resulting, for instance, in a strong national bourgeoisie as in Egypt.

Secondly, I attempted to show that the importance of Islam was restricted to the ideological sphere. Islam has been, and still is, of immense importance in legitimizing the power of the ruling élite or class in Egypt as well as in Saudi Arabia. To a large extent, the 'Ulamā' has become an instrument in the hands of the ruling circles of the two societies. There are, of course, obvious differences between Egypt and Saudi Arabia. The comparatively limited influence of Islam and the 'Ulamā' is most conspicuous in the case of Egypt. On the other hand, I tried to show that the different regimes of Egypt could not neglect Islam as an important ideological element.

Saudi Arabia is generally considered to be the prime example of an Islamic state. However, one has to be careful not to overestimate the importance of Islam and the 'Ulamā' in the Kingdom. I have attempted to show how the impact of Islam and the 'Ulamā' was generally restricted to areas of minor importance, such as the segregation of the two sexes in the educational system and the like.

Finally, I dealt briefly with the so-called Islamic renaissance or Islamic revival. I found that the militant Islamic groups in Egypt to a very large extent can be interpreted as a political youth revolt. In Egypt, the groups are basically concerned with political and social questions, even though their jargon is religious. In Saudi Arabia, the Islamic opposition is more purely religious in its demands. Islamic fundamentalism may be an expression of a (widespread?) frustration and lack of understanding or acceptance of the present social situation in Saudi Arabia. And as such, it can be interpreted as a reaction to the extremely rapid economic and social changes in the Kingdom over the past 20 years or so. If that is correct, the Islamic fundamentalists may represent a potential threat to the ruling class in Saudi Arabia if they ever get a popular following. However, the Saudi Arabia of the 1980s is not the Iran of the 1970s. The Saudi regime seems to have a much broader and more popular legitimacy. Also the ruling class (and social categories) of the Kingdom hold very strong economic, political and, not least, ideological power positions *vis-à-vis* the masses. In all these respects, Saudi Arabia differs from Iran in the 1970s.

In conclusion, I have shown that Islam has had no significance in relation to what I define as the "fundamental changes" of Egypt and Saudi Arabia. On the other hand, I have shown that Islam is important in legitimizing the political (and economic) power of the ruling class of the two countries. Finally I have shown that the Islamic opposition is only of possible future significance in Saudi Arabia, even though I have argued that there is a clear difference between the Kingdom and Iran in the 1970s.

One final question remains: To what extent can the observations of the paper be generalized to other Muslim countries? At least, I think they can be generalized to other Sunnī Muslim societies of the Arab world. Iran, as a Shī'ī Muslim society, represents a more tricky case in relation to generalizations and so do Indonesia, Bangladesh, etc. I hope, nevertheless, that the conclusions of this paper have contributed to place Islam in its "proper" societal position and thus provide a better understanding of the role of Islam in Sunnī Muslim Arab countries.

11

WHEN MUSLIM IDENTITY HAS DIFFERENT MEANINGS: RELIGION AND POLITICS IN CONTEMPORARY AFGHANISTAN

Asger Christensen

'For Islam, honour, and homeland' (*Islam de para, namūs de para, votan de para*) is the expression used when refugees and guerillas belonging to Afghanistan's largest ethnic group, the Pakhtun,[1] explain their opposition to the present regime in Kabul and its Soviet allies. Together these three categories define the conceptual realm which provides meaning and *raison d'être* for the Afghan resistance struggle: the defence of territory and cultural tradition against interference from an opponent considered to be infidel (*Kāfir*). Yet, although the majority among the Pakhtun and other ethnic groups in Afghanistan appear to agree to defend their beliefs and way of life against the Kabul regime and the Soviet forces of occupation, this does not mean that there exists a consensus, even within the separate ethnic groups, concerning the conceptualization of the cultural tradition which is defended. The Afghan resistance, and in particular that of the Pakhtun, is split into a large number of political parties and groups, each with different views of what they regard as proper Islam, and with respect to the kind of society they envisage in a liberated Afghanistan. In what follows I shall attempt to outline how the very same categories — Islam, honour, and homeland — which provide the impetus for resistance are also the ones which must be considered, if the political and organizational fragmentation of the resistance is to be explained.

Diversity within Islam

Islam contains no distinction between a religious and a secular sphere of life, but instead strives to create a total way of life based on the guidelines, directives, and prohibitions given by God in the Qur'ān or contained in the legends about the life of Muhammad, the *hadīth*. However, the fact that the overwhelming majority of Afghans consider themselves Muslims and regard the Qur'ān and *hadīth* as supreme authorities on all aspects of life does not make Islam in Afghanistan an unequivocal or static phenomenon.

The presence of both of the major Muslim sects, Sunnī and Shī'ī, reflects the basic diversity within Islam in Afghanistan. Neither Sunnī nor Shī'ī constitite monolithic systems of belief. Instead, both contain internal sectarian differences, such as Imāmīs and Ismā'īlīs among the Shī'ī, or those which separate the different Sūfī *tariqa* and also distinguish the followers of these from other believers among the Sunnī. Moreover, the adherents of both Sunnī and Shī'ī Islam come from culturally diverse ethnic groups, who practise distinct versions of a Muslim way of life. All of these versions contain elements which deviate from or even contradict the message of the Qur'ān and *hadīth*, but people experience this condition very differently, and the practical consequences which they draw also vary considerably.

The Pakhtun provide an example of this kind of diversity. They regard themselves as descendants from a common ancestor named Qays, who lived at the time of Muḥammad, and who was converted to Islam by the Prophet himself. The Pakhtun thus associate and equate their very origin and identity with Islam, and they contrast this with all the other ethnic groups in Afghanistan, who are not original Muslims, but later converts. At the same time, however, this notion of common descent also constitutes the basis of a tribal social order, whose norms and modes of conduct deviate from Islam in several important respects.[2] This schism is part of Pakhtun cultural consciousness and is clearly expressed as when the tribal notions of honourable behaviour, *pakhtūnwālī*, are contrasted with the sayings of the Qur'ān in the proverb "Pakhtun half use the Qur'ān, half *Pakhtūnwālī*" (*Pukhtāne nīm Qur'ān mani, nīm pukhtūnwālī mani*).[3] Most Pakhtun do not consider this conflict particularly problematic, and many just appear to accept it as a fact of life, while others experience it as a fundamental existential dilemma and strive to solve it in different ways. Some attempt to do this by practising a personal life-style that places greater emphasis on the precepts of Islam, or by attaching themselves to a religious figure respected for his piousness and learning from whom they receive spiritual guidance, e.g. one of the leaders (*Pīrs*) of a Sūfī *tariqa*. Yet others who wish to resolve this contradiction seek a political solution through a transformation of society which brings it into correspondence with what they view as proper Islam.

Such differences of opinion concerning the relationship between what is understood as proper Islam and the existing social order can be found within all sections of the Afghan population. They were also present in people's attitudes towards the increasing "modernization" and "westernization" of Afghan society.

Instead of providing unity of belief and a shared unequivocal conception of how society should be, the role of Islam as the basic conceptual frame of reference and the ultimate source of legitimation implies that social and political affairs are understood and discussed in religious terms. The concepts of Islam have always been sufficiently ambiguous to allow different interpretations and thus allowing mutually conflicting political views to be seen as religiously legitimate by their exponents. The result is that attempts to mobilize people for political action through religiously legitimated appeals or to convince them of the correctness of certain kinds of conduct, invariably occur in a context of conflicting appeals, which likewise are held to be derived from Islam.

Afghan history contains many examples of political confrontations based on different interpretations of Islam.[4] One of the most illustrative of these conflicts took place during the expansion and consolidation of Afghan state authority in the reign of Amīr 'Abd ur-Rahmān (1882 – 1901). In addition to harsh military and administrative measures his attempts to strengthen the authority of the state also involved a religious policy that entailed the propagation of a new interpretation of Islam (cf. Ghani 1978). The main feature of this interpretation was the attempt to combine state authority with religious legitimation by defining the good Muslim as identical with the good subject who accepted this authority. Through a combination of repression and rewards the state managed to gain the support of a number of prominent religious personalities who together promoted this version of Islam. But at the same time this version was rejected by others, who proclaimed the ruler heretic, and who thereby lent religious legitimation to a widespread popular resistance against the attempts of the state to expand and strengthen its control.

The situation today exhibits certain parallels to that of the reign of Amīr 'Abd ur-Rahmān. Ever since it seized power by the *coup d'état* in April 1978, the new "revolutionary" regime has striven to appear Muslim. Its decrees and other official proclamations have all been introduced by an invocation of God, and like its nineteenth century predecessor, it has repressed and eliminated part of the religious establishment while at the same time attempting to ally iself with those religious figures willing to provide the regime and its policies with religious legitimation. However, the extensive popular opposition to the new regime demonstrates that this policy has been far from successful. Most people instead identify themselves with the resistance and consider it the legitimate representative of Islam.

Honour — autonomy and rivalry

One of the most important reasons for this state of affairs is the same which prompted the resistance against the centralizing policies of Amīr

'Abd ur-Rahmān, and it is expressed in the second of the categories that
the Pakhtun use to explain the current resistance struggle — their
honour. For the Pakhtun, honour is associated with the maintenance of
autonomy and integrity, be it in relation to other members of the local
community or to outside powers such as the state. While the notions of
honour (*nang*) appear most elaborated among the Pakhtun, where they
constitute the core of the tribal value system *pakhtūnwālī* (cf. Janata &
Hassas 1975), the association of honour and autonomy is also shared by
other rural ethnic groups in Afghanistan.

The attempt to strengthen state authority at the expense of local
autonomy at the end of last century, and to introduce such measures as
taxation and military conscription, met with open resistance from
practically all ethnic groups in the country (cf. Kakar 1971). But
although the central government succeeded in expanding its influence
considerably compared to its predecessors, there nevertheless remained
considerable sections of the rural population who managed to retain
much of their former autonomy, and who, moreover, have been able to
do so right up to the present.

The current resistance struggle began as a number of mutually isolated
and unrelated attempts to defend this local autonomy against the
increasing interference from the new "revolutionary" regime. Clashes
between the local population and inexperienced, newly-appointed
officials, who often acted in a dogmatic and highhanded fashion, were
seen by the government as 'counter-revolutionary' resistance and met
with military reprisals. The result was, that as early as the summer of
1978, a few months after the *coup d'état* and before the reforms
affecting the rural population had been made public, the actions of the
new regime had already generated a growing popular resistance. In the
beginning of October this resistance reached such a high level in the
province of Kunar in Eastern Afghanistan, that the Afghan army had
difficulties in handling the situation and had to be supported by Soviet
military advisers (Christensen 1983: 11). The dependency of the new
regime on Soviet civil and military aid — a dependency which deepened
and became more manifest as the resistance increased — thus made it
appear foreign dominated and un-Islamic to many Afghans long before
the Soviet invasion in December 1979.

However, as mentioned above, the Pakhtun notion of honour
comprises yet another dimension. Just as the maintenance of honour
leads to resistance against the imposition of outside control, it is also a
source of local rivalry for influence, leadership and control over
resources.

The notion of honour is closely linked with the idea that all (male)
Pakhtun are equal (*siāl*) because of their common descent. Honour is

preserved by asserting equality *vis-à-vis* other Pakhtun, be they close or distant kinsmen. The realization of this involves above all the maintenance of the autonomy and integrity of the household (*korunei*) through the ability to protect (and control) the women, the house, and the land belonging to it; these three categories are united in the same concept of honour — *nāmūs*. In the eyes of Pakhtun society, then, it is not enough that the individual is a Pakhtun merely through descent; he also has "to do Pakhto" (*pakhtō kavöl*) by upholding *nāmūs* in order to preserve equivalence and status as a real Pakhtun tribesman.

Equality thus has a dual nature for the Pakhtun: On the one hand it is something which is ascribed and given, yet on the other hand it also has to be confirmed through achievement. This duality constitutes the source of the ambiguity, tension, and frequent hostility that pervade the relations between even close collateral agnates, because the effort to maintain equality by upholding honour and autonomy may be pursued either through co-operation with others or by competition and efforts at dominance (Christensen 1984: 72).

The ambiguity inherent in the relationship between patrilineal kinsmen is clearly expressed in the concepts used by the Pakhtun. Despite the oft-stated ideal of solidarity between agnates, the verb *siālī kavöl*, which literally means "to do equality", also means "competition", and the term for patrilateral cousin, *tarbur*, has the connotation of "enemy", while *tarburwālī* denotes the rivalry often existing between collateral agnates.

Hence, political relations are shaped by and take place within an organizational context of a patrilineal descent system with a strong normative emphasis on solidarity, but where at the same time the actual relations between agnates are crucially influenced by variable interests, which may either bring them together as allies, or separate them as competitors and opponents. The result is that landholding descent groups sharing the same village or local community are usually split into rival factions headed by "big-man" type of leaders, who compete with each other in building and consolidating a following among both kinsmen and non-kin. Political allegiance crosscuts patrilineal descent relations, and the political groupings confronting each other consist of more or less unstable factions and coalitions of factions having coincident interests. While patrilineal descent groups are not mobilized in any consistent pattern of balanced opposition (cf. Barth 1959), descent segments of varying size nevertheless do emerge within the overall context of this factional rivalry (cf. Christensen 1982: 37 ff).

Variations in this factional mode of politics are also found outside the areas inhabited by the Pakhtun (c.f. Azoy 1982; Canfield 1973), and this pattern of political orgnization has implications which reach beyond that of local-level politics. One is that despite resentment of state interference, the rivalry caused by the attempt to uphold autonomy and honour also lends an ambiguous character to the relationship between local populations and the state.

Thus, throughout this century, successive Afghan regimes, all of which had tried to gain control over what they regarded as the Pakhtun *yaghistan*, or "land of rebels" (Caroe 1958: 347), have managed to achieve a degree of influence by means other than direct military intervention. By measures such as direct financial subsidies, the granting of administrative functions to favoured individuals, or by a generally privileged treatment compared to that given to others, the regimes have been able to forge alliances with persons and groups at the local level. As a result of the pervasive rivalry and the attendant competition for the prestigious position of local political leadership, there will always be some people among those aspiring to local leadership who will find it advantageous to ally themselves with which ever regime is in power. For the local leader, however, such alliances do not necessarily entail acceptance of the wider implications of state authority. His ties to government and administrators are more likely to be founded on tactical considerations concerning the benefits and support which can be derived from the state, and the followers who can be attracted by his acting as middle man between them and the state authorities.

Although still uneven and often marginal, the influence of the state apparatus in Afghanistan has nevertheless been felt in practically every corner of the rural hinterland since the period of state consolidation at the end of the nineteenth century. Since the state is something to be reckoned with, participants in the competition for local leadership generally attempt to establish ties with the state authorities in their province, and, if possible, at the political centre in Kabul as well. These ties can be used to reinforce the leader's authority and to provide benefits for his allies and followers. The means used to establish such friendly relations, and to obtain easy access to provincial authorities, include hospitality and bribes to different officials, as well as collaboration with them in various matters. In addition, an increasing number of the families of local political importance have members employed in government service as bureaucrats, teachers, and army officers whose connections with the regime in power or with rival cliques and groupings in the capital may yield immediate or future results.

The frequent political upheavals and changes which have taken place in Kabul during this century have been accompanied by corresponding realignments between the state and local leaders in the provinces.

Following such changes, the leaders most closely attached to the former regime have usually been discarded as allies. Their successors instead promote and favour new constellations of rising local leaders, often comprising the rivals of the previously dominant ones (cf. Christensen 1982: 42 ff).

Such forms of political organization and processes have provided the framework of both the support for and the opposition to the new "revolutionary" regime after the *coup d'ètat* in April 1978. Allegiance and opposition to the new regime thus cuts across class divisions, and in the rural areas both supporters and opponents are made up of factions comprising feudal landowners, small landholders, tenants, and the landless (Christensen 1983: 6 ff).

Support for the new regime appears in particular to have come from those factions which before the *coup-de-état* were the underdogs in the competition for local political influence, and which did not have closer relations with the previous regime. Some of the families heading these factions had members who had joined the People's Democratic Party of Afghanistan and who have received promotion within the administration and army. As the new regime did not have any organizational foothold among the rural population, its influence in the countryside following the coup was critically dependent on such alliances with local factional leaders. In the years following the seizure of power, the new regime has consistently striven to maintain and expand these alliances, using such means as frequent meetings in the capital with local leaders, bribes and gifts, or promises to refrain from interference in local affairs.

The pattern of local factional rivalry has another important implication besides that of creating conditions for alliances between local leaders and the state. Factional rivalry also prevents the resistance groups from uniting within a more encompassing framework, since few factional leaders are prepared to relinquish their autonomy and submit to the authority of someone whom they consider their equal. In cases where resistance forces have united, this has been achieved through religious and not secular leadership. Both religious figures such as *Sayyids, Ākhundzādas, Mīāns, Pīrs, Maulawīs,* and occasionally even village *mullās* have frequently managed to transcend their customary role as spiritual teachers, mediators, and magico-religious healers and have been able to use their spiritual reputation and following as a means of exercising political influence. But their ability to function as political leaders and to rally people by invoking appeals to Islam has always been subjected to the inherent diversity of attitudes, interpretations, and interests which exist in Afghan society; therefore their leadership remains partial and incomplete as well as relatively unstable. It is partial and incomplete because their message and version of Islam are not accepted by everybody. As the same time it is relatively unstable, because only part of their following may be motivated by a shared religious attitude. Others may have joined mainly for more mundane political considerations, which make their continued support dependent on the success of the religious cum political leader, and on his ability to safeguard their interests. Thus, even though religious leaders may be able to build broader followings this does not mean that factional rivalry is neutralized or superseded; rather, factionalism is transferred to another level of organization, where it is expressed in the support for different religious leaders.

The divided resistance

Within the current resistance movement, political divisions founded on different interpretations of Islam exist among both Sunnī and Shī'ī. Within each of these major sects the many political groupings appear to be divided into two main categories, of which only those among the Sunnī will be discussed here.[5]

The political groups and parties constituting the first of these main categories have evolved from traditional religous forms of organization and leadership like the Sufi *tariqas*. Thus, members of the leading Mujaddedi family within the *Naqshbandiyya tariqa* now head the National Liberation Front (*Jabha-e najād-e melli-e Afghānistān*), while members of the Gailani family from the *Qaderia tariqa* constitute the leadership of the National Islamic Front (*Mahaz-e melli-e islāmī-e Afghānistān*). Formerly these families played an important role in the religious and political life of Afghanistan, and both are related by marriage to the exiled royal family. The members of each party are largely drawn from the religious followers of the Sufi *tariqa* out of which evolved the party; since both *tariqa* have a considerable number of adherents among the Pakhtun in Eastern Afghanistan, this is also the region where they are most influential. The two parties thus represent different segments of the traditional religious and political establishment. Both seek to unify the resistance into a broad national front, and they favour the restoration of the monarchy and the establishment of a pluralist political system, while at the same time stressing the need for a strengthening of Islam.

The second main category is composed of so-called "fundamentalist" organizations like the Islamic Party (*Hizb-e Islāmī*) headed by the former student of engineering, Gulbuddin Hekmatyar, and the Islamic Union (*Jamiyyat-e Islāmī*) which is lead by Burhannudin Rabbani, who formerly held a teaching position in theology and Islamic law at the University of Kabul. These parties both want a radical transformation of Afghan society to make it conform to their conception of Islam: each regards itself as the leading force in this process. They look upon the Sūfī background of the National Liberation Front and the National Islamic Front as something which is ideologically suspect. At the same time they consider the leaders of these parties to be partly responsible for the present situation in Afghanistan because of their former association with the monarchy, whose policies the "fundamentalists" view as excessively liberal.

These "fundamentalist" parties represent a new phenomenon in Afghan politics. Like their opponents on the Afghan left the "fundamentalists" considered as a political movement are mainly the creation of a radicalization which took place among parts of the intelligentsia and urban middle class since the late 1960s as a reaction to frustrated aspirations of employment, political influence and economic development. But Marxism and "fundamentalist" Islam share more than their being alternative and opposed ideological solutions to the same social problems. Besides a common historical background, their urban origins and their radical, uncompromising dogmatism make both of them basically unacceptable to the rural population.

Thus, as early as the middle 1970s "fundamentalist' Islamic revolutionaries tried to mobilize the rural population against the Daud regime, but without success, despite the financial and military support they allegedly received from the then president of Pakistan, Ali Bhutto. Nor did this change before the *coup d'état* in April 1978. "Fundamentalist" agitators, which were named *Panj Pīrei* by the local population, after the madressa of Panj Pir outside Peshawar where they had been educated, were active preaching against the government in the province of Kunar in 1977 and early 1978. But although the authorities were unable to catch them, the *Panj Pīrei*, failed to attract sufficient followers to pose any serious problem. The local mullās looked upon them as a threat to their own position, while people in general either ignored them or considered them somewhat heretical.[6]

It was only after the *coup d'état*, when interference in local affairs and increasing repression by the new regime had created a growing opposition in the countryside, that the "fundamentalist" groups managed to gain popular support.

All the resistance organizations mentioned above as well as others are to be found among the Pakhtun, but far from all Pakhtun resistance leaders are members of such organizations. Many local leaders among the Pakhtun are not prepared to relinquish their autonomy and submit to the authority of the religious leadership of these organizations. The Pakhtun conception of their own original Muslimness introduces a certain ambiguity in their relative ranking *vis-à-vis* religious figures, and they tend to consider themselves as being on a par with people of religious status. Although individual religious figures may acquire considerable prestige because of their piety, learning, or divine descent, they are not automatically considered superior or entitled to wield authority over the lives of others. This situation and the fact that the following of the religious leaders in the current resistance struggle may be based on either shared ideology or more practical political considerations would seem to indicate that, in addition to the two ideological tendencies within the resistance described above, there exists a third: that of the those Pakhtun tribesmen who do not view the discrepancies between Islam and *paktūnwālī* as particularly problematical, and who consequently do not feel the need of spiritual guidance and political leadership by religious figures.

Homeland — emerging national consciousness

As we have seen, the major resistance organizations, like the four mentioned above, are based either on common ideology or derive from more immediate and mundane political interests. From their headquarters in Peshawar in Pakistan these resistance organizations, and a couple of others besides, maintain international contacts with governments or kindred Islamic organizations both in Pakistan and in the Arab world. These contacts provide them with access to some of the resources, money, and to a certain extent also weapons, so badly needed by the active resistance groups inside Afghanistan. In exchange for material support, the resistance organizations expect political allegiance from the groups who receive it. Thus, although the overall context is different, the position of the major resistance organizations and of their leadership nevertheless to a large extent derives from their ability to assume what is essentially the traditional role of successful local leaders: that of the middleman or broker who creates a following through patronage. This kind of dependency, and the resulting organizational fragmentation of the active resistance struggle, is deeply resented by many Afghans, who regard the resistance organizations in Peshawar as being too self-seeking and therefore refer to the six largest of them as *spag dukanān* — the six shops.

Yet, at the same time there is a tendency towards increased cooperation between some of the active resistance groups inside Afghanistan. A new generation of leaders have emerged from the resistance struggle and they have in many cases replaced or overshadowed the traditional local leadership. Some of the most able of these leaders have managed to maintain relations with a resistance organization in Peshawar, which gives them access to resources and arms without allowing this to compromise their freedom of action, and they have succeeded in uniting all or most of the resistance groups in a particular province or region. This tendency is most developed in areas dominated by non-Pakhtun ethnic groups, whereas the Pakhtun resistance apparently remains fragmented. The most prominent examples of such unification, cutting across both political and ethnic divisions, are the resistance fronts headed by Massoud in the Panjshir valley, Sabiullah in the region around Mazir-i Sharif, and Ismail Khan and Allahuddin in the provinces of Herat, Ghor, Farah, and Nimruz in Western Afghanistan.

Whereas resistance groups formerly used to restrict their actions to that particular locality or region which they considered their homeland, the existence of a degree of co-operation between the three large fronts of Northern and Western Afghanistan, as well as the sentiments expressed by Afghan refugees in Pakistan, indicate that the struggle is increasingly seen as one of national liberation.

Conclusion

In the preceding discussion I have tried to show how the concepts of Islam, honour, and homeland which constitute the *raison d'être* of the current Afghan resistance struggle are also the sources of its ideological and organizational heterogenity. Although the three categories are simultaneously present in political discourse and can be used to define a shared cultural tradition and way of life for the Pakhtun, they do not constitute a consistent ideology or system of meaning.

This lack of consistency is inherent in the categories, and exists on different levels. First of all, the precepts of Islam and the notions of *pakhtūnwālī* differ in ways which cannot be resolved without compromising one of the systems. Secondly, the concepts of Islam leave room for interpretation and accommodation to different views of how the believers should order their existence. Thirdly, *pakhtūnwālī* also contains ambiguity, since the maintenance of honour may pose the dilemma of choice between autonomy and agnatic solidarity, both of which are considered important values by the Pakhtun. Finally, the dilemma of choice posed by the notion of honour generates factional rivalry, which in turn provides a social setting which admits of various solutions to the ideological inconsistencies to function as alternatives.

Viewed from this perspective, Pakhtun culture in the sense of a unified, consistent, and shared system of meaning does not exist.

Culture and ideology instead have to be understood as heterogenous systems of meaning which contain inherent contradictions, ambiguities, and dilemmas, all of which are resolved in different ways by the members of the society in question. Moreover, such alternative ideological versions are always associated with and defined by specific interests, which they in turn serve to legitimate.

12

AFGHANISTAN:
THE DEVELOPMENT OF THE MODERN STATE

Asta Olesen

In Afghanistan, the development of the modern state and centralization of power has, during the last 100 years, been characterized by various "legitimization of power" models.[1] The Afghan state has been confronted by obvious legitimization problems due to the peculiarities of Afghan society: a population of ninety-nine per cent Muslims, of which a great proportion, particularly the State-supporting ethnic Pashtuns, have tribal backgrounds, deep-rooted egalitarian traditions and great ethnic heterogeneity.

The different models of legitimization of power represent, first, the attempt of superimposing a centralized State apparatus on the tribes and autonomous ethnic groups of the Hindu Kush mountains and Turkestan plains and secondly, means of overcoming conflicts between a centralizing power on the one hand and the tribes and 'Ulamā' on the other. Subsequently, the budding bourgeoisie only complicates the struggle for power.

This analysis of the development of the Power apparatus will therefore focus on the unsteady equilibrium between politics and the social basis which has been for longer or shorter periods, represented by the following models.

"Tribal State" model vs. Islamic model

Until the 1880s Afghanistan could, at best, be described as a "tribal kingdom". In dealing with the Pashtun tribes which formed the military and the political backbone of the kingdom, the Afghan monarchs were subject to the same limitations of authority as the tribal chieftains of those basically egalitarian tribes. The actions and decisions of the rulers had to conform to *Pashtūnwālī* (tribal code of the Pashtuns), to the Sharī'a and especially to the decisions of the *Jirga* (tribal councils), which were based on the concept of communal authority. Hence, the central power which politically and militarily originated from and was

based upon the Pashtun tribes, had not yet been able to supersede
structural limitations of the tribal state with its inherent disintegrating
effects.[2]

This situation presented itself in a dichotomy in the legitimation of
transmission of Power:

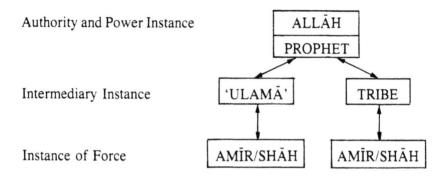

Authority and Power Instance

Intermediary Instance

Instance of Force

Islam as adhered to by the tribesmen did not have the Sharī'a as its
judicial basis (in case of differences, the Sharī'a was normally
superseded by Pashtūnwālī) and there was no local tradition which
enforced allegiance to the monarch.[3] Legitimacy of power, although
ultimately derived from Allāh, was mediated through the tribe in which
the authority was rooted in Pashtūnwālī and the internal equality of the
Jurga, i.e., a "tribal-state" model of legitimacy. For the Pashtuns, the
putative genealogical links to the Prophet through apical ancestor Qays
made both this model and bypassing of the 'Ulamā' acceptable and
compatible with Islam since the Muslim identity was inherent in being
Pashtuns.[4] However, within the power struggle between the tribes and
the rulers, the latter increasingly attempted to claim legitimacy on the
basis of the "Islamic Model", by appealing to a source of legitimacy
external to the tribal system.[5] Eventually a confrontation between these
two models of legitimacy could not be avoided in the sphere of practical
politics, as during the reign of Amīr 'Abd ur-Rahmān (1880 – 1901).

The problem facing Amīr 'Abd ur-Rahmān and the central State
when he assumed power in 1880 was not to *maintain* ideological
hegemony but rather to *create* it; this was achieved through breaking
the structural limitations of the "tribal state" and replacing it with the
"modern" State apparatus. This policy was to break the independence
of traditional power groups in society, the royal lineage, tribal leaders
and the religious establishment and to turn them into groups whose
basic economic and political interests were those of the State. As a
whole, the socio-economic structure of Afghan society did not change;
the policy was aimed only at restructuring power relations between the

ruling groups of society and the State. However, for such an enterprise to succeed and to be not entirely dependent upon the use of physical force, i.e. army and police, some justification of legitimacy of power *vis-à-vis* the total population was essential. The Amīr's political and economic policy was to replace the 'tribal-state' model by an Islamic model of legitimacy of power. To base the legitimacy of this rudimentary modern-type State upon Islam was the most obvious, if not the only choice open to the Amīr. Islam was the only common denominator in a very heterogeneous society with strong popular traditions. Islam's ultimate authority could not be challenged; moreover, the Islamic tradition also contained the possiblity of sanctioning an absolute monarchy.

Since the religious establishment as a group claimed a monopoly on the interpretation of Islam, it was obvious that this policy could not succeed without subjecting this group to State control. It was also inevitable that Islam should gain an even stronger position in society than it had hitherto enjoyed as it was being utilized as *the* State ideology. In establishing hegemony of the State-sanctioned interpretations of Islam, the whole educational system was reorganized as were the legal, executive and legislative powers. Religious beliefs and practices were controlled and standardized to comply with the 'State-Church' of Hanafī Sunnī Islām. By applying orthodox Sunnī doctrine in religious policies, no challenge to religious interpretations by the clergy was possible. However, the discourse into which these religious concepts were integrated was determined by the secular, political goals of the central State, and not by any religious goals.[6] Amīr 'Abd ur-Rahmān's achievements in providing Afghanistan with some of the forms and symbols of the modern State were essential in its transition from a tribal empire, but the Amīr still retained many of the attributes of a tribal chieftain. An important source of revenue lay in the fertile non-Pashtun regions; around half of this area provided a surplus to be distributed in tribal fashion as subsidies and to finance the centralizing institutions of the State.[7]

"Nation and Islam" — a semi-unitary model

The intellectual climate in the Muslim World changed during the first two decades of the twentieth century, and this was also the case in Afghanistan. Pan-Islamic and anti-colonial sentiments greatly influenced the political groups around the court and for two decades (1910 – 1930) there was a power-struggle among the following groups:

(1) An Aligarh-inspired, pro-British group consisting mainly of big merchants.

(2) A strongly pan-Islamic, nationalistic and anti-British group, influenced by the Young Turk movement, and consisting mainly of intellectuals.[8]

(3) A "traditionalist" group of conservative religious outlook and strongly anti-British consisting of tribal and religious leaders commanding strong support from the population.

The anti-British sentiments formed the basis for an alliance between the nationalists and the traditionalists within the so-called "War Party" — an alliance which, in spite of its short duration, resulted not only in the Third Anglo-Afghan War, but also in the replacement of the "old regime".

With the assumption of power by King Amanullah in 1919,[9] the nationalists acquired direct influence and, through the king, the direct authority over the power-apparatus. The effects soon became visible in the form of a far-reaching reform policy aimed at changing the structure of the State and the whole outlook of society.

The Nizāmnāma of 1923, the first comprehensive legal code of Afghanistan, was designed to lead to the development of secular law-making and gradually to provide for the separation of secular from canonical jurisprudence (Schwager, 1932:110). The Young Turk influence on Afghan nationalists was obvious in legal as well as in all other reforms of Amanullah's reign. In formulating the Nizāmnāma, Turkish legal experts were mainly employed while Turkish codes were the source of inspiration.

For the first time in Afghanistan, the concept of Nation (millat) was applied and granted a position as the source of legitimacy of power (Article 4) which was followed by another characteristic of modern nation states such as guarantees for civil rights (free press, free speech, free education, security of property, etc.) and making the king subject to existing laws. These legal reforms were followed by educational, cultural, political and economic reforms which, like the contemporary measures in Turkey and Iran, aimed at breaking the power and influence of tribal and religious leaders and turning the society into a modern Western style nation-state.

However, in spite of the Turkish model and Turkish assistance, King Amanullah's legal reform policy differed from that of Mustafa Kemal in essential fields. Although Afghanistan was to be transformed into a modern nation-state, it was unlike Turkey as yet impossible to dispense with Islam as a supporting source of authority and legitimacy (Article 4: The King will pledge to rule in accordance with the principles enunciated in Shari'a and in the constitution). Hence the Nizāmnāma ("governing regulations" presumably in deference to the usage which reserves the term *qanūn* for Sharī'a, Poullada, 1973:93) did *not* establish the legality of the State independently of Islam. The new model of the legitimation of transmission of Power was semi-unitary:

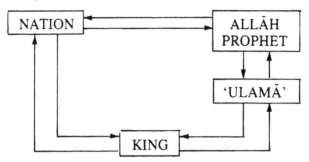

The problem of secular versus the religious law was handled in article 21: "all cases will be decided in accordance with the principles of Sharī'a and of general civil and criminal laws". This apparent inconsistency was reconciled by public declarations that the Nizāmnāma and all legal codes were designed so as to be compatible with the dictates of Sharī'a (Poullada, 1973:96). These attempts to propagate secularization of the legal system on the basis of Sharī'a were made with the assistance of liberal 'ulamā' who approved the new legislation by issuing *fatwā* to the effect that the legislation was not contrary to Sharī'a and was, therefore, valid law.

Consequently, the whole reform policy of the 1920s involved attempts to find religious justification for (apparently) secular measures. While the Turkish example served as a guideline for practical politics, the British-Indian influence (Aligarh — Sayyed Ahmad Khan) had greater influence on the ideological climate of Afghanistan during Amanullah's reign.

While 'Abd ur-Rahmān had used Islam to legitimize the absolute monarchy, the chief ideologue of the Amanullah period, the king's father-in-law, Mahmud Tarzi, attached Islam to nation-state and monarchy. 'Abd ur-Rahmān focused on judicial concepts and dogmas in Islam while Amanullah's policy was to apply the faith and ethics of Islam. Since it was by the grace and will of God that the Afghans had accepted Islam, Afghanistan was consequently a God-given country; hence, love for the fatherland (watan) was religiously determined. Although all Muslims belong to umma, this consists of many political units, of the Fatherland where people constitute themselves in nations (millat). Thereby pan-Islamism and nationalism did not contradict each other. If the Fatherland were equal to a Being, then the Nation was its meat and bones and the King its soul. Therefore, it was a religious duty

for any Muslim to serve not only his Fatherland and his Nation but also
his Government and Monarch: "for a Fatherland without a Nation, a
Nation without a Fatherland, and both without a Government and a
Government without a King would be equal to an inorganic structure.
Equally so, defence of Fatherland, promotion of education, modernism
and patriotism were turned into religiously derived duties."[10]

King Amanullah enjoyed considerable support when he assumed
power and after the "victorious" Third Anglo-Afghan War whereby
Afghanistan gained full independence Amanullah was hailed as a great
Muslim leader. His supporters were, as mentioned, a very diversified
group of nationalist "modernizers" and anti-British "traditionalists".
But Amanullah's all-embracing reform programme soon alienated the
traditionalist group of tribal and religious leaders. First of all, the
reforms, particularly the educational reforms and import of technical
expertise were expensive and had to be financed by increased taxation,
Secondly, turning Afghanistan into a modern nation-state necessitated
abolishing the political (and economic) position of tribal leaders as
administrative links between tribes and the government. Thirdly, the
introduction of secular law and education signalled the end of the power
and authority of religious leaders who, even under the iron-fist of Amīr
'Abd ur-Rahmān, had retained their monopoly in these vital fields.
And, finally, although Amanullah's policy on women did not have
much practical effect, the propagation of it still meant that, for the first
time, the patriarchal family structure existing in all social groups was
being questioned or threatened as the population saw it.

At first liberal 'ulamā' had sanctioned the reform policy and the King
had also tried to change the outlook of the 'ulamā' by forbidding
Afghan mullās to study at the orthodox religious school of Deoband in
British India — though many of his original "traditionalist" supporters
were strongly influenced by Deoband. However, from 1924 onwards,
conflicts and tribal rebellions occurred. As the clergy over the
following years experienced encroachment upon their privileges, the
traditional alliance between tribal and religious leaders against the
central state was re-formed with the downfall of the Amanullah regime
as the ultimate result.

In spite of four decades of centralizing policy and attempts to expand
and modernize the Afghan State apparatus, the question of legitimacy
was still urgent. Amanullah's nation-state could not exist without the
approval of tribal and religious groups.

Re-establishment of the Social Order, 1929 – 63

The accession to the throne of Nadir Khan showed that the tribes, in
spite of Amīr 'Abd ur-Rahmān's measures, had retained their force not

only as king-breakers but also as king-makers. The skilful handling of tribal politics in combination with traditionally-accepted Mohammadzai claims to the throne, were the means whereby Nadir Khan ousted the Tajik bandit-king Bacha Saqqao, who had exploited dissatisfaction to topple Amanullah but had no chance himself to retain power in view of lack of support from Pashtun tribes.

While the Nizāmnāma of 1923 had been an attempt to provide the ruler and the State with a legitimacy based on the concept of nation rather than on political realities of the tribes, Nadir Shah's constitution of 1931 was a recognition of the actual distribution of power in the kingdom. However, Nadir Khan was not a "traditionalist" in the Afghan context. On the contrary, since the reign of King Habibullah he had belonged to the Nationalist-Modernist camp. But, where Amanullah was a *radical* modernizer, Nadir Shah was a *gradual* modernizer. Consequently, the constitution "embodied a hodgepodge of unworkable elements, extracted from the Turkish, Iranian and French constitutions including the 1923 Constitution of Amanullah, plus many aspects of Hanafī Sharī'a of Sunnī Islam and local customs ('ādat), several of them, in fact, contradicting the Sharī'a."[11]

The Constitution of 1931 established the legitimacy (and here specifically in the line of Nadir Shah's family, the Musahiban) on the basis of the Nation (Article 5), created a facade of parliamentary government while actual control remained in the hands of the king and the judiciary system basically reverted to the religious leaders. Hence the constitution which was to be in force until 1964 was a showpiece of appeasement to various power groups in the society.[12]

The formal framework, the stress on nation, theoretical guarantee of individual equality and civil rights and outward forms of constitutional government was a concession to the new urban classes who had supported Amanullah. At the same time the supremacy and orthodoxy of the Hanafī school of jurisprudence was recognized. Complete autonomy of Sharī'a courts was guaranteed but with the monarchy's right of final approval. The religious leaders were granted freedom and influence they had not known since before Amīr Abd ur-Rahmān. In 1931 the first national 'ulamā' (Jamiyyat ul-'Ulamā') was founded and it was entrusted with the interpretation of existing law; all proposed governmental regulations and laws were to be submitted to the 'ulamā' in order to ascertain their compatibility with Islam. As far as the tribes were concerned, they were basically left in peace from government economic and political pressures during the following twenty years. However, the ultimate power of the tribes was formally recognized. Where King Amanullah had wanted to abolish the whole (tribal) jirga concept, it was now laid down that a national Loya Jirga was to be convened at least once every three years, and no new taxes could be imposed or radical changes made without the consent of this extra-legal body. Thus, in the view of the monarchy, the tribes represented the national consensus of the Afghans and, by unwritten law, only the Loya Jirga could make changes in the constitution. As if these concessions were not sufficient Nadir Shah granted certain frontier tribes such privileges as complete exemption from taxation and conscription into the army in return for their support in bringing Nadir Shah to the throne.

The model of the legitimation of transmission of power according to the Constitution of 1931 was very complex if not inconsistent as appears from numerous inconsistent, unclear or contradictory formulations. While Article 5 stated the Nation to be source of legitimacy of the monarchy, Article 27 declared that the parliament was organized "in conformity to the decision and the will of His Majesty the King and approbation of the Jirga of 1930, gathered at Kabul". Parliamentary authority therefore emanated from the King and the will of the Afghan people, as represented by the Jirga.[13] These formulations and the extra-legal status of the Jirga meant that the parliament was subjected to the tribal concept of Jirga, hence, the king was a constitutional monarch as well as a tribal chieftain. The third source of legitimacy of the monarch was Islam. Article 6 stated that the king swears "to rule according to the Sharī'a of Muhammad and the fundamental rules of the country (and to strive) for the protection of the glorious religion of Islam, the independence of Afghanistan and the rights of the nation . . ."

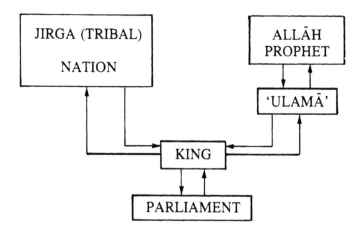

With the change of power and the establishment of a new *modus vivendi* between the traditional power groups in society and the State, a long peaceful period started. Although no major political changes took place, the reign of Nadir Shah and his brothers (1933 – 1953) was characterized by considerable socio-economic development, as Afghanistan increasingly opened up for foreign experts and the State encouraged private enterprise and trade.

The social and economic development weakened the influence of the tribes while the urban classes were steadily growing in number and, ultimately, in influence. The first sign of this came with the brief "spring" of 1949 – 1952 where the urban classes started pressing for parliamentarism and civil rights in the form of Wikh-i-Zalmaiyān movement. However, the first encroachments upon the power of tribal leaders and clergy since King Amanullah did not appear until the premiership of Prince Daoud Khan, 1953 – 63. These encroachments were the enforcement of taxation on tribes, the unveiling of women, and increased education. The state was given a very active role in pushing social and economic development while holding back political development. It is important to note that these policies, in the spirit of Amīr 'Abd ur-Rahmān, were not carried out until the repressive State apparatus, police and the army, were strong enough to cope with tribal unrest[14] and the economic basis of the State had significantly improved through foreign development aid; the decade of Daoud Khan was significant in strengthening the state apparatus and extending its activity and control in the country.

It was not until 1964 that any attempts were made to accommodate the Afghan State and constitution to the changing socio-economic structure of the society. The new constitution was approved in 1964, signalling the end of authoritarian rule and establishing the framework for a parliamentary democracy. The constitution prescribed the tripartite division of powers and the establishment of a parliament consisting of an Upper House (Meshrano Jirga) and a Lower House (Wolesi Jirga), the latter being formed through general suffrage in free, secret and direct elections including votes for women. In 1965 a Press Law was passed granting, in principle, extensive freedom of press.

The constitution formally turned Afghanistan into a modern, democratic nation-state, and Islamic Sharī'a became subordinate to secular law, although cases where no secular laws applied were referred to Hanafī Sharī'a as a last resort. The constitution of 1964 as a whole signalled a shift of power from the monarch to the growing urban classes. However, through the two houses of parliament, traditional tribal and rural leaders as well as the conservative clergy had acquired a new forum for the struggle for political power.

Instance of Legitimation

Instance of Power

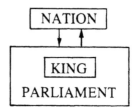

The democratic experiment failed due to lack of co-operation between the cabinet (urban educated people appointed by the King) and the parliament which, through the elections in 1964 and 1969, gave true representation to the heterogeneous population of the country.

The king's failure to promulgate a Political Parties Law gave no secure parliamentarian basis for the cabinet which, as a consequence, remained powerless.

What was achieved by the new constitution regarding legitimacy of power was that the traditional and tribal legitimacy which the Mohammadzai ruler still enjoyed was supplemented by and made second to the legitimacy of constitutionalism appealing to the urban classes.

Nation-Party: a Unitary Model

The failure of the parliamentarian regime in Afghanistan brought about the Palace Revolution in 1973 whereby Prince Daoud Khan, with the help of the military, abolished the monarchy and proclaimed himself as the president of the republic. The coup of 26 Saratan (17 July) brought attention to the existence of two new power groups in Afghan politics: the army, which for the first time acted in its own right, and a small group of basically urban, educated leftists, both of whom in despair of the parliamentarian chaos lent their support to Daoud Kahn.

A new republican constitution was formulated in 1977 and although it evoked the same constitutional legitimacy as the 1964 Constitution, some major changes had come about. First of all, there was the constitutional institutionalization of the one-party system which, together with undermining the partition of power, paved the way for authoritarian rule. While the 1964 Constitution had declared the parliament as manifesting the will of the people and representing the whole of the nation (*instance de puissance*), the constitution of 1977 pointed out the Loya Jirga as the "paramount power of the will of the people". This, however, was not comparable to the position of the Loya Jirga in the 1933 Constitution where it served the function of providing tribal legitimacy to the monarchy. The 1977 Loya Jirga had only a minimal tribal component — basically it was formed by loyal bureaucrats.[15] The 1977 Constitution thus alienated the traditional rural power groups and cut them off from formal influence, and as far as the clergy was concerned, the new constitution and the new penal code and civil law added yet another step to the secularization of Afghanistan.

When his initial supporters among the urban Left were alienated after a short period, President Daoud, like Amīr 'Abd ur-Rahmān, relied upon a strong and loyal army and bureaucracy to silence any challenge to his authoritarian rule. Where former rulers had failed when losing the tribal support, President Daoud's downfall was brought about by the very army he had built up since the 1950s.

People-Revolutionary Council — a Unitary Model

The Saur Revolution in 1978 which brought the People's Democratic Party to power in Afghanistan was carried out by the help of vital units of the military. However, a civilian government composed of PDPA members, amongst them only a few military officers, immediately took power. The initial "Basic Lines" published in May 1978 sketched a 30-point programme for the new government which was closely related to the party platform as formulated by the PDPA in 1966 following "non-capitalist development strategy", i.e., a strategy for less-developed countries *gradually* to mature to socialism. However, in March 1979 a more detailed and specific outline for a new constitution was formulated and that clearly reflected the radicalization process which had taken place in the government after the purge of the Parcham-group of the PDPA.[16] The Party and the Revolutionary Fatherland Front, central concepts in the non-capitalist model, were completely ignored, and instead a more centralized and authoritarian structure was designed compatible with Hafizullah Amin's megalomaniac attempts to quell all divergent opinions even inside the party. In the "Basic Lines" of May 1978, Afghanistan was declared a "Democratic Republic" and the source of legitimacy of power was the People (as opposed to the concept of Nation in preceding constitutions of this century); "the Revolutionary Council and Government . . are formed on the basis of the will of the free and toiling people of Afghanistan and represent the sovereignty of the democratic classes and strata of the people of Afghanistan (Basic Lines — preamble).

According to the Law for Regulating Government Duties, promulgated by the Khalq government, 31 March 1979, the Revolutionary Council was granted supreme state power of the country; it should approve the constitution of the country, and also hold the legislative power. The president of the Revolutionary Council, elected by the RC among its members, was Head of State and the armed forces; he appointed the prime minister and approved other ministers, as well as members of the High Court. The government personified the highest executive power of the country and was responsible before the RC and president of the RC. It was not described how the Revolutionary Council was selected or composed. Hence, the model for the legitimation of the transfer of power:

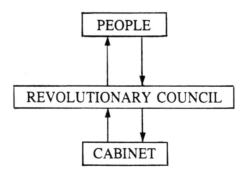

It is clear that the model not only centralized all power in the Revolutionary Council, particularly in the hands of the president of the Revolutionary Council, but did not even give lipservice to any of the power and interest groups of the society. The whole question of legitimacy is unrelated to tribal, religious or parliamentarian traditions. In this situation only repressive force could maintain the position of the government as it could not benefit from traditional tribal loyalties — even the republican president Mohammad Daoud had been able to command ethnic loyalties. Khalq being an almost exclusively Pashtun party, ethnic loyalties to it did not last very long. The social base of the party being mainly schoolteachers and small bureaucrats, etc., was numerically small, and consequently the military component of the party was the most important part. It had been its saving grace in the conflict with Parcham. Another fact is that all democratic rights which the Basic Lines of 1978 were supposed to defend were neither described nor ensured by decrees and in 1979 "democratic rights" were not even mentioned.

With "brotherly assistance" in ousting Hafizullah Amin and the return to power of Babrak Karmal, in December 1979, the way was opened for a reformulation of the revolution as well as for a new constitution more in line with the original "non-capitalist" strategy.

People-Party — a Unitary Model

By April 1980, the Karmal government had formulated an interim constitution which was to be in force until a Loya Jirga, elected on the basis of free, secret, direct and equal ballots, had adopted the new constitution. The State of Afghanistan belongs to the working people (Ch. 1, Article 1) whose power is based on the National Fatherland Front (Article 3) under the leadership of the PDPA. The PDPA will be the guiding and mobilizing force of society and State (Article 4). Thus, with this interim constitution, the party is granted its leading role according to "non-capitalist strategy" and the National Fatherland Front serves as an umbrella organization for the wide spectrum of progressive interest groups and organizations of the country (workers, peasants, tradesmen, nomads, women, youths and representatives of all nationalities, tribes and clans).

Model of the transfer of the legitimization of power:

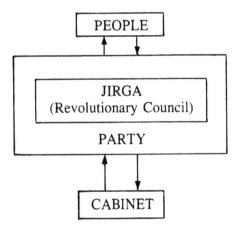

Until there are elections of delegates for the Loya Jirga, the Revolutionary Council will act as the highest organ of state power. By granting the party and National Fatherland Front a vital position in the power structure a broader constitutional base of the State is sought. Although the Revolutionary Council as compared with Amin's constitution is still supreme, the reference to a future Loya Jirga is a clear attempt to gain legitimacy through this representative and originally tribal/rural concept (even though nothing is stated about its specific composition). Equally so, the National Fatherland Front is an attempt to achieve a broad "democratic" representation of a hetero-geneous population within the framework of a political system dominated by *one* guiding party, and so is the reviving of the jirga institution at local level of administration.

So much for achieving constitutional, democratic and 'traditional' (tribal) legitimacy among the diverse groups of society. A special effort is made to appease religious groups although no concession is made to Islam in the constitution which like those of 1977 and 1978 is entirely secular. Chapter 1, Article 5 states that respect, observance and preservation of Islam will be ensured and that freedom of religious rites are guaranteed. However no citizen is entitled to exploit religion for anti-national and anti-state propaganda — and the government will help the clergy and religious scholars in their patriotic duties and obligations.

In other words, the role of Islam as a source of legitimacy is completely abandoned and freedom of religion is guaranteed as long as it has no dangerous political potentials. In the legal system, Islam is granted an ever-diminishing role through formulations that in cases where the law is not clear the courts will apply Sharī'a *and* the principles of democratic legality and justice.

In spite of these concessions to Afghan traditionalism, the 1980 Constitution is still based on a unitary model of legitimacy. However, in order to achieve a broader base of legitimacy it has been necessary to pay at least some lipservice to Islam but even more important, to ensure representation (at least in theory) of broader sections of the society through the National Fatherland Front and the constitutional assembly of Loya Jirga (yet to be seen) as well as to revive the jirga concept in local administration. However, in spite of these important changes as compared to 1978, the legitimacy of the present regime is still very weak indeed, and has not even military might to reinforce its own repressive power.

In this connection, it is important to evaluate the claims to legitimacy of the multitude of resistance groups. Generally speaking, they claim legitimacy on all those sources represented in Afghan constitutions. A number of groups claim to work for the establishment of an Islamic State in Afghanistan, but it is highly doubtful that this would enjoy very wide popular support. Another range of groups appeals to a mixture of nation-state and Islam; groups dominated by mostly Western-educated intellectuals forward the idea of a constitutional parliamentarian system on the Western nation-state model; finally, the anti-Soviet Afghan left calls for a democratic or at times federal system, with legitimacy rooted in the Afghan people.

Recruitment to these groups is also based upon a mixture of loyalties: religious, tribal, ethnic, regional or patron-client relations, as well as political-ideological loyalties.

The heterogeneity of this picture points out the difficulties any Afghan government under peaceful, democratic conditions would face in choosing a power structure which would ensure a general legitimacy *vis-à-vis* such a heterogeneous population.

13

LABOUR ORGANIZATION IN LIBYA

Maja Naur

Religion, Conflicts, and the State

To a Muslim, social and political development is unthinkable without Islam. To a Western social scientist, religion is separate from the material sphere. In Europe the separation of the religious and the secular power had taken place several hundred years before the rise of the working class. Within the totality of Islam, there is an emphasis on consensus. In the West there is a recognition of conflicting interests in society which have gradually become organized in separate labour market institutions. Let me here use the organization of the labour market in Libya as an example of an Islamic state in which the state ideology is no longer legitimated by reference to Islam, but where the new organization of production could not have taken place without a general acceptance of the notion of society inherited from Islam.

Before proceeding further, let me first discuss the concept of the state in Libya. It has become surprisingly popular among left-wing social scientists[1] to use the term "state" in a European sense even when Middle Eastern societies are analysed. According to the European notion, the state is twofold: it is both an administration and a sphere. These two very different notions are meaningful when applied to the Western nation-state. But they are not necessarily meaningful in a Middle Eastern context. In Libya the state can be confined to a very small group of persons. By this I do not wish to go on "perpetuating a cardinal error in the study of the Near East by reducing its structural analysis to the level of personal intrigue and manipulations".[2] I make no attempt to replace structural analysis with ideological manipulation by an Oriental state. What is claimed is that in the period concerned (1969 – 1981) the Libyan state was in a socio-economic position which allowed for far-reaching political aims.

The dominant feature of the trade unions in present-day Arab countries is their Western-inspired origin. The industrial labour force began to organize during the colonial period and was often directly organized by the imperial powers. After independence the character of the state changed and the cultural heritage of Islam became more obvious. The trade unions were converted from being organized as interest groups to becoming part of the state apparatus. Although the change in the position of the trade unions was rarely explained with direct reference to Islam,[3] one can argue that it was easier for the population to accept an incorporation of the trade union movement into the state apparatus because of the Muslim cultural heritage. This does not mean to say that the incorporation was a consequence of its being a Muslim state. What is suggested is that the opposition from the growing, but still small, industrial labour force has been limited because it has never managed to develop an organized labour consciousness. An awareness of a common political interest would have been contrary to the basic tenets of Islam and, equally important, it would have been contrary to the interests of the state. Let me comment shortly on both aspects.

The Qur'ān is the basis of Sharī'a law, and thus the law of Muslim society is divine. After the liberation from the European powers, Sharī'a law once again became the basis of law in most Arab states. According to religious tenets, it is not possible for man to intervene in what is given by God. Law is not, as it was when introduced in the West at the time of the Renaissance, based on humanism where man is at the centre as regulator of society. In Islam there is no room for positive law made by man. Although the Qur'ān does not deal explicitly with labour organization, present-day labour laws are supplementary to the principles given in Sharī'a. The laws may not contradict the original principles, for that would constitute a break with the fundamental principle of the totality of Islam. Given the totality of Islam, there is a strong emphasis on consensus. Conflicts are seen as a disturbance of the Islamic Umma.[4] Conflicting interests have either to be incorporated and become part of the harmonious whole or be eliminated. Thus the state can refer to Sharī'a law when it suppressed labour conflicts. The state may also win the argument when there is accord between Islam and the state ideology. The action is thus seen as the legitimate right of the regime.[5] Within the totality of Islam there is no separation of religion and politics. In several post-colonial Arab countries, regimes emerged based on a strong state apparatus which suppressed the independent labour movement. In doing so, they were actually putting themselves in a similar position as under the caliphate, the difference being that the regimes now had to limit themselves to national (territorial)[6] boundaries. In Islam there is a tradition of centralization of power in which the people at the periphery are allowed extensive freedom as long as they pay tribute to the centre. Actually Islam arose from a social context of disharmony in which tribal rivalry disrupted the prevailing social order. When Muḥammad went to Medina, his intent was to bring harmony to the people of the Arab peninsula. Prior to Islam, there was little awareness among Arabs of their belonging together. They were probably more conscious of the differences among tribes.[7] It was a lack of a coherent social structure in Medina which made Islam possible. The legitimizing principle shifted from kinship to religion as a consequence of the introduction of Islam. The chief means for unification in one community was that everyone was to acknowledge Muḥammad as "messenger of God" and was to observe the Islamic forms of prayer. Islam therefore became both the unifying and the legitimizing base of the new social order.[8] With this origin a statehood emerged which sought to bring harmony among rival tribes; consequently Muslim societies reject conflict as part of a "modern" complex society. To accept diverging interests would be equivalent to recognizing a secularization of society: a separation of religion and politics. Within this perception of society, the state may over-react (by Western standards) where a labour conflict is seen as a threat to the fundamental principle of the state ideology as well as to the regime. Modern thinkers on Islam and trade unions[9] argue that there is no contradiction between Islam and trade unions: they are both fighting for justice; and a state which does not provide justice is not an Islamic state. However, for the Muslim labour force it is important to question whether an independent trade union movement is possible within an Islamic state. Thus the questions to be raised in this study of the development of labour organization in Libya are: how has the changing state apparatus been legitimized? What is the historical and cultural heritage of this legitimation? Has the state actually managed to reorganize the labour force in agreement with the state ideology? And, finally, what has the change meant for the objective interests of the labour force?

The Legitimation of the State Ideology in Libya

In May 1973 Qadhāfī, in answer to the question about secularism in the Arab world, stated paradoxically that in Islam there was no such thing as secularism, "for the Islamic religion itself is secular".[10] He gave two major reasons for his statement: first, although this dialectial way of putting the relationship between Islam and secularism may appear to be contradictory, he simply meant that Islam has no clergy as does Christianity. He therefore saw no need for the separation of Church and State since for him the Church as such had no separate existence. Secondly, Qadhāfī maintained that since Islam was not just a religion of rite and rituals but also a practical way of dealing with mundane legislation and guiding people in their everyday life, it was secular in that respect as well. However, he argued in February 1976 that if secularism implied that a state was non-religious (la-dīniya), then he rejected that form of secularism because to him, the laws and legislation of a nation had to be based on universal, ethical standards of divine origin.[11] To Qadhāfī the separation of Islam and the State is neither possible nor desirable.

For Qadhāfī the unity of the Umma had to be maintained. Interest groups, be they party, class, sect or tribe, work on behalf of their own interests and consequently, he argues in *The Green Book*,[12] they tend to divide society. "If a class, party or sect dominates a society, the whole system becomes dictatorship." He thus rejects the idea of balanced group interests although he states "a class or a tribal coalition is better than a party coalition because the people consist originally of a group of tribes". He continues that the

> party that is formed in the name of the class automatically becomes a substitute for that class and continues until it becomes a replacement of the class hostile to it. Any class which becomes heir to the society inherits, at the same time, its characteristics. That is to say that if the working class crushes all other classes, for instance, it becomes heir to the society. The heir bears the traits of the one he inherits from, though they may not be evident at once. As time passes, attributes of other eliminated classes emerge in the very ranks of the working class. And the possessor of those characteristics takes the attitudes and points of view appropriate to the characteristics. Thus the working class turns out to be a separate society, showing the same contradictions as the old.[13]

It is obvious that Qadhāfī here rejects the party system imposed on Libya during the post-colonial period[14] as well as the Soviet model of proletarian dictatorship.

In the new ideal society of the "Authority of the People", Qadhāfī reviews the old society, although he does not break with the fundamental principle of consensus within Islam. He believes that the legislation of any nation should be based on two sources: custom and religion.[15] Custom to him is the "expression of the natural life of human society".[16] Religion, on the other hand, supersedes custom because it provides permanent ethical standards which transcend a particular society or epoch. Moreover, he believes that religious law includes customary law and complements it.[17] Positive law, by contrast, is man-made; it is neither religious nor customary. "I as an individual do not accept to be subjected to positive law, and cannot accept imprisonment, or sentence to death, or even be fined in accordance with laws written by a group of individuals (mortal like myself) against me.''[18] In *The Green Book* he speaks of a universal law based on ''natural principles''. The Third Universal Theory, writes Qadhāfī, is simply the outcome of man's effort to resolve the problem of democracy irrespective of the specific historical epoch or the particular society in which he lives.[19]

The new organizational structure given in *The Green Book* states:

> First, the people are divided into basic popular congresses. Each basic popular congress chooses its secretariat. The secretariats together form popular congresses, which are other than the basic ones. Then the masses of those basic popular congresses choose administrative people's committees to replace government administration. Thus all public utilities are run by people's committees which will be responsible to the basic congresses, and these dictate the policy to be followed by the people's committees and supervise its execution. Thus, both the administration and the supervision become popular, and the outdated definition of democracy — *Democracy is the supervision of the government by the people* — comes to an end. It will be replaced by the right definition — *Democracy is the supervision of the people by the people*. All citizens who are members of those popular congresses belong, professionally and functionally, to categories. They have, therefore, to establish their own unions and syndicates in addition to being, as citizens, members of the basic popular congresses or the people's committees. Subjects discussed by basic popular congresses or the people's committees, syndicates and unions, will take their final shape in the General People's Congress, where the secretariats of popular congresses, peoples committees, syndicates and unions meet. What is drafted by the General People's Congress, which meets annually or periodically, will, in turn, be submitted to popular congresses, people's committees, syndicates and unions. The people's committees, responsible to the basic popular congresses, will, then, start executive action. The General People's Congress is not a gathering of members or ordinary persons as is the case with parliaments. It is a gathering of the basic popular congresses, the people's committees, the unions, the syndicates and the professional associations. (pp. 29 – 31).

Syndicates, associations and unions are parts of the Basic Popular Congresses and do not function as separate interest groups. Qadhāfī sees production as containing ''raw materials, an instrument of production and a producer''.[20] The three to him are equal and comparable, and equal attention has to be paid to all three.[21] How it is to be done in practice is not mentioned. It is stated that workers shall become partners in the process of production and ''he who produces is the one who consumes''.[22] The slogan ''partners not wage workers'' became the basis for the new state ideology, and even the first slogan to be seen in Tripoli on arrival at the airport. Nobody shall, according to the Third Universal Theory, be in the position to benefit from other people's work. On the way to the final step when the new socialist society reaches the stage where "profit and money disappear", Qadhāfī sees

> the threatening power of the trade unions in the capitalist world as capable of turning capitalist societies of wage-workers into societies of partners.
>
> It is probable that the outbreak of the revolution to achieve socialism will start with the appropriation by the producers of their share of what they produce. The objective of the workers' strikes will shift from the demand for the increase of wages to the demand for sharing in production. All that will, sooner or later, take place under the guidance of *The Green Book*.[23]

Although the model of the "Authority of the People" is part of the "Third Universal Theory" and intended for society as a whole there are two exceptions. The first, and most important in Libyan society, is that only Libyans are eligible for partnership in production. Within the official figure of almost forty per cent non-Libyan,[24] which almost per definition is too low since clandestine labour is omitted, a very large part of the population is excluded from partnership in production. Forty per cent are still wage-workers. Secondly, almost one-third of the labour force — that in the private sector — is excluded from partnership according to Article 1 in the "Decision of the General People's Committee on the Insurance of the Administrative Regulation of Companies and Establishments Owned by Society" which states:

> The provisions of the regulation shall apply to the society-owned companies and establishments which are set up to undertake any industrial or commercial activity as well as services.
>
> They shall not apply to the companies or establishments where a foreign body shares in their capital. This is in accordance with the provisions of the Libyan Commercial Law or the other laws effective in the Socialist People's Libyan Arab Jamahiriya.[25]

State Mobilization of the Labour Force

Qadhāfī sees trade unions as a product of the capitalist world, and it is therefore not surprising that the new regime in their first years of power after the revolution prohibited trade unions. During the Fascist period, working conditions had been regulated by the Italian labour code for Africa.[26] Labour union legislation of the co-operative kind had been introduced in Libya in 1935 and applied only to Italians; only at the very end of the occupation — August 1943 — came a decree specifying the conditions of labour and the wages of Libyan workers. Under the British military administration, the British organized the labour force. During the colonial period the trade unions in Libya, as in other occupied Arabic countries, were heavily influenced by the Western political system. In 1951, the year of independence, trade unions were granted legal recognition.[27] Although there were several trade unions working actively in Libya under the king, their actions as a free trade union movement came to an end with the general strike in 1961. Twenty trade union leaders were arrested and severe restrictions were put on the labour movement.[28] The industrial base was small in the economy and the support for an institutionalized labour movement was limited. Norman's study on labour and politics in Libya and North Africa concludes that "the labour movement has been active in Arab Africa in a nationalist context rather than an industrial one".[29] Later developments showed that the labour movement was not the main force behind the revolution, as was the case elsewhere in the Arab world, e.g. in South Yemen. Though in Libya the religiously legitimate but pro-Western king had allowed a free trade union movement, it was stopped when it became a threat to the state.

After the revolution in 1969 trade unions were abolished and in 1972 workers were forbidden to strike.[30] However, many of the section leaders who were active before the revolution are today the founders of what has become the Producers' Union. Thus, from being a trade union in opposition to the monarchy, the movement has become part of the power base and one of the most powerful organizations in Libyan society. Together with the International Centre for the Study of *The Green Book*, the Partners' Unions are the reproducers of the state ideological apparatus. The two can be said to be second only to the Revolutionary Command Council.[31] In production the Producers' Union is the overall policy-making body which, at an earlier stage, prepared for the workers' final take-over of production and the creation of the revolutionary committee.

In describing the distribution of power in Libyan society, the leader of the international department of the Producer's Union, Salem Jalloud,[32] mentioned three pillars of the people's power by which he gave the official self-understanding of the Libyan regime: (1) People's meeting, (2) People's committees, and (3) the Producers' Union. On the historical background for mobilizing the labour force after the revolution, Jalloud referred to five steps in the development from trade unions to the workers' take-over of production in 1977: (1) trade unions to 1969, (2) the revolutionary regime abolished the trade unions in

1971, (3) in 1970 – 71, 150 courses were held to train people selected from various factories, (4) meetings with leaders and military training between 1971 and 1977, and (5) the take-over in 1977. The structure as well as some of the personnel from the former trade unions were used to transform society after the revolution. The people selected from each of the production units were known to be the most revolutionary and had the most education. They were brought together to receive a combination of "revolutionary and military training", and "nobody knew if there was only one or several from the same production unit". At the time of the training it was a centralized and secret organization. They never attended the same courses, and there was no internal communication while they "met and discussed with the leaders of the revolution". "They became militarily and culturally prepared for the final take-over."[33] When Qadhāfī in a speech empowered the workers to take over the factories from *both* the private *and* public sectors (which are unique to Libya), the world thought it was a spontaneous action by the leader of the revolution.[34] That is far from the truth. It was a carefully planned take-over, prepared down to the last detail, where everybody knew exactly where to go. The trained revolutionaries gave reports containing detailed information on who was appointed in each factory, by name, nationality, position, etc. The organization of the labour force had reached its climax at the take-over, and Jalloud expressed satisfaction when he concluded that "The revolutionary committees are the product of the training . . . Qadhāfī discussed with the producers . . . Nobody was in between. The political education of the people means that they now understand Qadhāfī's objectives." Concerning the organization, "The first person who comes is the leader of that meeting . . . There is no fixed place for the meeting of the revolutionary committees . . . They are everywhere, and nobody knows where . . . There is a known and unknown number."

In the second half of the 1970s, Qadhāfī felt that the Libyan people had become apathetic, and parallel to the restructuring of production, the revolutionary committees (*lijan thawriya*) were put into action. Their function was to act as revolutionary watchdogs over the political activities of the popular committees and the secretariats of the popular congresses,[35] which in the production units are the Producers' Congress and the people's committees. In effect these revolutionary committees have become extremely powerful: they can select the candidates for the popular committees, can bring "subversive elements" to trial, have the power of censorship, and have published since January 1980 a weekly entitled *al-Zahf al-Akhdar*, which propounds the views of the regime. One can easily argue, consequently, that the revolutionary committees have become an undeclared political party through which the regime implements and enforces its policies.[36] This description would, however, be unacceptable to the regime as it has continuously been against the formation of political parties. It seems, however, that the regime now concedes that a countrywide institutional set-up, be it a party or otherwise, may be effective for carrying out the "revolutionary aims". Thus an unofficial one-party system has begun to emerge in spite of Qadhāfī's previous vehement attacks on party politics.

The State and the Libyan Labourers

Although the new organizational structure appears on the surface to have given more power to the producers, it may not turn out to be the case. Based on a survey I carried out in Libya in 1980 the new organization is described in detail in an earlier publication.[37] Let me limit myself here to the procedure for setting the wages and dealing with conflicts in order to show the influence of the new state ideology on the Libyan labour organization. Whatever the customs, religion or laws of a society, the function of setting the wages and solving conflicts are the most important problems for the workers; one way or the other, these functions must be carried out.

According to a 1980 document of the Producers' Union, this organization set the level of minimum wages and defined the criteria for production and scale of incomes.[38] However, the function of setting the minimum wages seems to have been transferred to the Secretariat of Labour and Civil Service.[39] Likewise, it is the Secretariat of Labour and Civil Service which takes action if a work dispute cannot be settled in the production unit. Within the system of partnership, the labourers, be they Libyan partners or foreign wage-workers, have to put their case to the Basic People's Congress and beyond that to the General People's Congress outside the establishment. However, most work disputes last a matter of hours, days, or at most weeks, and there is no guarantee that the Basic Popular Congress or the General People's Congress will meet at that time. In fact, *The Green Book* prescribes that the General People's Congress "meet annually or periodically". Either production will stop or immediate action has to be taken, and then it becomes a question of who is to be involved. The Secretariat of Labour and Civil Service is responsible for solving the problem. Thus the Producers' Union has ceased to function as a labour organization working on behalf of the partners.

In 1980 more than 70 per cent of the labour force was employed in state-owned establishments. The state thus serves as an employer, although according to the notion of "non-wage workers but partners in production", it would not be referred to as an employer. Salem Jalloud mentioned at the Producers' Union that there was no centrally-directed control of the Revolutionary Committees. This accords with the Producers' Union's self-definition of being an overall political organization not dealing with traditional trade union matters such as negotiating on behalf of the labour force. Thus, in case of a conflict, the Producers' Union cannot be used as a trade union. There is nowhere the labourers can go for help. The system of partnership has limited the power of the labour force to working within the boundaries of the production unit. The state has taken over the position of both the trade union and the employer's union. Furthermore, the state sets the rules for both as well as "taking care of" their respective interests.

The position of the Secretariat of Labour and Civil Service is not to be confused with the increasing state intervention that takes place in West European countries. To define the behaviour of the state as intervention requires a legal set of rules to be followed by the accepted partners in a negotiation. That is not the case in Libya. The regime has never accepted conflicting interests, and the way to solve divergence is to build a strong state legitimized by reference to a divine or a universal concept of a society in consensus. Thus the state is not "intervening" in a free labour market, but has gradually regained control over a non-secular, Muslim society.

Secondly, the Basic Popular Congress and the General People's Congress are the forums for the common interests of society. Thus, within the Basic Popular Congress and the General People's Congress, the problems of farmers, producers, civil servants — all the professional associations, union and syndicates — have to be resolved during the meeting. Within the distribution sector of the Libyan economy, in which only 7.8 per cent of the work force works in manufacturing, they might end up being in the minority. At least the manufacturing section (if united as a group) would have difficulty in being heard by, for example, the public sector which employs 44.9 per cent of the people (of which 33.8 per cent are Libyans).[40] In reality it is also this overwhelmingly large sector which has been put in the position of representing the labour force in case of conflict within the unit. The system requires a consensus which might not always be the case. As the secretariat of Labour and Civil Service also distributes the economic resources for investment, it is in the position to put substantial pressure on the labour force.

Thirdly, there may be quite a substantial list of issues which have to be negotiated in the limited period of time for a meeting within the Basic Popular Congress or the General People's Congress. It might be difficult to reach a conclusion for every single one of the many issues, and each will feel that his specific problem is of utmost importance. One might expect that the debates may be quite heated or — still worse — the issues might not be raised for discussion, and they will have to be settled outside the democratic and open forums given in *The Green Book*.

Fourthly, one may question the suitability of the form under which negotiations in both the Producers' Congress (within the establishment) and in the Basic Popular Congress (within the munipality) takes place. To make decisions on complicated issues requires detailed information as to the background of the production dispute, the consequences of each of the different solutions put forward, etc. It is rare to find large gatherings of people who have collected sufficient information for rational decisions. If there are many issues to be discussed — as may be expected at the meeting of the Basic Popular Congress or the General People's Congress — it may require a substantial amount of time to obtain the necessary information. Here we will leave out the question of availability of information as well as concrete background experiences aside — although these could also be inadequate. Here I merely want to emphasize that the democratic system put forward in the Third Universal Theory is very time-consuming. Furthermore, it gives large gatherings of people — ideally the whole population — the advantage of having the possibility of expressing themselves on broad political issues, but it is hardly a forum for making concrete decisions concerning specific and complicated issues.

Fifthly, in the case of conflict in production, the partners will not have an institution to which they can be directed for advice. In a completely decentralized system — which is the formulated aim of the Authority of the People in the Third Universal Theory — every case becomes outstanding. In different establishments, the same or a similar problem may be solved very differently if there is no reference to or communication with other similar cases. It adds to the variety of society but hardly to the feeling of equality.

Sixthly, concerning income distribution and the notion of justice, it can be said that Libya is one of the leaders in the Arab world. The increasing income gap experienced under the king, even after oil was exported in large quantities, fell dramatically after the revolution. Measured both directly and indirectly (with the fall in infant mortality as the social indicator), it is clear that incomes have been distributed more equitably.[41] With respect to economic justice, the state has performed in the interests of the labour force. However, in my survey[42] it was found that on average the non-Libyans received 26 per cent less in income than the Libyans when education was kept constant.

Seventhly, my survey carried out in 1980 on income distribution in two production lines shows a remarkable similarity in income levels irrespective of the location of the unit.[43] The largest difference was between the Libyans and the non-Libyans, and this applies to all the establishments. This indicates that income setting is *not* left to the partners at the Producers' Congress in the individual establishment. The result is what should be expected when incomes are centrally settled. Thus, political decentralization has not reached the economic sphere of production. The partners, and to a certain extent the foreign labour force, are caught in the dilemma of having gained better economic conditions and a seemingly decentralized political system in control of production on the one hand, and having lost their institutional framework for reaching central economic decisions on the other.

Although the Third Theory given in *The Green Book* claims that it will become universal, the system is only applicable to 60 per cent of the labour force in Libya. According to the official statistics given above, non-Libyans occupy 40 per cent of the labour force which means that a substantial proportion of the workers are excluded. In a single establishment, the largest in my sample,[44] the partners had decided at the Producers' Congress that both Libyans and non-Libyans should be eligible for profit-sharing. Thus, the partners can decide to equalize Libyan wages with the foreign workers, but the fact that it has only taken place at one factory (out of 16) shows that it was an exceptional case. A pre-condition for a universal principle of governing is that it should be applied to all the inhabitants of the country. The official argument for excluding foreign workers[45] from partnership in production was given by Ahmed Shahati[46] during a seminar on partnership — Tripoli, May 1984 — where he stated that "the non-Libyans could not be expected to defend the Jamahiriya[47] in the event of an external threat. They might in such a situation be more loyal to their country of origin." Thus the argument for excluding pagans in the foreign work force accords with traditional Islamic categorization in which there is a division between (1) Muslims, (2) other people of the Book (Orthodox Christians, Zoroastrians and the like), and (3) pagans. However, to extend the exclusion to all Muslim foreign workers[48] — and thus to the members of *Dār al-Islām* — is a sign of a national, territorial definition of the state and is alien to the notion of society within Islam.

Let me conclude that the new organizational structure leaves power in the hands of the central regime. The new state ideology is being used to legitimize the new regime, which is, of course, its purpose. Finally, let me add that whether the notion of society springs directly from Islam or from a universal principle claiming to be natural law, they are both based on consensus. As such it is culturally acceptable in Libya to merge the labourer's and the leader's interests into a single institution within the state apparatus. Only the future can tell if the cultural heritage and the fact that the regime, through income equalization, is living up to the Islamic notion of justice will be sufficient to prevent unrest within the declining oil economy.

14

CULTURE AND MINORITIES IN THE
ARABO-ISLAMIC IDENTITY OF ALGERIA

Tuomo Melasuo

Over twenty years have passed since Algeria became independent after a long and hard liberation war against France. During these two decades the country has gone through deep social, economic and political transformations. The most important aspects of the development efforts have centred on heavy industry, especially to the so-called "industrie industrialisante", on agriculture and the "agrarian revolution" and on the building of the state apparatus.

The development efforts are based on two options; the building of the state and the economy along "modern" western models and the "modernization" of society along "standard" Arabo-Islamic ideology from the Near East.

The evolution of Algeria has been remarkable but not without its problems — as that of any society. In the economy the main problems have been caused by the low integration of new heavy industry with the rest of the economy and its low degree of production, as well as the slow progress of the agrarian revolution which has kept Algeria dependent on food imports.

Social developments of the country have also been quite radical, causing new difficulties especially in the everyday life of the Algerians. Urbanization and rural exodus have totally transformed the predominantly rural Algeria of 1962. This phenomenon is reinforced by very strong demographic growth, and it is one reason for increasing unemployment. The poor functioning of urban infrastructure and the rise in prices of basic commodities all add to the difficulties of everyday life. These malaises are reinforced as well in the domain of culture. In the schools and in administration the use of standard, Near East imported Arabic is causing new problems for the common Algerian in his everyday life.[1]

In the second half of the 1970s many observers believed that Algeria's problems would reveal themselves through radical, opposition activities by the peasant population. The outbreak of frustrations in the field of cultural identity was a surprise for many. The political, economic and social difficulties were channelled into the field of culture thus adding to its own problems. Hence the problems in the cultural field reflect the ensemble of difficulties in Algerian society; they are primarily political, related to the particular trends in modern Algerian development. They concern not only the situation of the Berbers but the self-image of the whole Algerian society. We can distinguish four interconnected areas where these problems of identity take form. (1) The question of proper cultural identity, primarily the relation between Arabo-Islamic and Berber identities. (2) The religious situation and the role of Islam in the state, the role of modern "integrism", the so-called Muslim Brothers, the Algerian reformist 'Ulamā's and the more traditional forms of Islam in Algeria. (3) The project of the new Family Law, especially the situation of women, taking into consideration the controversial demands of Islam and Algerian socialism. (4) Basic civil democratic liberties, especially in culture, religion and daily life.

The impasses in these four areas led to the spring 1980 Kabylian Berber protest movement. In many respects this has been one of the most, if not the most important political phenomenon in independent Algeria.[2]

Historical Background

We do not know the actual number of *berberophones* in Algeria. The most realistic and reliable estimates exceed 20% of the population, perhaps between 3.5 and 4 millions.[3] The Berbers are considered as being the original peoples of North Africa extending over the area from Egypt to the Atlantic and from the Mediterranean to the Niger River.[4] In Algeria they live mainly in Kabylie, east of Algiers, in Aurès-province in the south-east of Northern Algeria, and in the Mzab and Hoggar areas of the Sahara.

After the spread of Islam and the Arab conquest in the seventh century the Berber populations were Islamized relatively quickly concurrently with a long and complex period of mixing between the Berbers and newly-arrived Arabs. Many Berber "tribes" were Arabized, and some Arab groups became Berberized.[5] Hence we must be careful of discussing Algerian Berbers and Arabs using ethnic or racial terms; instead we should perhaps limit ourselves to calling them *berberophone* and Arabized populations. It is clear that we are dealing more with a question of a process of cultural Arabization than with the demographic and "biological, physical" transformation of whole Maghreb population.

Since the beginning of Islamic penetration of the Maghreb the Berbers have through the centuries participated actively and fully in the Arabic cultural life of Algeria. Even if there have been tensions between the *arabophone* and *berberophone* populations we can say that no serious problems existed between them.[6] The *berberophones* took part in the resistance against French conquest in the nineteenth century even though their actions were separate from the rest of the Algerians.

Since the 1840s the French started to create the so-called "Kabyle Myth". This stressed the differences between *berberophone* and *arabophone* populations, trying to use the old method of "divide ut regnes". Furthermore, it tried to show that the Kabyles were closer to European and to French culture than to Arabo-Islamic; thus they were said to be easier to "frenchify", to assimilate and to colonize.[7] The paradoxical point is that the elements of this myth took root in Algerian society and still exist today. In reality the French Berber-policy had very little practical importance. We could mention the creation of the chair of the Berber language in the University of Algiers and of the Kabyle radio channel after the Second World War.[8]

Berbers participated in the Algerian modern political and national movements from the beginning of the early twentieth century.

The activities of the political movements coincided with the cultural questions — the first main requirement demanded political rights with the retention of Muslim civil status.[9] Until the Popular Front period in the 1930s the political movements spoke about the Algerian Muslims. But under extremely strong pressure of French assimilation and the obstacles set against Arabic culture in Algeria it became natural for these political movements to define the cultural identity of Algeria in Arabo-Islamic terms. This stress on Algeria's place in Arabo-Islamic civilization was the only means of forming a strong enough counter-weight to French pressure. In this situation, the particular local cultures were simply not strong enough to fight against French influences.[10]

In the early 1930s there arose the Algerian Muslim 'Ulamā' Association which guided the reformist movement in the country. The 'Ulamā' movement stressed the importance of classical Arabic and pure, reformed, original Islam against the more local and traditional Maghreb forms of the religion.

Since the Second World War the national movements have spoken about the Algerians as Arabo-Berbers,[11] and at the end of the 1940s there was the so-called "Berber crisis" inside the most radical national movement. Even if the causes of this crisis were not ethnic or cultural but more connected to a political power struggle the ethnic problems

remained traumatic for the whole national movement.[12] When the
National Liberation Front emerged in spring 1954 its main task, besides
that of making war against the French, was to bring unity among the
Algerian political formations. The myth of unity was almost institutionalized during the war period, which was more than natural in such a
hard situation.

Thus, the evolution of Algerian political life was hardly appropriate
to the emergence of cultural pluralism. Since the beginning of the
liberation war the main support, even if modest, to the Algerians came
from the Arab world. If we take into the consideration the general
atmosphere of the 1950s and early 1960s in colonized countries and
especially in the Arab world we can understand how the stress on the
Arabo-Islamic identity of Algeria helped to maintain its positions on the
Front.

Since independence there were serious problems from 1963 to 1965
in Kabylie where armed dissident movements challenged the new
government. This, of course, did not facilitate solving the problems of
minority culture.

As for the questions of Islam and women, we can note that during the
last decades of colonialism these issues developed almost along the
same lines as that of culture. The main goal was to defend Algerian
society against colonialism and not to discuss these matters within
Algerian society itself. In the domain of religion the national
movements required the application of the principle of the separation
between religion and the state. This applied also to Islam and in general
the movements were quite moderate in their planning for the role of
Islam in the future Algeria.[13] The question of women was more
complex. Almost from the beginning of the colonial period, the
Algerians wanted to close off their society from the white settlers. This
was especially true concerning family life. The Algerian passive social
resistance against colonialism stressed those phenomena which traditionally wanted to restrict women's possibilities to participate in
activities outside the family.

The 'Ulamā' movement, when trying to modernize and reform
Algerian Islam and Arabo-Islamic culture, demanded educational
opportunities for both sexes. Algerian women had an active life in the
liberation war which led many to suppose that independence would
bring about radical changes in those areas as well.

Cultural Debate

From the beginning of Algerian independence until the late 1970s the
Berbers were not even mentioned in the official documents of the

country.[14] This Berberness was quasi-officially understood an anti-Algerian, as opposing national unity or as serving foreign (mostly French) imperialism. However, we should notice that 'unofficially'' the Berber language and culture were studied at the University of Algiers from 1965 to 1972.[15]

Neither the National Charter nor the Constitution of 1976 gave consideration to the Berber elements in Algerian culture, and this caused deep frustration, the problems being discussed more and more openly.

The interdiction of Mouloud Mameri's lectures on ancient Kabyle poetry in the University of Tizi Ouzou brought matters to a head in March 1980. There were student and popular demonstrations in Algiers and in Tizi-Ouzou, the University of Tizi-Ouzou was occupied, disorders and struggles with the police occurred and lasted over two months with more and more structured demands made by the Berbers. During this period the Berber movement was consolidating itself and took part in the debate on cultural policy started earlier by the state apparatus, broadening and radicalizing it at the same time.[16]

We can distinguish four items in this debate brought on by the Berber movement. (1) The recognition of the Berber language and culture, of the need for it to be taught and studied, of the Berbers' role in Algeria's cultural patrimony. (2) The recognition of Algerian popular culture, especially ''colloquial'' Maghrebin and Algerian Arabic. (3) The interpretation of Algerian history, the role of the Berbers, the importance of the Arabs and Arabic civilization. (4) The basic civil liberties, especially in the fields of arts and expression.[17]

A key problem in independent Algeria has been the content of the Arabization process. In the schools, press, administration, radio and TV the government has advanced the use of so-called standard Arabic.[18]

The problem is that this Arabic is quite different from the colloquial Algerian Arabic. At the same time, the imposition of this standard Arabic introduced a certain quite particular interpretation of Arabo-Islamic culture. It refers more to modern Arabic nationalism, to the so-called Arabism than to the cultural pluralism of the Near East.[19] In fact, when the Algerian government affirms that Algeria is and remains Arabo-Islamic it has never seriously tried to define what it means. It is more an affirmation than an attempt to give a dynamic content to this cultural concept.

Both the language and the ideology behind Arabism remain quite foreign to the majority of Algerians. Still, we can notice that in the schools, but especially in the modern electronic means of communication knowledge of this standard Arabic is advancing in Algeria as in other Arab countries. With the success of Eygptian songs the Cairo dialect has started to be understood in every family. This official stress on standard Arabic remains strange to people and is often considered élitist. It is one of the factors which incensed public opinion.[20]

The essence of the Berber movement was the demand for recognition of Berber language and culture as an integral part of Algerian reality. The main stress was put on demands concerning the study and teaching of the Berber language and culture in the universities. It is somewhat surprising how strongly this "academic" demand had been emphasized, as also the role of Berber arts in the national culture.[21]

In August 1981 the so-called Yakouren-seminar was organized in Kabylie. This unofficial seminar produced a large document dealing with the actual situation and future possibilities of Berber culture in Algeria. Central to it was the demand that Berber cultures should develop equitably in Algeria.[22]

In spring 1981 a major and well-informed public debate occurred in the Algerian press about the country's cultural identity. Many eminent persons such as Ahmed Taleb Ibrahimi, the current foreign minister, Mostafa Lacheraf, the Algerian ambassador to Unesco, and Mohammed El Mili, former director of the APS and ambassador to Greece, took positions in favour of cultural pluralism and recognized Arabo-Berber identity for the country.[23] At the same time, informal instruction in Berber language and culture was begun in many universities and even an unoffical "Movement for the Popular Culture" was tolerated.[24]

In summer 1981 the Central Committee of the FLN party drafted a general outline for the country's cultural policy in *Rapport sur la Politique Culturelle*. This report was a disappointment for the *berberophones*. Even if it mentioned the Berber they were considered more as belonging to the Algerian past, they were simply "folklorized", rather than recognized as a dynamic, actual factor in today's Algerian culture.[25]

But in September 1981 the Ministry of Higher Education promised the creation of Berber studies in four Algerian universities. The problem was that the universities in Berber provinces were excluded and that the Berber studies departments would form part of the Institutes of Arabic Language and Culture which were traditionally illdisposed towards Berber cultures.[26] It seemed that the government remained undecided and afraid to work out a clear solution to this difficult question.

The second item in this cultural debate concerned the role of Algerian Arabic and popular culture. To some extent the movement required a *droit de cité* for the Algerian spoken Arabic instead of the imposition of standard Arabic from the Near East. Similarly, the stress put on popular culture was a reaction against the transnational interpretation of Arabo-Islamic culture associated with standard Arabic. In this context there occurred a more general discussion about the state and the conditions of cultural life in Algeria. The Algerian writer Kateb Yacine stated that culture is not a bureaucratic dossier which one opens and closes when necessary; it required a more dynamic and open basis in order to be really creative.[27]

The Berber movement also disagreed with the official interpretation of Algerian history. According to the movement, it did not adequately take into consideration the history before the Arab conquest. The movement asserted that the official interpretation showed the earlier history of the Berbers as a forerunner of the Arab conquest — the Berbers were seen as having waited for centuries in order to find their own historical fulfilment. Later on, the Berber movement demanded that their own role during the history of the Arabic period should be more objectively integrated into the national patrimony. They were against the romantization of the Berber past and of the "folklorization" of their present reality. The movement demanded that the role of Berbers as a dynamic and actual element of Algerian society should be totally integrated into the past and present.[28]

The fourth element of this cultural debate from 1980 on has been the question of civil liberties, especially in the fields of culture and expression. In this the Berber movement cited the general state of cultural activities in Algeria which have been so much controlled by the government that all possibilities for creative expression have disappeared. It should be noted that in this, as also in the question of popular culture, a great number of the *arabophones* agreed with the Berber movement and supported it.[29]

Also discussed was the view that the government had been overestimating the threat posed by cultural movements and particularly the Berber movement. In the press debate the cultural authorities aforementioned stood for pluralist liberties in the fields of arts and sciences. During this debate the government organized national conferences for writers, painters and others so that they could debate the problems of their fields. These discussions were condemned as élitist and said not to have involved the masses. The whole atmosphere was somewhat controversial, with the government saying that there was complete freedom of expression in Algeria and the Berber movement insisting that there was not.[30]

The debate around the four main cultural questions is not closed. Since 1980 it has also had political implications for the nature of Algerian socialism and the development strategies in Algerian society.

Besides the official FLN party there exist at least three activist tendencies especially among Algerian youth. On the official side the UNJA is backing the FLN and has a socialist orientation. The UNJA approaches, at least partly, the Berber movement which it has tried to integrate on its own lines.

At least one important section of the *arabophones* oppose the UNJA as well as the Berber movement. The *arabophones* have difficulties in being employed in Algerian higher administration which functions mostly in French or English. In this situation they do not wish to make concessions concerning the status of Arab identity. The most radical opponents of the Berber movement are the so-called Muslim Brothers, which is a new "integrist" or "fundamentalist" wave of Islamic renewal. Their aim is to transfer Algeria into the "real Islamic" state where all public and civil life should be subordinated to their strict interpretations of the Qur'ān and the Sharī'a. Hence, they strongly oppose Algeria's socialist orientation and especially the agrarian revolution.

But the whole situation is not so simple. The Berber movement has also been attacked for its anti-socialist policy and blamed for being a tool of imperialism. They have been accused of having contacts with the French anti-Algerian circles and with exiled Algerian opposition groups. The demands for rights for Berber language and culture have been interpreted as a neo-colonial plot for the restoration of French as the main language in Algeria.

In this complex situation, where the power struggle inside the state's top administration must also be included, it has been said that President Chadly Benjedid has managed to consolidate his own position in power and to remove the remaining members of Boumedienne's Revolutionary Council. It seems to be clear that the government is making some concessions to the Berber movement especially in order to step up the struggle against the fundamentalist Muslim Brothers. These are considered as a more important threat to the Algerian régime.[31]

At the party congress of December 1983, President Chadly recognized that the history of today's Algeria covers 25 centuries and started when the people began to call themselves Amazighs, that is free men, Berbers. This was considered a new and definitive step on the way to recognizing Berber culture. When the rearrangement of the government was introduced in spring 1984 one of the main tasks of the new government was to neutralize the Islamic protest movement by recognizing the role of the Berbers in the creation of the Algerian nation and to avoid the kind of troubles Morocco and Tunisia had in the beginning of 1984.[32]

Religion

Long after Algerian independence, Islam in the country was almost completely guided by the state. The 'Ulamā' movement from the 1930s was entirely integrated into the national movement. During the time of colonialism it had in a very remarkable way strengthened the Algerian Arabo-Islamic identity by working for a reformed Islam. Because of both these aspects its position towards the traditional *confréries, tariqa* — brotherhoods — and towards maraboutism was officially negative. There were no organized, autonomous Islamic movements in Algeria during the first years of independence.[33]

Since the early 1970s Islamic pressures have slowly started to revive. Especially in the countryside the maraboutist tradition remains strong and the brotherhoods are said to have renewed their support.[34]

In 1976 the government made some concessions to Islam; the official rest day was changed to Friday and, more importantly, Islam was declared the state religion in the new Constitution.[35] The political game is almost the same in the case of Berber culture. The concessions to Islam are, at least partly, the means by which the government fights for socialist and agrarian revolution. In 1962 there were about 800 mosques in Algeria, now there are about 5000 official mosques and an uncounted number of small private prayer-rooms.[36] It has been said that the fundamentalist movement gets financial support from those who oppose socialism and especially the agrarian revolution including funds from abroad. It also seems that the Algerian middle class is leaning more and more towards Islam. This is due to the wave of neo-moralism caused by rapid westernization and especially by the fact that religion has been the most easy mode of expressing political opposition against socialism.[37]

In November 1982 the fundamentalists organized an unofficial and unauthorized demonstration in the centre of Algiers just in order to show their strength. There were ten thousand people at this demonstration which was the largest in independent Algeria.[38]

In April 1984 a fundamentalist leader died and 25,000 men took part in the funerals in Algiers.[39] Even if the fundamentalists have increased their support their influence is largely limited to the big towns. In the countryside they have very little importance.

In general, the discussion concerning religion in Algeria is concentrated mostly on Islam. There are organized Christians and Jewish confessions in Algeria, but they have not been discussed in this debate on Islam.

Code de la Famille

Family law has been lacking in Algeria since independence. Several times the idea of this legislation has been discussed but the government was always obliged to withdraw it from parliament.[40]

The reason why this has been so difficult is the legal situation of women. Traditionally all four principal rites of Islamic law interpretations have been used in Algeria. The Mālikī school, dominant in the Maghreb, has applied the most strict interpretation of the woman's position.[41] During the colonial period the women's question was included in the programme of national movements, even if modestly; for instance, all of them demanded education possibilities for both sexes and it was usual that even the 'Ulamā' families sent their daughters unveiled to schools.[42]

Women took an active part in the liberation war and this opened new possibilities for them. Thus, Franz Fanon, when writing about the social changes caused by the Algerian liberation war, supposed that the liberation of women would be very quick. But Fanon paid too little attention to the peasant, rural character of the liberation war and he was unable to see the wave of puritanism which took place in the first years of independence.

The National Charter of 1976 defines Algerian women as completely equal to men in rights and the duties. But the draft of the Family Law which was submitted to parliament in September 1981 neglected the principles of the National Charter and was based much more on the Qur'ān. According to this draft, a woman needs the man's permission before being allowed to work outside the family.[43]

The discussion in the Algerian parliament raised a lively debate about family law in the country. Street demonstrations of women were organised and lists of petitions circulated. Since the beginning of Berber activities in spring 1980 the question of women had been included in the debate on civil liberties and national identity. In the course of demonstrations and petitions, rights for free information were stressed; others were opposed to the fact that the projected law was prepared in great secrecy.[44]

In late May 1984 the new Family Law was passed in parliament after one month of official discussions. In his speech the Minister of Justice strongly defended the "feminist" position. The new law, confirmed by President Chadli on 9 June 1984 was a compromise between "traditional and modern" pressure groups. It eliminates inequalities between the sexes, but polygamy is retained, with the first wife having the right to divorce. In general, the wife's position in marriage is improved. In the case of divorce, a woman's rights as to her children are strengthened as is her economic situation. It has been said that the use of the term divorce instead of repudiation has had enormous consequences in Algerian life.[45] It is worth noting that the new Family Law especially stresses the interests of children when dealing with relations between husband and wife.[46]

Conclusions

Questions related to cultural identities have been appearing more and more not only in Algeria but throughout the Arab and African worlds. Signs of this are found in the renewal of Islam and in the events in Iran. More generally, the rapid westernization which is often included in development strategies and processes has also touched the very cultural identity of peoples and societies. Today, more than twenty years have passed since Arab and African countries achieved independence. During these two decades the questions related to cultural identity have had sufficient time to mature and to become real social issues. We can suppose that the questions discussed in Algeria during the last several years will repeat themselves in other parts of Africa in the near future.

But these questions of cultural identity are relevant also for Europe. The regional movements, the new religious phenomena and even "the Greens" in Europe can be considered as cultural expressions. We might suggest that the rapid structural and economic transformations since the Second World War, and their strong homogeneous pressures, have provoked a certain crisis between "modernization" and cultural identities of people all over the world.

In Algeria this question of cultural identity and the actual debate around it have been considered the most important issues since independence.[47] In fact, the most vocal participants have been the youth, which in the case of Algeria has had no direct personal experience of colonialism or the war of liberation. They base their political and cultural opinions and analysis on the realities of independent Algeria.[48]

The Berber question is not limited only to the situation of the Berber minority but concerns the image of the whole Algerian society. It has been said that the cultural debate about the Berbers started to demystify the whole value system born during colonialism and the liberation war.[49]

It has also been stated that the official interpretations of Algerian history, of the role of national movements and of the current state explain the homogenization pressures of today.[50] The debate on these questions is a means by which the present generation tries to define its own interpretations of Algeria's past, of its relations to Islam and of the nature of the society that will ensue.

The very question of the Berbers has changed since 1980. In December 1983 teaching and studying of Berber language and culture positively began in the University of Algiers.[51] The problem is that there are very few competent experts in Algeria on Berber matters and during the twenty years of "bad conditions" most of the highly-qualified Algerian Berber researchers moved abroad, especially to France.

In general, Berber studies have experienced a rise in quality during recent years. This is particularly true for linguistic research, where about twenty doctoral theses have been presented; often these deal with those linguistic questions neglected by "colonial Berber science". In many ways this current research is creating the basic tools for the maintenance and florescence of Berber cultures in the future.

The other phenomenon is that "the Berber question" has become internationalized. Today it is discussed in Morocco, Algeria and France as well as in Mali and Niger. Specially for the Tuareg, the example of the "Kabylian Spring" has been significant. This question will influence the immediate future of the Maghreb. But the political character of the problem in Algeria still remains essential.[52]

In Algeria the Berber question has received some concessions from the government. But the Berber language is still considered suitable only for arts and perhaps for popular cultures. It is "folklorized", while communications in the more serious matters of arts and sciences are in Arabic. We can now say that the dilemma is formulated more in the context of classical Arabic *and* popular Arabic as well as Berber, rather than pitting them against each other as was the case just a few years ago.[53] We can presume that these debates on the concepts of Islam, Arabism and Berber cultures, which are certainly the main elements of Algerian identity, will go on for years because they are the crucial factors in the political struggle for social and economic development.

NOTES

Notes to Introduction

1 Cf. Ernest Barker, Preface to F. J. C. Hearnshaw (ed.), *Medieval Contributions to modern civilisation*, New York, 1949, 6.
2 'The role of the individual in history' in C. T. McIntire, *Herbert Butterfield: writings on Christianity and History*, New York 1979, 18.
3 Cf. R. Allen Brown, *The origins of modern Europe*, London 1972, 8.
4 See further M. Sharon, *Black banners from the east*, The Magnes Press, The Hebrew University of Jerusalem, Leiden 1983, 38ff.
5 See L. Gardet, 'Fitna', *Encyclopaedia of Islam*, 2nd edn., and B. Lewis, 'Islamic concepts of revolution' in P. J. Vatikiotis (ed.), *Revolution in the Middle East*, London 1972, 35ff. (also in B. Lewis, *Islam in History*, London 1973).
6 See further A. K. S. Lambton, *State and government in medieval Islam*, Oxford University Press, London, 1981, 69ff.
7 H. A. R. Gibb, 'The heritage of Islam', *IJMES*, I (1970), 12 – 13.
8 *Al-Siyāsa al-shar'iyya*, ed. A. S. Nashshar and A. E. 'Atiya, 2nd ed., Cairo 1951, 174 (Fr. tr. *Le traité de droit publique d'Ibn Taimiya*, by H. Laoust, Beirut 1948, 173 – 4), cited by A. Hourani, *Arabic thought in the liberal age 1798 – 1939*, Oxford University Press, London 1962, 4.
9 The term *mujāhid* still evokes memories of the past, whether it is used in West Africa to designate those who undertake operations against communities which are not Islamic, in Afghanistan to signify those who fight against a government supported by infidel foreigners, or dissident forces in Iran aiming at the overthrow of a regime which they consider to be unjust.
10 Lewis, 'Politics and war' in J. Schacht and C. E. Bosworth, *The legacy of Islam*, Oxford 1974, 173 – 4.
11 Lambton, op. cit., 201ff.
12 *Arabic thought in the liberal age 1798 – 1939*, 369.
13 Cf. Lewis, 'Islamic political movements', *Middle East Insight*, 17.
14 For an account of "modernist" movements see Fazlur Rahman, 'Revival and reform in Islam' in P. M. Holt, A. K. S. Lambton and B. Lewis (eds.), *The Cambridge History of Islam*, Cambridge 1970, ii, 641ff.
15 Cf. Lewis, 'Islamic political movements,' 17.
16 See further M. Arkoun, *Pour une critique de la raison islamique (Islam d'hier et d'aujourd'hui*, 24), Paris 1984.
17 Cf. G. R. Elton, *The practice of history*, Flamingo ed., London 1984, 119 – 20 (first published Sydney University Press, 1967).

Notes to Chapter 1

1 Hourani, A., *Europe and the Middle East*, London 1980, pp. 8 f.
2 Ullmann, M., *Die Medizin im Islam*, Leiden & Köln 1970, pp. 115 ff.
3 Fück, J., *Die arabischen Studien in Europa*, Leizpig 1955.
4 *Arabica* 27/1980:154 ff., P. Kemp. I would like to add that in the French
   colonies sociologists were no less supporting colonialism than Orientalists,
   see E. Burke, 'The Sociology of Islam: The French tradition', in *Islamic
   studies: a tradition and its problems*, ed. by M. H. Kerr, Malibu 1980
   (Seventh G. Della Vida Biennal Conference), pp. 73 ff.
5 Andrae, T., *I myrtenträdgården*, Stockholm 1947, p. 16.
6 1919, see S. Kahle in *Västmanlands-Dala Nation Skriftserie*, 13, 1977, p.
   20.
7 op. cit., pp. 38 ff.
8 op. cit., pp. 107, 111.
9 Waardenburg, J. D. J., *L'Islam dans le miroir de l'Occident*,
   's-Gravenhage 1961 (diss.), p. 313.
10 For the existence and importance of the rich merchants, see S. D. Goitein,
   'The rise of the Near-Eastern bourgeoisie in early Islamic times', in
   Cahiers d'histoire mondiale 3/1956 – 57:583 – 604.
11 Sperber, M., *Zur Analyse der Tyrannis*, Wien 1975, pp. 108 f.
12 op. cit., p. 32.
13 Said, E., *Covering Islam*, New York 1981, p. 141.
14 Cf. J. van Ess, 'The emergence of *Kulturgeschichte* in Islamic studies', in
   Islamic studies: a tradition and its problems (see note 4), p. 51:
   "Historical texts are part of literature; as historians, we are not working
   with facts, but only with the interpretation imposed on these facts. The
   civilizational and conceptual framework of a text, its *Sinnzusammenhang*,
   is not given to us in advance, but has to be gained out of the text itself, in
   constant confrontation of the text with our own tradition; otherwise a
   scholar will almost inevitably produce a framework more characteristic of
   himself than of the phenomenon he wants to explain. *Kulturgeschichte*
   without texts is construction. Becker's antipathy for the "French garden"
   was timebound. There is no valid historical research without philology.
   We need Herder as well as Hegel."
15 Schiøler, Th., *Roman and Islamic water-lifting wheels*, Odense 1973.
16 al-Hamdānī, *Kitāb al-Ǧauharatain al-'atīqatain al-mā'i'atain aṣṣafrā'
   wa'l-baidā'*, *Die beiden Edelmetalle Gold und Silber*, hrsg. und übers.
   von Christopher Toll, Uppsala 1968 (diss.).
17 Fück, op. cit., p. 34.
18 As is well known, there are two kinds of Arabic but the division is not
   horizontal, between Classical and Modern Arabic, but vertical, between
   Classical (written) Arabic and spoken Arabic, neither of them being more
   modern than the other. This emphasizing of the modern as the most
   important aspect of our studies is shown also in the title of this paper which
   is taken from the programme "Contemporary Islamic Studies", within

which this symposium is held. Now, "contemporary" either refers to "studies" in which case it is a truism and thus redundant (except in the title of my paper where, actually, it is meaningful: what is the purpose of Islamic studies today?) or it refers to "Islamic", meaning "studies of Contemporary Islam" As many of the papers presented to this symposium show, the studies of contemporary Islam begin with the Qur'ān and the Prophet Muḥammad, i.e., with the 7th century A.D.

19   Cf. the theory of Karl Popper: "In Popper's view the generative act in scientific discovery or in the solution of a problem is the formulation of an hypothesis, i.e., an imaginative conjecture about what the truth of the matter might be. . . .In the outcome science is not a collection of facts or of unquestionable generalisations, but a logically connected network of hypotheses which represent our current opinion about what the real world is like." P. Medawar, 'The philosophy of Karl Popper', in *Art, science and humanism*, ed. R. B. McConnell, London 1983, p. 92.

20   Lessing, G.E., *Nathan der Weise*, from 1779; cf. H. Arendt, 'On humanity in dark times; Thoughts about Lessing', in her *Men in dark times*, Pelican 1973. Djaït, H., *L'Europe et l'Islam*, Paris 1978, p. 79. Cf. also the quotation from P. Feyerabend at the end of note 26.

21   *Classicisme et déclin culturel dans l'histoire de l'Islam*, Symposium de Bordeaux, 1957, p. 49.

22   Eco, U., *Il nome della rosa*, Milano (1980) 1981, p. 495. And Niels Bohr "never regarded achieved results in any other light than as starting points for further exploration", P. Feyerabend, *Against method*, London 1975, p. 24, n. 1.

23   op. cit., p. 34.

24   See O. Löfgren in *Encyclopaedia of Islam/Encyclopédie de l'Islam*, 2. ed., s.v. al-Hamdānī, and Chr. Toll in *Dictionary of scientific biography*, 6, New York 1972, pp. 79 f., and *Arabica* 31/1984, pp. 306 – 17.

25   Cf. J. van Ess, op. cit. (in note 14), p. 51: "It is distance which makes the task of a Western Orientalist easier; it permits him to see things more sharply, provided that his being aware of otherness blends with that indispensable sympathy, without which understanding is not possible. More sharply he will then also see himself; axioms and notions which a European or an American normally take for granted might become questionable to him once he discovers their alternatives in a value system which, in many respects, is built upon assumptions similar to his own. In the last instance, a Western Orientalist does Oriental studies for himself.[139]

([139] Or, to avoid a current misunderstanding: for his own "society.")

26   In the humanities, many scholars have turned from imaginative to descriptive scholarship because they think that descriptive scholarship looks more scientific, natural science being for some reason considered as more important. This is a misapprehension, of course, since science, too, is concerned not only with factual truths but also with general truths which are arrived at only by creative imagination (cf. above, note 19). For the affinity of science with art, see *Art, science and human progress*, ed. by R. B. McConnell, London 1983, where P. Medawar says (p. 95): "Some

people think the idea that science is conjectural in character in some way diminishes science and those who practise it; but to my mind nothing could be more diminishing than the idea that the scientist is a collector and classifier of facts, a man who cranks some well-oiled machine of discovery. Popper's conception of science is, in my opinion, a liberating one; I feel enlarged, not diminished, by the thought that any truth begins life as an imaginative preconception of what the truth might be, for it puts me on the same footing as all other people who use the imaginative faculty.'' A result of the prevalence of descriptive scholarship has been an interest in method that sometimes seems greater than the interest in the matter itself (this has a parallel in the tendency to value pedagogics higher than the knowledge to be taught). For a criticism of method, see P. Feyerabend, *Against method*, London 1975, e.g., p. 45: "Methods . . . tend to *preserve the status quo* of intellectual life . . . the semblance of absolute truth is nothing but the result of an absolute conformism."

27 Rundgren, F., "Vetenskapen som livsform', in *Kungl. Vitterhets Historie och Antikvitets Akademiens Årsbok 1972*, pp. 149 – 56, with the quotation from N. Söderblom's speech on p. 155.

Notes to Chapter 2

1   Cf. the preamble to the Declaration. This point is also often stressed in the commentaries.
2   For the term "cognitive universe" and for the process of "incorporation", cf. Berger P. and Luckmann, T., *The Social Construction of Reality*, New York 1967, esp. pp. 36 ff. and p. 115.
3   Cf. the sample of quotations given by Edward Mortimer, in the article 'Islam and human rights' in: *Index of censorship 5/83*, p. 5.
4   The attitude considered is the one connected with what M. Arkoun calls ''le discours islamique contemporain''.
5   Cf. "Versachlichung" in Marxist terminology.
6   Cf. Norman Anderson, *Law reform in the Muslim World*, London 1967.
7   Cf. the Constitution of Egypt, Art 2.
8   The quotations follow the translation of Changiz Vafai.
9   *Time* magazine, 21 May 1984.
10 *Arabia*, Feb. 1984, pp. 31.
11 *Impact* 13 – 26 Jan. 1984, pp. 9 f.
12 I allude to the reports from the embassies in Muslim countries, those from Amnesty International and from the US State Department.
13 Very good examples of the apologetic tendency in the Muslim discussion on Human Rights can be found in the conference report "Human Rights in Islam" (1982) from the seminar in Kuwait in Dec. 1980, where many of the most distinguished jurists of the Muslim World participated. Almost everyone stressed the theme how much better the Sharī'a was, if applied

correctly, than other legal systems in (early) history. This is a rather pointless argument, since the UN Declaration owes its existence to the consciousness of the oppression and tragedies of the past.

Notes to Chapter 3

1 *Minbar al-Islam*, No. 9, Cairo, 1963, pp. 194 – 5.
2 *Al-Ummah*, a monthly Islamic comprehensive magazine, published by the Presidency of Sharī'a, Kataz, No. 24, p. 17.
3 *Al-Ahram*, Cairo, 7Y, 1976, p. 12.
4 'On the Jewish Question' in K. Marx and F. Engels *Collected Works*, Vol. 3, Moscow, 1975, p. 157.
5 'The Holy Family, or a Critique of Critical Criticism, against Bruno Bauer and company', in K. Marx and F. Engels *Collected Works*, Vol. 4, Moscow, 1975, p. 111.
6 see note 4, p. 151.
7 *Minbar al-Islam*, No. 1, Cairo, 1964.
8 Ulvan Abdullah Nasikh, *An Education of Children in Islam*, Vol. II, Cairo, 1981, pp. 1088 – 92.
9 see note 7.

Notes to Chapter 4

1 Ann K. S. Lambton: *State and Government in Medieval Islam*, O.U.P. 1981; *La notion d'autorité eu Moyen Age, Islam, Byzance, Occident*, ed. P.U.F. 1982; Pouvours, *Les Régimes Islamiques*, P.U.F. 1980/12; *L'Islam et l'Etat dans le monde d'aujourd'hui*, sous la direction d'O. Carré, P.U.F. 1982. M. Arkoun; 'Autorieté et pouvoir en Islam', in *Critique de la Raison Islamique*, Maisonneuve & Larose, 1984, pp. 155 – 92.
2 For a critical approach of recent theories, cf. Paul Udrière: 'Le sens du sacré et le metier de sociologue', in *Archives des sciences sociales des religions*, 1984/57/1, pp. 115 – 39.
3 On this concept, see my *Critique*, op. cit., pp. 162 – 75.
4 On this concept, cf. M. Arkoun: op. cit., pp. 43 – 64.
5 I have given a description of this concept in 'L'Islam dans l'histoire', in *Maghreb-Machreq* 1983/108, pp. 3 ff.
6 Cf. M. Arkoun: *Lectures du Coran*, Maisonneuve & Larose 1983, pp. 145 – 56.
7 Cf. *sura al-tawba* and my analysis in *Les sciences de l'homme et de la société appliquées à l'étude de l'Islam* (to be published).
8 On this concept, cf. Hans Robert Jansen: *Pour une esthétique de la reception*, Gallimard 1979.

9 A. Abel: 'Le calife, presence sacrée', in *Studia Islamica* 1957/VII; and Ann K. S. Lambton, op. cit., p. 264 ff.

10 An Ideal-Type of Islamic Authority can be described with the portraits of these mythical Figures, or transfigured historical personalities; this Ideal-Type can then be distinguished from that given by the literature of Mirrors for Princes.

11 edited and translated by Ch. Pellat, Maisonneuve & Larose 1976.

12 Cf. H. Laoust: *La profession de foi d'Ibn Batta*, Damas 1958.

13 For a more developed critique on Uṣūl, cf. M. Arkoun, *Critique*, op. cit., pp. 65 – 100, and for the Shī'ī position *ibid.*, pp. 129 – 54. We must notice that *uṣūl* literature came after the elaboration of the *corpus juris*, mainly on a pragmatic basis: this fact underlines the ideological function — *après coup* — of the *uṣūl*.

14 On the anthropological opposition oral/written, cf. J. Goody: *La raison graphique*, Gallimard 1980.

15 Cf. M. Arkoun; 'Pour une autre pensée religieuse', in *Islamo-christiana* 1978/4.

16 Ibn Taymiyya has given a clear definition of this concept, in Ibn Taymiyya: *Naqd al-Manṭiq*, p. 90.

17 I write Tradition with a capital T to refer to the idealized sacred legacy of texts used by each community.

18 Literarization is a general phenomenon which all historians have to master, but the modern historian is supposed to be more conscious of the difficulty and to pay great attention to the critic of each concept used to describe the past.

19 This opposition has not yet been well analysed as a sociological and ideological issue.

20 C. Castoriadis: *L'institution imaginaire de la société*, Seuil 1975.

21 Cf. P. Ladrière, op. cit. and the books of F. A. Isambert analysed in this article: *Le sens du sacré*, ed. Minuit 1982.

22 Cf. M. Arkoun: 'Logocentrisme et verité religieuse dans la pensée islamique', in *Essai sur la pensée islamique*, Maisonneuve & Larose, 3rd ed. 1984, pp. 185 – 232.

23 Expression used by P. Bourdieu.

24 Cf. my *Lectures*, op. cit., pp. 87 – 144.

25 On this concept, cf. M. Arkoun, *L'Islam, hier, demain*, 2nd ed. Buchet-Chastel 1982.

26 The concept of deconstruction is related to the concepts of systems of thought and epistemology well developed by J. Derrida and M. Foucault.

Notes to Chapter 5

1 See Duri, A. A.: *Al-Zuhri. A study on the beginning of History Writing in Islam*, (BSOAS, XIX (1957)), and E. Ladewig Petersen: *'Alī and Mu'āwiya in early Arabic tradition*, Copenhagen 1964.

2   Imam Khomeini: *The Islamic Government. Islam and Revolution, Writings and Declarations of Imam Khomeini*, translated by Hamid Algar, Berkeley 1981, p. 40.

3   al-Balādhurī: *Futūḥal-Buldān*, ed. Cairo 1959, pp. 22 f.

4   Ibid., p. 24.

5   Cf. *The Qur'ān*, Sura 112.

6   Among others Petra and Palmyra.

7   Djudjām, cf. E.I.² vol. 2, p. 573 s.v., (C. E. Bosworth).

8   Montgomery Watt: *Muhammad at Mecca*, Oxford 1953, and Maxime Rodinson, *Mahomet*, Paris 1961, both passim.

9   Think of the contents of his first revelations.

10   Montgomery Watt: op. cit., p. 45.

11   ibn Ishāq, p. 230 ff.

12   Ibid., pp. 281 ff.

13   Ibid., pp. 286 ff.

14   Ibid., pp. 341 ff.

15   M. J. Kister: 'The Market of the Prophet', *JESHO*, vol. 8, (1965), pp. 272 ff.

16   The battle of Badr was fought in March 624.

17   al-Wāqidī, vol. 1, pp. 19 ff.

18   al-Wāqidī, vol. 1, pp. 86 f.

19   ibn Ishāq, p. 342.

20   M.J. Kister; 'Some Reports concerning Mecca from Jahiliyya to Islam', *JESHO*, vol. 15, (1972), pp. 61 ff.

21   Richard W. Bulliet: *The Camel and the Wheel*, p. 92.

22   Bell: *The Qur'ān*, p. 171.

23   Ibid., p. 177, note 1.

24   E.I.². s.v. "Dhimma" (Cl. Cahen).

Notes to Chapter 6

1   Azraqi, I, p. 109.

2   Ibn Sa'd, *Tabaqāt*, I, p. 74.

3   Serjeant "*Hāram* and *Hāwtah*, the sacred enclave in Arabia", in *Melanges Taha Husain*, Le Caire 1962, p. 42.

4   Sīra, p. 343; Serjeant, p. 50; H. M. T. Nagel, "Some consideration concerning the pre-islamic and the islamic foundations of the authority of the Caliphate", in *Studies on the first century of Islamic society*, ed. G. H. A. Juynboll, 1982, p. 180.

5   H. M. T. Nagel, art. cit., p. 180 ff.

6   Sīra, p. 313.

7   Ibid., p. 506.

8   Ibid., p. 299 ff.

9   Ibid., pp. 670; W. M. Watt, *Mahomet à Médine*, p. 52.

10 Sīra, pp. 692 – 693.
11 Ibid., pp. 716 – 717.
12 Ibid., p. 743.
13 Ibid., pp. 747 ff.
14 Ibid., p. 763.
15 Ibid., p. 759.
16 Ibid., p. 814.
17 Tabarī, III, p. 242. Kināna est entrée dans l'apostasie.
18 Sīra, p. 817.
19 Ibid., p. 816.
20 Ibid., p. 933 ff; Ibn Sa'd, *Tabaqāt*, I, p. 291 ff.
21 Tabarī, III, p. 283.
22 Sīra, p. 965.
23 Sīra, p. 423.
24 Sīra, p. 922.

Notes to Chapter 7

1   For a detailed discussion on Shāh Walīy Allāh's contribution in various
    fields see the present writer's hitherto unpublished monograph, *The
    Muslim Revivalism in Post-Awrangzeb period — A study of Shāh Walīy
    Allāh's Contribution*.
2   Shāh Walīy Allāh, Al-Budūr al-Bāzighah, pp. 32 – 3.
3   Ibid., pp. 115 – 16 et seq.
4   Ibid., pp. 61 – 2.
5   Ibid., pp. 62 – 3.
6   For a fuller discussion on the role of five wisdoms in the social and
    cultural development, ibid., pp. 69 – 90.
7   Ibid., p. 90.
8   Ibid., p. 91.
9   Ibid., pp. 63 – 4.
10 Ibid., p. 64.
11 Shāh Walīy Allāh, *Hujjat Allāh al-Bālighah*, Cairo, 1322, Vol. I, p. 37.
12 Ibid: hiya l-hikmatu l-bāhithatu 'an siyāsati hukkāmi l-muduni wa-
    mulūkihā wa-kayfīyati l-rabti l-wāqi'i bayna ahli l-aqālīm.
13 *Hujjat Allāh al-Bālighah*, Cairo, 1322, Vol. I, p. 34: hiya l-hikmatu l-
    bāhithatu 'an kayfīyati hifzi l)rabti l-wāqi'i bayna ahli l-madīnati wa-a'nī
    bi-l-madīnati jamā'atan mutaqāribatan tajrī baynahumu l-mu'āmalātu wa-
    yakūnūna ahla manāzila shattā.
14 *Al-Budūr al-Bāzighah*, p. 95.
15 *Hujjat Allāh al-Bālighah*, Vol. I, p. 34.
16 *Al-Budūr al-Bāzighah*, p. 96 ff.
17 For details see, *Hujjat Allāh al-Bālighah*, Vol. I, pp. 35 – 36.

18 *Hujjat Allāh al-Bālighah,* Vol. I, p. 35.
19 Ibid.
20 Ibid.
21 Ibid. Also *Budūr,* pp. 97 – 8.
22 *Budūr,* pp. 96 – 7.
23 Ibid., pp. 110 – 11.
24 *Hujjat Allāh al-Bālighah* Vol. I. p. 361; also *Budūr,* p. 111.
25 *Al-Budūr al-Bāzighah,* pp. 111 – 12; see also *Hujjat Allah al-Bālighah,* Vol. I. p. 36. He seems to be more clear in *Budur* than in *Hujjah.*
26 *Budur,* pp. 112 – 13.
27 *Hujjah,* op. cit. p. 37.
28 Ibid. Vol. I. p. 37.
29 *Budur,* p. 95 – 6.
30 Ibid: fa-hwa l-khalīfatu l-a'zamu wa-laysa fawqahū khalīfah.
31 It is not a verbatim translation of Shāh Walīy Allāh's passage; it is only a reproduction of the contents.
32 *Budūr,* pp. 113 – 14
33 These categories have been discussed by Shāh Walīy Alāh in *Hujjat Allah al-Balighah,* vol. II, p. 110.
34 Cf. Ibid. Vol. I p. 37.
35 Ibid. Vol. II, p. 111.
36 man yuti'i l-amīra fa-qad ata'a-nī wa-man 'asā l-amīra fa-qad 'asā-nī. Reported by Muslim, al-Sahih Cairo, 1955, vol. III, p. 1466, Kitab al-Imārah.
37 innamā l-imāma junnatun yuqātalu min warā'ihī wa-yuttaqā bihī fa-'in amara bi-taqwā -llāhi wa-hadā fa-'inna lahū bi-dhālika ajran wa-'in qāla bi-ghayrihī fa-'inna 'alayhī minhu. (Ibid., p. 1471).
38 man ra'ā min amīrihī shay'an yakrahuhū fa-l-yasbir fa-'innahū laysa ahadun yufāriqu l-djamā'ata shibran illā māta mītatan jāhilīyatan (Ibid., p. 1477).
39 *Hujjah* Vol. II, p. 112.
40 Muslim, *al-Sahih,* Cairo, 1955, Vol. III, p. 1478.
41 Shāh Walīy Allāh, *Izālat al-Khaf',* Lahore, 1976.
42 Cf. *A History of Freedom Movement,* Vol. I. pp. 495 – 6.
43 Shāh Walīy Allāh, *Izālat al-Khafā',* op. cit.
44 *Hujjat Allāh al-Bālighah,* Vol. II, p. 111.
45 al-muhimmu fi l-khilāfati ridā l-nāsi bihī wa-jtimā'uhum 'alayhī wa-tawqīruhum iyyāhū wa-'an yuqīma l-huddūda wa-yunādila dūna l-millati wa-yunfidha l-ahkāma (Ibid.).
46 Qur'ān, 4: 141.
47 *Izalat al-Khafa',* Vol. I. pp. 3 – 4; also *Hujjat Allah al-Balighah,* Vol. II, p. 111.
48 Ibid.
49 Qur'ān, 4:5.
50 *Izālat al-Khafa',* op. cit., p. 4; also *Hujjah,* op. cit.
51 Ibid.

52 *Izālah*, op. cit., p. 4.
53 *Hujjah*, op. cit. also, *Izālah*, op. cit.
54 *Izālat al-Khafa'*, op. cit.
55 Ibid; also, *Hujjah*, op. cit.
56 Ibid.
57 *Izālah* op. cit.
58 Ibid.
59 *Hujjah*, op. cit.
60 *Izālah*, op. cit.
61 *Hujjah*, op. cit.
62 Ibid.
63 *Izālah*, op. cit., pp. 4 – 5.
64 Ibid.
65 *Hijjah*, op. cit.; also *Izalah*, op. cit.
66 Ibid.
67 *Izālat al-Khafā'*; Vol. I, pp. 4 – 5.
68 Ibid.
69 *Izālat al-Khafa'*, Vol. I, pp. 4 – 5.
70 *Hujjat Allāh al-Balighah*, Vol. II, p. 111.
71 Ibid. Vol. II, pp. 111 – 12.
72 Ibid. This sense has been conveyed by several *Ahadīth* reported by Muslim — *al-Sahīh*, Kitab al-Imārah, op. cit. pp. 1470 – 80, 1482.
73 *Hujjah* op. cit. p. 112. This *Hadīth* has also been reported by Muslim, op. cit. p. 1469.
74 *Budūr*, pp. 92 – 4, 101 – 3.

Notes to Chapter 8

1 However, this term has been used in the Qur'ān where the Book permits the division of people among diverse tribes, clans and 'nations', p. xlix, Vol. 49.
2 A. 'Abdel Malek, 'Idéologie et renaissance nationale' in *l'Egypte Moderne*, ed. Anthropos, Paris, 1975, p. 491.
3 Ibid., p. 489.
4 For more information on this new class see: M. Mozaffari, *La naissance de la bourgeoisie commerçante*, Institute of Political Science, Aarhus, 1981.
5 A distinction must be drawn between the term *Mellat* and *Ra'iyyat*. Sociologically, the first applies to the urban middle classes while the second comprises the modest layers and in particular the peasantry.
6 For example B. Etienne, 'Essai sur le prone politique dans l'Islam contemporain', in *Revue française de Science Politique*, August 1983.
7 I take the liberty to refer the reader to my article 'Le typologie des conflits au Moyen-Orient', in *Tiers-Monde: diplomatie et stratégie*, Economica, Paris, 1983.

8   A. Cabral, *Palvaras de Ordem Gerais* (Bissau: PAIGC Secretariado
    General, 1976), p. 34.
9   See: A. Mozaffari, *Le régime de la propriété foncière en Iran*, Institute of
    Political Science, Aarhus, 1981.
10 According to Barrington Moore, the author of the book entitled *Injustice:
    The Social Bases of Obedience and Revolt* (New York, Pantheon, 1979),
    for the call for rebellion to be obeyed two conditions are necessary: (1) a
    large number of the repressed must be persuaded that the change proposed
    to them has chances of succeeding; (2) the groups of the discontented must
    have arrived at the conclusion that their present situation is the worst
    possible, and that any other alternative would in any case be not as bad. In
    the Iranian case, these two conditions were fully met.

Notes to Chapter 9

1   One can see the Lebanon as an exception to the rule of the importance of
    the state in the Middle East. The absence of an effective state-apparatus —
    also before the civil war — can be used as a point of comparison to other
    Middle Eastern nations.
2   The concept of the state as an *instrument* of the dominant class has been
    much discussed among Marxist writers, also concerning the societies of
    advanced capitalism. By instrument I do not mean to imply a mechanistic
    one-to-one relation (cf. Miliband 1977:71 – 3).
3   To label the governing class in Syria, as in many similar societies, is not
    without problems. Some analysts (Amin 1978:8) would use the term
    "state bourgeoisie". Roberts (1980:5) claims that this term can be used
    only where surplus is appropriated by the governing class through political
    sanction, and then used exclusively as the property of the governing class.
    Hinnebusch (1983:185) calls those controlling the state "neo-
    patrimonial". "Intermediate" has the advantage, I think, of giving the
    rulers links both to subordinate and dominant classes.
4   The relative autonomy of the state is pertinent also to the state in advanced
    capitalist nations (cf. Miliband 1977:68 & 73). But the relative autonomy
    of the state in nations like Syria is greater because (1) the dominant classes
    are divided and hence relatively weak and (2) factions within the dominant
    classes survive through the State's repression of the subordinate classes. It
    is also possible to "read" the relative autonomy of the state in Syria in
    terms of the state being "a source of economic power as well as an
    instrument of it: the state is a major 'means of production' " (Miliband
    1977:109).
5   Some Syrians claim that the Muslim Brotherhood was well aware of the
    behind-the-scene manipulations by its supporters, but that their analysis of
    the situation made them think they could gain advantage thereby. In this
    view the Muslim Brotherhood was not naive; rather, they were making
    tactical moves in their political struggle.

6 Methodologically it can be problematic to gain insight into the symbolic language of politics. I have used an inductive method derived from participant observation while doing social anthropological fieldwork in Syria between 1978 – 80. The symbolic language of the power-holders can be studied through the mass-media, that of organized dissidents through their secret pamphlets. But the relation between "ordinary people" and these contesting symbols can only be gained through direct participant observations.

7 These two political myths are basic to Syrian politics, but they are not the only ones. In northern Syria, for example, the semi-pastoral groups along the Euphrates river nourish the myth of the just Hārūn al-Rashīd rule in Iraq. The Iraqi president is depicted in myth-like stories to be a modern Hārūn al-Rashīd, walking around at night listening to people's problems to be able to understand and solve the injustices of his own rule. Others in the north nourish the myth of the essential democracy of the consulting-advising rule in Saudi Arabia. The various Saudi princes are shown in stories to receive ordinary people and redress their grievances. These myths are, I feel, not so much a discourse in comparative politics (i.e. statements about how politics *are* in other countries) as statements about *ideals* in political life. Different Syrian ethnic and religious groups or classes put forward different types of myths through which a discourse about political goals, ideals and struggles is formulated. A more comprehensive study of political myths in the Middle East would be extremely valuable.

References

Ahmad, E., 1983 'Post-colonial systems of power' in *Arab Studies Quarterly* vol. 2, no. 4, pp. 350 – 63.

Alasdair, D., 1982 'The Assad regime and its troubles' in *MERIP* no. 110 vol. 12, no. 9, pp. 3 – 11.

Alavi, H., 1982 'State and class under peripheral capitalism' in *Introduction to the Sociology of 'Developing Societies'* eds: Alavi & Shanin, The Macmillan Press Ltd., London, pp. 289 – 307.

Amin, S., 1978 *The Arab Nation: Nationalism and Class Struggle*, Zed Press London, 116 pp.

Hinnebusch, R.A., 1984 'Syria under the Ba'th: state formation in a fragmented society' in *Arab Studies Quarterly* vol. 4, no. 3, pp. 177 – 99.

Miliband, R., 1977 *Marxism and Politics*, Oxford University Press, 199 pp.

Roberts, H., 1980 'Is Algeria socialist?' in *Gazelle Review* 8, Ithaca Press, London, pp. 1 – 10.

Turner, B.D., 1978 *Marx and the End of Orientalism*, George Allen and Unwin, London, 98 pp.

Van Dam, N., 1978 'Sectarian and regional factionalism in the Syrian political elite', in *The Middle East Journal* vol. 32, pp. 201 – 10.

Vatikiotis, P.J., 1972 'The Politics of the Fertile Crescent; in *Political Dynamics in the Middle East*, eds: Hammond & Alexander, American Elsevier Publishing Company Inc. N.Y., pp. 225 – 63.

Notes to Chapter 10

1 It is worth noting that others seem to share, at least partly, this point of view, though using other words. Cf. P. J. Vatikiotis, "Islamic Resurgence: A Critical View", in: A. S. Cudsi & A. H. Dessouki (eds.), *Islam and Power*, London 1981, p. 192: "Islam, in short, may dominate the highly inter-personal basis of the traditional social order, but remains removed from the impersonal arrangements required by a modern society".

2 This is another way of expressing one of the basic theoretical assumptions of the Althusser-inspired social science, saying that in a given society the economic structure is determinant in 'the last instance'. This concept does not imply, however, an economic reduction. It only points out the importance of the economy. As it is known, the Althusserian concept of 'social formation' is open to the possibility of either the political or the ideological structures being dominating at a particular historical time, cf. especially: E. Balibar, "On the Basic Concepts of Historical Materialism", in L. Althusser, *Reading Capital*, London 1972, esp. pp. 204 – 24; L. Althusser, *For Marx*, Copenhagen 1969, and others.

3 Cf. for example, Ch. Mouffe, "Hegemony and Ideology in Gramsci", in Ch. Mouffe (ed.), *Gramsci and Marxist Theory*, London 1975, pp. 168 – 204; C. Buci-Glucksman, *Gramsci and the State*, London 1980, pp. 47 – 68; B. Jessop, *The Capitalist State*, Oxford 1982, pp. 142 – 52.

4 Cf. J. Saul, "The State in Post-Colonial Societies: Tanzania", *The Socialist Register 1974*, London 1974, esp. p. 351.

5 Cf. Poulantzas, *L'Etat, le pouvoir, le socialism*, Paris 1978; Poulantzas, *Fascisme et dictature*, Paris 1970; Poulantzas, *Political Power and Social Classes*, London 1973.

6 The same line of argument is found in R. Owen, "Explaining Arab Politics", *Political Studies*, Vol. 26, December 1978, pp. 507 – 12.

7 The same basic point of view is found in M. Ayoob, "Conclusion: The Discernible Patterns", in M. Ayoob (ed.), *The Politics of Islamic Reassertion*, London 1981, p. 289.

8 Vatikiotis, op. cit., pp. 194 and 172.

9 Cf. A. E. H. Dessouki, "The Islamic Resurgence: Sources, Dynamics and Implications", in A. E. H. Dessouki (ed.), *Islamic Resurgence in the Arab World*, New York 1982, pp. 14ff; Ayoob, op. cit., pp. 271ff.

10 Dessouki, op. cit., pp. 17 and 8; further A. S. Cudsi & Dessouki, "Introduction", in Cudsi & Dessouki (eds.), op. cit., p. 5.

11   Cf. also N. M. Ayubi, "The Politics of Militant Islamic Movements in the
      Middle East", *Journal of International Affairs*, Vol. 36, No. 2, 1982/83,
      pp. 271 – 83.
12   R. H. Dekmejian, "The Anatomy of Islamic Revival", *The Middle East
      Journal*, Vol. 34, 1980, pp. 3ff; Vatikiotis, op. cit., pp. 190f; and others.
13   Cf. B. Tibi, "The Renewed Role of Islam in the Political and Social
      Development of the Middle East", *The Middle East Journal*, Vol. 37, No.
      1, 1983, pp. 7ff.
14   Cf. table 8.8 in R. Mabro, *The Egyptian Economy, 1952 – 72*, Oxford
      1974, p. 189. I reckon only 'industry & electricty' as totally capitalist. To
      that, I have added an unspecified part of the following categories:
      'construction', 'transport & commerce'. Finally, I consider 'agriculture'
      totally pre-capitalist in 1952.
15   This assertion is based on my own analyses in G. Rye Olsen, *En analyse af
      den egyptiske stat*, Aarhus 1979, esp. pp. 31 – 61, and G. Rye Olsen,
      "Statens rolle i den egyptiske industriudvikling efter 1952", in G. Rye
      Olsen (ed.), *Industripolitik og industriudvikling i den tredje verden*,
      Aarhus 1982, esp. pp. 162ff.
16   The literature on Egyptian economic development is extensive. I therefore
      restrict myself to emphasize the excellent work by John Waterbury, *The
      Egypt of Nasser and Sadat. The Political Economy of Two Regimes*,
      Princeton 1983.
17   This rough estimate is based on "Economic Bulletin", *National Bank of
      Egypt*, Vol. 33, No. 1, Cairo 1980, table 6/1b.
18   Cf. Olsen, 1979, op. cit., pp. 150ff; Olsen, 1982, op. cit., pp. 187ff.
19   P. J. Vatikiotis, *The Egyptian Army in Politics. Pattern for New Nations?*,
      Bloomington 1961, p. 193, also pp. 191 – 9.1
20   P. J. Vatikiotis, *Nasser and his generation*, London 1978, pp. 205ff;
      Waterbury, op. cit., p. 61.
21   So does Vatikiotis, 1961, op. cit., p. 202.
22   Hence, on 4 August 1961, Nasser's close friend Muhammad Haykal
      published an article in the *al-Ahram* concerning this topic, cf. M. H.
      Haykal, 'Communism and ourselves: Seven differences between Commu-
      nism and Arab Socialism", in K. H. Karpat, *Political and Social Thought
      in the Contemporary Middle East*, New York 1970, pp. 156 – 161; see
      also Malcolm Kerr, "The Emergence of a Socialist Ideology in Egypt",
      The Middle East Journal, Vol. 16, Spring 1962, No. 2, pp. 127 – 44.
23   It seems as if a number of academics had a full-time job "proving" this;
      cf. Abd El Fattah J. S. Badour, "Socialism and the Salient Features of
      Arab Socialism", *The Egyptian Political Science Review*, No. 63, Cairo,
      Jan-Apr. 1967, pp. 26 – 38; Muhammad Abdullah El Araby, "Economics
      in the Social Structure of Islam", *The Egyptian Political Science Review*,
      No. 11, Cairo, Feb. 1962, pp. 3ff; Salah-Eldin Abdel-Wahab, "The
      Concept of State in Islam", *The Egyptian Political Science Review*, No.
      23, Cairo, Feb. 1963, pp. 4ff; M. Abdullah El-Araby, "The Concept of
      State in Islam", *The Egyptian Political Science Review*, No. 12, Cairo,
      March 1962, pp. 3 – 19; Fadil Zahy Mohammad, "The Theory of the

State according to Arab Political and Islamic Thought", *The Egyptian Political Science Review*, No. 42, Cairo, Sept 1964, pp. 25 – 30.

24 Cf. A. H. Dessouki, "The Development of Offical Ideology in Egypt", *Indian Journal of Politics*, Vol. XIv, Nos. 1, 2 and 3, 1980, pp. 55; also Dekmejian, *Egypt under Nasir. A Study in Political Dynamics*, London 1972, pp. 132ff.

25 Cf. N. N. M. Ayubi, "The Political Revival of Islam: The Case of Egypt", *International Journal of Middle East Studies*, Vol. 12, 1980, p. 489.

26 Ayubi, "The Politics of Militant Islamic Movements . . .", op. cit., p. 271.

27 A. E. H. Dessouki, "The Politics of Income Distribution in Egypt", in G. Abdel-Khalek & R. Tignor (eds.), *The Political Economy of Income Distribution in Egypt*, New York 1982, pp. 62 and 75.

28 Dessouki, "The Development of Official Ideology . . .", op. cit., p. 60.

29 M. Berger, *Islam in Egypt Today. Social and Political Aspects of Popular Religion*, Cambridge 1970, pp. 44ff.

30 B. M. Borthwick, "Religion and Politics in Israel and Egypt", *The Middle East Journal*, Vol. 33, No. 2, 1979, pp. 155ff; G. R. Warburg, "Islam and Politics in Egypt: 1952 – 1980", *Middle East Studies*, Vol. 18, No. 2, 1982, pp. 135ff; Berger, op. cit., pp. 45ff, 60f, 128.

31 Warburg, op. cit., p. 137.

32 R. S. Humphreys, "Islam and Political Values in Saudi Arabia, Egypt and Syria", *The Middle East Journal*, Vol. 133, No. 1, 1979, p. 12; cf. also A. Dessouki, "The Resurgence of Islamic Organizations in Egypt: An Interpretation", in A. S. Cudsi & A. H. Dessouki (eds.), *Islam and Power*, London 1981, p. 110.

33 R. Springborg, "Egypt, Syria and Iraq", in M. Auoob (ed.), *The Politics of Islamic Reassertion*, London 1981, pp. 35 – 6.

34 Ibid., p. 36; Dessouki, "The Islamic Revival . . .", op. cit., pp. 17ff.

35 Cf. F. Ajami, "In the Pharaohs' Shadow: Religion and Authority in Egypt", in J. P. Piscatori (ed.), *Islam in the Political Process*, Cambridge 1983, p. 15, also pp. 13ff.

36 Dessouki, "The Islamic Revival . . .", op. cit., p. 17.

37 Ajami, op. cit., p. 15.

38 Cf. for example S. E. Ibrahim, "Anatomy of Egypt's Militant Islamic Groups: Methodological Note and Preliminary Findings", *International Journal of Middle East Studies*, Vol. 12, 1980, pp. 423 – 53; Humphreys, op. cit.; Dessouki, "The Resurgence . . .", op. cit.

39 Cf. also Dessouki, op. cit., p. 116.

40 Cf. Ayubi, "The Politics of Militant . . .", op. cit., p. 280; also Ibraham, op. cit., pp. 435ff. As will appear, I do not distinguish between the different Islamic groups in Egypt. For an overview and discussion of some of these and especially the Muslim Brotherhood, cf. for example: Ayubi, "The Political Revival of Islam: The Case of Egypt", *International Journal of Middle East Studies*, pp. 488ff; Ibraham, op. cit.; H. Hanafi, "The Relevance of the Islamic Alternative in Egypt", *Arab Studies*

Quarterly, Vol. 4, Nos. 1 & 2, 1982, pp. 54 – 74; S. E. Ibraham, ''An Islamic Alternative in Egypt: The Muslim Brotherhood and Sadat'', *Arab Studies Quarterly*, Vol. 4, Nos. 1 & 2, 1982, pp. 75 – 93; K. A. Kheir, *The Moslem Brothers. Quest for an Islamic Alternative*, (MA thesis, The American University in Cairo), July 1983.

41   Ayubi, ''The Politics . . .'', op. cit., p. 280.

42   Cf. Ibrahim, ''Anatomy of Egypt's . . .'', op. cit., pp. 447; Ayubi, ''The Politics . . .'', op. cit., p. 280; Ayubi, ''The Political Revival of Islam . . .'', op. cit., pp. 493ff.

43   Cf. Hanafi, op. cit., pp. 71ff; Ibraham, op. cit.

44   Ibraham, op. cit., pp. 447f; Ayubi, ''The Political Revival of Islam . . .'', op. cit., p. 495.

45   According to Dr A. M. Saad Ali, *al-Ahram*, in an interview in Cairo, November 1983.

46   Hanafi, op. cit., p. 73.

47   This point of view is found in a number of works, cf. for example: J. S. Birks & C. A. Sinclair, ''The Domestic Political Economy of Development in Saudi Arabia'', in T. Niblock (ed.), *State, Society and Economy in Saudi Arabia*, London 1982, pp. 198ff; G. M. Rumaihi, ''The Mode of Production in the Arab Gulf before the Discovery of Oil'', in T. Niblock (ed.), *Social and Economic Development in the Arab Gulf*, London 1980, pp. 49 – 60.

48   I reckon the following among the capitalist economic sectors: ''oil production and refining'', a lesser part of ''manufacturing'', ''construction'', ''wholesale and transport''. I am including only a smaller part of the sectors last mentioned, as it is probably most correct to reckon them as part of small-scale production, i.e. as non-capitalist sectors, cf. Y. A. Sayigh, *The Economies of the Arab World*, (Vol. I), London 1978, p. 155. The statistical information is drawn from R. Knauerhase, *The Saudi Arabian Economy*, New York 1975, pp. 82 – 3. This information is further elaborated in my: ''Saudi-Arabien: Industripolitik i en olieøkonomi'' (Saudi Arabia: Industrial policies in an oil economy'', in G. Rye Olsen (ed.), *Industripolitik og industriudvikling i den tredje verden*, Aarhus 1982, pp. 246ff.

49   Numerous works deal with the Saudi development policy, cf. for example R. El Mallakh, *Saudi Arabia. Rush to Development*, London 1982; Knauerhase, op. cit.; Olsen, op. cit., pp. 250 – 69.

50   The following information is drawn from Olsen, op. cit., esp. pp. 269 – 71, and El Mallakh, op. cit., p. 29.

51   W. B. Quant, *Saudi Arabia in the 1980's*, Washington 1981, p. 89, also pp. 87 – 9.

52   D. Pipes, ''This World is Political: The Islamic Revival in the Seventies'', *Orbis*, Vol. 24, 1980, No. 1, p. 26.

53   R.R. MacIntyre, ''Saudi Arabia'', Ayoob, op. cit., pp. 27f.

54   Ibid., p. 28.

55   F. A. Sankari, ''Islam and Politics in Saudi Arabia'', in Dessouki, 1982, op. cit., p. 185; cf. also B. Tibi, ''Zum Verhältnis von Politik, Religion

und Staat in islamisch legitimierten Monarchien", *Orient*, Vol. 21, No. 2, 1980, pp. 170f.

56   Cf. Al-Farsy, *Saudi Arabia. A Case Study in Development*, London 1982, pp. 66 – 9.
57   G. Shanneik, "Die Modernisierung des traditionellen politischen Systems in Saudi Arabien", *Orient*, Vol. 21, No. 3, 1980, p. 317; Sankari, op. cit., pp. 183ff.
58   Cf. Shanneik, op. cit., p. 317; Sankari, op. cit., p. 185.
59   MacIntyre, op. cit., p. 14.
60   Ibid., p. 27.
61   J. P. Piscatori, "Ideological Policies in Saudi Arabia", in J. P. Piscatori (ed.), *Islam in the Political Process*, Cambridge 1983, p. 61.
62   Ibid., p. 60.
63   Ibid., p. 59; cf. also A. M. Sindi, "King Faisal and Pan-Islamism", in W. A. Beling (ed.), *King Faisal and the Modernisation of Saudi Arabia*, London 1980, esp. p. 186.
64   Sankari, op. cit., p. 188.
65   Cf. R. Lacey, "Saudi Arabia: A More Visible Role in the Middle East", *The World Today*, Vol. 38, No. 1, 1982, p. 7.
66   Piscatori, op. cit., p. 61.
67   *The Middle East*, No. 63, January 1980, pp. 10 – 11; J. Paul, "Insurrection at Mecca", *Merip Reports*, No. 91, Oct 1980, pp. 3 – 4; Sankari, op. cit., p. 190.
68   Ayubi, op. cit., pp. 274ff; cf. also J. Reissner, "Die Besetzung der grossen Mosche in Mekka 1979", *Orient*, Vol. 21, No. 2, 1980, pp. 198ff.
69   Ibid., p. 274.
70   *The Middle East*, op. cit., p. 10; Ayubi, op. cit., p. 275.
71   Cf. for example Dessouki, 1982, op. cit., p. 16.
72   For a more elaborated argumentation, see my "Saudi Arabia: The Form of Regime, its Social Basis and Political Change", *Cooperation & Conflict*, No. 3, 1984.
73   As is probably well known, this point of view is not new in the debate of economic development in Muslim societies, cf. for example M. Rodinson, *Islam and Capitalism*, Harmondsworth 1974.

Notes to Chapter 11

This article was presented at the Symposium on "Islam: State and Society" held at the University of Aarhus from 31 August to 1 September 1984. Fieldwork was conducted during 1977 to 1978 in the Kunar Province and a supplementary shorter visit was undertaken in February-March 1981 to Afghan refugees in Pakistan and to Kunar. The research has been funded by the Danish Research Council for the Humanities.

1 The Pakhtun, who are also called Pashtun or Pathan, number about 6 million of the approximately 15 million inhabitants of Afghanistan. Their main settlement areas are in the Eastern and Southern parts of the country overlapping the border with Pakistan's North-West Frontier Province and Baluchistan, where an additional 6 million Pakhtun are living.
2 The relationship between formal Islamic injunctions and *Pakhtūnwālī* is described by Boesen (1979/80) and Anderson (1980).
3 Other proverbs expressing the same conflict can be found in Enevoldsen (1967) and Anderson (1980).
4 Concerning such confrontations among the Pakhtun see Caroe (1958, p. 299ff and 198ff) and Spain (1963, p. 86ff).
5 The political and ideological divisions among the Shī'ā Hazara have been described by Roy (1983).
6 Besides referring to their proponent's ideological connections to "fundamentalist" Islam in Pakistan, the name *Panj Pīrī* also carried the connotation of heresy, because it was used with the implication that the Islamic revolutionaries followed the fifth (: *panj*) Pīr instead of one of the four established legal schools within Sunnī Islam, i.e. the Hanafī, Malikī, Shāfī'ī or Hanbalī.

References

Anderson, J.W., 1984 'How Afghans define themselves in relation to Islam'. In: M. N. Shahrani and R. F. Canfield (eds.), *Revolutions and Rebellions in Afghanistan — Anthropological Perspectives*. Berkeley.
Azoy, G.W., 1982 *Buzkashi — Game and power in Afghanistan*. Philadelphia.
Barth, F., 1959 'Segmentary opposition and the theory of games: A study of Pathan organization'. *Jour. of the Royal Anth. Inst.* vol. 89.
Boesen, J.W., 1979/80 'Women, honour and love — Some aspects of Pashtun women's life in Eastern Afghanistan', *Folk*, vol. 21/22.
Canfield, R.L., 1973 *Faction and conversion in a plural society: Religious alignments in the Hindu Kush*. Ann Arbor.
Caroe, O., 1958 *The Pathans 550 BC — AD 1957*. London.
Christensen, A., 1982 'Agnates, affines, and allies: Patterns of marriage among Pakhtun in Kunar, North-East Afghanistan'. *Folk*, vol. 24.
Christensen, A., 1983 'Afghanistan — ikke kontrarevolution, men befrielseskamp'. *Jordens Folk* vol. 18, no. 1.
Christensen, A., 1983 'Politik og religion i Afghanistan' IF — *Internationalt Forum* no. 3.
Christensen, A., 1984 ' "Udvikling" ovenfra — modstand nedefra: Socialisme of stammefolk i Afghanistan'. *Stofskifte — Tidsskrift for Antropologi* no. 10.
Enevoldsen, J., 1967 *Oh måne — skynd dig — stig op og skin*. Herning.
Ghani, A., 1978 'Islam and state-building in a tribal society: Afghanistan 1880 – 1901'. *Modern Asian Studies* vol. 12, no. 2.

Janata, A. & R. Hassas, 1975 'Ghairatman — der gute Pashtune: Exkurs über die Grundlagen des Pashtunwali'. *Afghanistan Journal* vol. 2, no. 3.

Kakar, H., 1977 *Afghanistan: A study in internal political developments 1880 – 1896*. Kabul.

Roy, O., 1983 'L'essor du khomeynisme parmi la minorité chiite'. *Le Monde Diplomatique* 18 April.

Spain, J.W., 1963 *The Pathan borderland*. The Hague.

Notes to Chapter 12

This paper was written for the symposium, but not read there, as Asta Olesen was in New Delhi at that time (Eds.).

1 In this article I am trying to adapt the "Legitimization of Power" model developed by Professor Mehdi Mozaffari (cf. Mozaffari 1987), which I gratefully acknowledge. However, Prof. Mozaffari accepts no responsibility for any errors in the application of his model to the Afghan material.

2 See, for example, Poullada (1970, 1973) and Bellew (1962).

3 Ghani (1978:269).

4 Ahmed (1980:106 – 7).

5 This became particularly pronounced during various confrontations with the imperialist Christian powers; for example, Amīr Dost Mohammad declared himself as Amīr al-mu'minīm (Commander of the Faithful) and Amir Sher Ali claimed divine sanction for his rule.

6 For a comprehensive discussion of the reign of Amīr 'Abd ur-Rahmān, see Kakar (1971, 1979) and the autobiography of the Amir (Mahomed, 1900).

7 Tapper (1983:35 – 6).

8 The Young Afghans consisted of a number of semi-secular, Western-oriented intellectuals and activists who voiced liberal aspirations similar to those of the Young Turks. For a closer view of the ideological background of the Young Afghans, see Schinasi (1979).

9 An important difference between King Amanullah and his contemporaries, Mustafa Kemal in Turkey and Reza Shah in Iran, was that while the latter two came to power by overthrowing previous long-established tribal dynasties, King Amanullah succeeded to power as a tribal chieftain himself (Tapper, 1983).

10 Schinasi (1979).

11 Dupree (1973:464 – 5).

12 Gregorian (1969:305).

13 Ibid: 302 – 3.

14 The authorities dealing with the Mangal unrest in 1959 and the imposition of taxes in the Kandahar region the same year were clear signals to the population, particularly the tribes, of the forces of the Afghan army (Dupree 1973:534 – 6).

15 The Loya Jirga was to be composed of members of the National Assembly, the Central Council of the Party, the Government and the High Council of

the Armed Forces, the Supreme Court, 5 – 8 representatives from each province, and 30 members to be appointed by the President.

16 For a discussion of the non-capitalist development strategy and its application (or lack of) in Afghanistan during Hafizullah Amin's rule see Olesen (1983).

References

Ahmed, Akbar S., 1980 *Pukhtun Economy and Society: Traditional Structure and Economic Development in a Tribal Society.* London.

Bellew, H. W., 1862 *Journal of a Political Mission to Afghanistan in 1857, with an Account of the Country and the People*, London.

Dupree, Louis, 1973 *Afghanistan.* Princeton.

Ghani, Ashraf, 1978 'Islam and State-Building in a Tribal Society: Afghanistan 1880 – 1901'. In: *Modern Asian Studies*, Vol. 12, No. 2: 269 – 284, London.

Gregorian, Vartan, 1969 *The Emergence of Modern Afghanistan: Politics of Reform and Modernization, 1880 – 1946.* Stanford.

Kakar, Hasan K., 1979 *Government and Society in Afghanistan: The Reign of Amir 'abd al-Rahman Khan.* Austin.

Kakar, M. Hasan, 1971 *Afghanistan: A study in internal Political Developments, 1880 – 1896.* Kabul.

Mahomed, Mir Munshi, 1900 *The Life of Abdur Rahman, Amir of Afghanistan*, I – II. London.

Mozaffari, Mehdi, 1987 *Authority in Islam: From Muhammad to Khomeini.* New York.

Olesen, Asta, 1983 'The Saur Revolution and the Local Response to it'. In: Breckle, S.N. and Naumann, C.M. (eds.): *Forschungen in und über Afghanistan. Mitteillungen des Deutsches Orient-Instituts*, Nummer 22, Hamburg.

Poullada, Leon B., 1970 'The Pushtun Role in the Afghan Political System'. *Occasional Papers 1.* The Afghanistan Council of the Asia Society.

Poullada, Leon B., 1973 *Reform and Rebellion in Afghanistan, 1919 – 1929: King Ammanullah's Failure to Modernize a Tribal Society.* Ithaca and London.

Schinasi, May, 1979 *Afghanistan at the Beginning of the Twentieth Century: Nationalism and Journalism in Afghanistan: A Study of Seräj ul-akhbär (1911 – 1918)*, Naples.

Tapper, Richard (ed.), 1983 *The Conflict of Tribe and State in Iran and Afghanistan.* London.

Notes to Chapter 13

1 Examples can be found in: Gorm Rye Olsen; *En analyse af den Egyptiske Stat*, Institut for Statskundskab, Aarhus Universitet, specialeopgave juni 1979 and Gorm Rye Olsen (ed., *Industripolitik & Industriudvikling i den tredie verden*, Politica, Arhus 1982.

2 Elia Zureik, 'Theoretical Considerations for a Sociological Study of the Arab State', *Arab Studies Quarterly*, 1981: 3 pp. 229 – 57.

3 Saudi Arabia is an exception to this general rule, as the state in rejecting trade unions argues that such an organization is incompatible with Islam, see Siegfried Mielke (ed.), *Internationales Gewerkschafts-Handbuch*, Leske & Budrich, Opladen, 1983.

4 In the classical notion of community in Islam, there has to be made a distinction between *Ummat al-Islām* and *Dār al-Islām*. The first has the social connotation of the Islamic faith and is unlimited in time and space while the second refers to the political and legal aspects of the sovereign state within its territorial boundaries. The Muslim anywhere in the world considers himself a member of *Ummat al-Islām* even if he is not a member of *Dār al-Islām*. A Muslim living in Europe or America will always be a member of *Ummat al-Islām*: he is linked together with all other Muslims through the Faith and Creed of Islam. *Dār al-Islām* in a modern sense is the specific society which today may be considered equivalent to an Islamic nation. One *Dār al-Islām* is distinguished from another by geography, jurisprudence, and history. See e.g. Abdo A. Elkholy, 'The Concept of Community in Islam', *Islamic Perspectives*, Studies in honour of Sayid Abul a'la Mawdudi, The Islamic Foundation, UK, 1979.

5 For a discussion see Jan Hjärpe, 'Hur Förstå Islams Politiska Roll I Dag?', Särtryck ur *Årsbok för kristen humanism*, 1983.

6 For a further analysis of a conceptual development towards a more territorial definition of *Dār al-Islām* see: Mamoucher Parvin and Maurie Sommer; 'Dar al Islam: The Evolution of Muslim Territoriality and its Implications for Conflict Resolution in the Middle East', *International Journal of Middle Eastern Studies*, vol. 11, 1980, pp. 1 – 21.

7 W. Montgomery Watt, *Islam and the Integration of Society*, Routledge & Kegan Paul, London, 1961.

8 Watt, op. cit.

9 Gamal El-Banna, *Islam and Trade Unions*, The International Islamic Confederation of Labour, undated publication, and *Arabia*, December 1983, p. 52, 'Why Islam Applauds Trade Unions'

10 Muammar al-Qadhāfī, *Al-Sijil, Bayanet wa Khutab wa Ahadith*, vol. IV, 1972 – 73, Tripoli, n.d. pp. 937 – 8. Here quoted from Marius K. Deeb, 'Islam and Arab Nationalism in Al-Qadhafi's Ideology', *Journal of South Asian and Middle Eastern Studies*, vol. II, no. 2, Winter 1978.

11 Deeb, op. cit. p. 17.

12 Muammar al-Qahdhāfī, *The Green Book*, Martin Brian & O'Keefe, 1976 – 9.

13 *The Green Book*, op. cit.

14 After the Italian capitulation in 1943, Libya came under British and French and later United Nations administration during which period parties emerged and continued under the king.

15 Muammar al-Qadhāfī, *Al-Sijil al-Qawani, Bayant wa Khutab wa Ahadith*, Vol. VII, 1975 – 6, Tripoli, n.d. pp. 484 – 6, here from Deeb, op. cit., 1978.

16 Ibid. p. 486.

17 Ibid.

18 Ibid. p. 487. Qadhāfī is here using "positive law" as man-made law in contrast to divine law, and not, as it is common in jurisprudence, as written law in contrast to divine or natural law not (yet) written.

19 *The Green Book*, op. cit.

20 Ibid.

21 A further discussion of Islam in revolutionary Libya can be found in Marius K. Deeb and Mary Jane Deeb, *Libya Since the Revolution*, Praeger, USA, 1982.

22 *The Green Book*, op. cit.

23 *The Green Book*, op. cit.

24 *Statistical Abstract of Libya*, Census and Statistical Department, The Socialist People's Libyan Arab Jamahiriya, 1981.

25 *Decision of the General People's Committee on the Insurance of the Administrative Regulation of Companies and Establishments Owned by Society*, Socialist People's Libyan Arab Jamahiriya, General Popular Committee. The regulation was given to the protection units in September, 1980.

26 John Norman, *Labour and Politics in Libya and Arab Africa*, Bookman Associates, Inc. New York, 1965.

27 Willard A. Beling, *Pan-Arabism and Labor*, Harvard Middle Eastern Monograph Series, Cambridge, Mass. 1961.

28 Norman, op. cit., chapter 14. More recently, Wogu Ananaba, *The Trade Union Movement in Africa, Promise and Performance*, C. Hurst & Company, London, 1979.

29 Norman, op. cit. p. 165.

30 Lorna Hahn, *Historical Dictionary of Libya*, African Historical Dictionaries no. 33, The Scarecrow Press, Inc. Metuchen & London 1981, p. 73.

31 The Revolutionary Command Council (RCC) contained ten young army officers who shortly after the revolution in 1969 emerged as the new regime. Today only five of them are left, and the council is not part of the official organization of rule, although in reality some of the members have a very strong voice. The remaining members are the leader of the revolution, Colonel Muammar al-Qadhāfī; Major Abdul Salem Jalloud; the general leader of the armed forces, Lt. Col. Abu Baker Yunis Jaber; Chief of Staff Lt. Col. Mustafa Al-Kharraby; and leader of the people's army, Major Al Khobeidly Al-Humaidi.

32 In December 1980, the author had an interview with the head of the International Department of the Producers' Union, Salem Jalloud, who is a half-brother of Abdul Salem Jalloud, member of the RCC.

33 Jalloud, op. cit.
34 Ruth First is among those who give the impression of a spontaneous and impulsive form of government in her book: *Libya — The Elusive Revolution*, Penguin African Library, Middlesex, 1974.
35 Michel al-Nimri, 'Libya fi'Asr al-Jamahir, al-Lijan al-Thawriya, Itar al-Thawra la-Siyasiya', *al-Safir*, August 19, 1980, p. 11, here from M. & M. Deeb, op. cit. 1982.
36 Ibid.
37 Maja Naur, 'Social and Organizational Change in Libya', *Current African Issues*, no. 2, 1982. The Scandinavian Institute of African Studies.
38 Document from the Producers' Union, Tripoli, 1980.
39 Information from a high ranking official in the Secretariat of Labour and Civil Services, Interview, December 1980. Note the change from ministries to secretariats which is in accordance with the new state ideology.
40 *Statistical Abstract*, Tripoli, August 1981, op. cit.
41 Maja Naur, 'On Income Distribution and the Changing Sector Size Distribution', Odense University (unpublished) 1983.
42 Naur, ibid. 1983.
43 Naur, ibid. 1983.
44 Naur, ibid. 1983.
45 The Arab Workers — excluding the Palestinians, who keep fighting for their homeland — can become Libyans and thus partners. However, few have done so as that involves the duty of military service.
46 Ahmed Shahati is the leader of the International Centre for the Study of *The Green Book*, and as such one of the main ideologues in the country.
47 ''Jamahiriya'' means the republic of the masses. The name of the country is today, The Socialist People's Libyan Arab Jamahiriya.
48 The official statistics given in *Statistical Abstracts*, op. cit., the non-Libyan Arabs 45.9% of the total of foreign workers, the Asians 30%. Thus the majority might be expected to be Muslims.

Notes to Chapter 14

1 Junqua, Daniel, 1981, 'La Question Culturelle en Algérie'. *Grand Maghreb*, No. 2, 10.6.1981, p. 3.
2 Chaker, Salem, 1982a, 'La Revendication Culturelle Berbère'. *Les Tempes Modernes*, No. 432 – 433, Juillet Août 1982, p. 437.
3 Chaker, Salem, 1981, 'L'Emergence du Fait Berber', Annuaire de l'Afrique du Nord 1980, Paris, 1981, p. 475. and Dejeux, Jean, 1983, *Identité nationale, idéologie arabo-islamique et revendication berbèrophone en Algérie*. Université du Turku. Histoire Politique, Publication E:1/1983, p. 10.
4 Chaker, Salem, 1981, op. cit. p. 474.
5 Déjeux, Jean, 1983, op. cit. p. 8.

6 Déjeux, Jean, 1983, op. cit., and Lazreg, Marnia, 1981, *The Kabyle-Berber Cultural Movement: A Historical Perspective.* Unpublished manuscript, New York, pp. 9 – 10.

7 Dejeux, Jean, 1983, op. cit. pp. 11 – 12.

8 Chaker, Salem, 1981, op. cit. p. 477.

9 For instance Melasuo, Tuomo, 1983a, 'Les Mouvements Politiques et la Question Culturelle en Algérie avant la Guerre de Libération'. *Cahiers de la Méditerranée* No. 26, CMMC, Université de Nice, p. 6.

10 Melasuo, Tuomo, 1983a, op. cit. p. 5.

11 Melasuo, Tuomo, 1983a, op. cit. pp. 9 – 10.

12 Harbi, Mohammed, 1980, *Le FLN. Mirage et realité. Des origines à la prise du pouvoir, 1945 – 1962,* Paris, pp. 60 – 5.

13 Melasuo, Tuomo, 1983b, *Les Mouvements Politiques Algériens et la Réligion avant 1954,* Paper presented to symposium ''Religion och Samhälle i Mellanöstern'', University of Lund, 8-10.6.1983, p. 20.

14 Déjeux, Jean, 1983, op. cit. p. 7.

15 Chaker, Salem, 1981, op. cit. pp. 479, 481.

16 Chaker, Rachid, 1982, 'Journal des événements de Kabylie', *Les Temps Modernes,* No. 432 – 433, Juillet-Août 1982, and Déjeux, Jean, 1983, op. cit.

17 Chaker, Rachid, 1982, op. cit., Chaker, Salem, 1981, op. cit., p. 482, Déjeux, Jean, 1983, op. cit., p. 18 and Junqua, Daniel, 1981, op. cit., p. 32.

18 Déjeux, Jean, 1983, op. cit. p. 10. I call ''standard Arabic'' the modern ''newspaper'' Arabic used in the Near East and based on classical Arabic.

19 Dejeux, Jean, 1983, op. cit., p. 20, Rodinson, Maxime, 1979, *Les Arabes,* Paris, pp. 22 and 138, and Stephens, Robert, 1971, *Nasser. A Political Biography,* London, p. 351.

20 Déjeux, Jean, 1983, op. cit., p. 10.

21 Chaker, Salem, 1984, 'La Question Berbère quatre ans après Tizi-Ouzou', *Grand Maghreb* No. 32, 23.7.1984, p. 42 – 44.

22 Chaker, Salem, 1982a, op. cit. annexe I.

23 'Culture et personalité algérienne. Reflexions autour du dossier de politique culturelle', *Revue de Presse,* Dossier No. 2, Alger, 1981.

24 Déjeux, Jean, 1983, op. cit. p. 26 and Junqua, Daniel, 1981, op. cit., p. 32.

25 Chaker, Salem, 1982b, 'De question constantes du discours dominant sur les langues popularies en Algérie'. *Annuaire de l'Afrique du Nord 1981,* Paris, p. 451, 456. and Déjeux, Jean, 1983, op. cit., p. 27.

26 Chaker, Salem, 1982a, op. cit., p. 442.

27 Déjeux, Jean, 1983, op. cit., pp. 26 – 7.

28 Chaker, Salem, 1981, op. cit., p. 475 and Déjeux, Jean, 1983, op. cit., p. 18.

29 Déjeux, Jean, 1982, 'Le débat culturel en Algérie en 1979 – 1982', *L'Afrique et l'Asie Modernes,* Paris, No. 133, pp. 17 – 18.

30 Chaker, Salem, 1982a, op. cit., pp. 442, 445, Déjeux, Jean, 1983, op. cit., p. 31, Harbi, Mohammed, 1981, 'Rationalité idéologique et identité nationale: l'Algérie entre le passé et le present', *Sou'al*, Paris, No. 1, pp. 48 – 50.
31 For these political connections see Chaker, Salem, 1984, op. cit., p. 44, Duteil, Mireille, 1984, 'L'Integrisme Islamique au Maghreb: le pause?' *Grand Maghreb* No. 29, 19.3.1984, p. 49. UNJA = Union Nationale de la Jeunesse Algérienne.
32 *Grand Maghreb*, No. 28, 6.2.1984, p. 8 and No. 29. 19.3.1984, pp. 8 – 9.
33 Melasuo, Tuomo, 1983b, op. cit., p. 5.
34 Murin, Sophie, 1982, 'L'appel du Muezzin'. *Autrement — Algérie 20 ans*, No. 38, p. 151.
35 Duteille, Mireille, 1984, op. cit., p. 49.
36 Murin, Sophie, 1982, op. cit., p. 147.
37 Duteil, Mireille, 1984, op. cit., p. 50.
38 Duteil, Mireille, 1984, op. cit., p. 49.
39 *Grand Maghreb*, No. 31, 11.6.1984, p. 8.
40 Junqua, Daniel, 1981, 'Vers une législation du "Statut Personel" en Algérie', *Grand Maghreb*, No. 6, 10.11.1984, p. 54.
41 Junqua, Daniel, 1981, op. cit., p. 53.
42 Melasuo, Tuomo, 1983a, op. cit., p. 16.
43 Junqua, Daniel, 1981, op. cit., p. 55.
44 Chaker, Rachin, 1982, op. cit., Chaker, Salem, 1982a, op. cit., p. 441, and Junqua, Daniel, 1981, op. cit., p. 56.
45 *Grand Maghreb*, No. 32, 23.7.1984, p. 7.
46 Code de la Famille, *El Moudjahid*, 20.6.1984.
47 Chaker, Salem, 1982a, op. cit., p. 437.
48 Chaker, Salem, 1982a, op. cit., p. 441.
49 Chaker, Salem, 1982a, op. cit., ibid.
50 Harbi, Mohammed, 1981, op. cit., p. 50.
51 Chaker, Salem, 1984, op. cit., p. 43.
52 Chaker, Salem, 1984, op. cit.
53 Chaker, Salem, 1982b,op. cit., p. 455.